Critical Essays on Arthur Miller

James J. Martine

G. K. Hall & Co. ● Boston, Massachusetts

Library of Congress Cataloging in Publication Data
Main entry under title:

Critical essays on Arthur Miller.

   (Critical esssays on American literature)
   Includes index.
   1. Miller, Arthur, 1915–   —Criticism and interpretation—Addresses, essays, lectures.
I. Martine, James J. II. Series,
PS3525.I5156Z62   813'   .5'2   79-2557
ISBN 0-8161-8258-2

This publication is printed on permanent/durable acid-free paper
MANUFACTURED IN THE UNITED-STATES OF AMERICA

For Patricia

CRITICAL ESSAYS ON AMERICAN LITERATURE

This series seeks to publish the most important reprinted criticism on writers and topics in American literature along with, in various volumes, original essays, interviews, bibliographies, letters, manuscripts sections, and other materials brought to public attention for the first time. James Martine's collection of criticism on Arthur Miller is a distinguished contribution to the series. It contains reprinted essays by such critics as John Simon, Brooks Atkinson, Walter Kerr, and Thomas Porter. In addition to a valuable bibliographical introduction and a new essay by Daniel Walden, Professor Martine includes a transcription of his own interview with Miller in February of 1979, one which reveals a great deal about Miller's life and creative process. We are confident that this collection represents a permanent and significant addition to American literary scholarship.

JAMES NAGEL, GENERAL EDITOR

Northeastern University

CONTENTS

INTRODUCTION

I. BIBLIOGRAPHY

The first of the bibliographic items worthy of mention is Martha Turnquist Eissenstat, "Arthur Miller: A Bibliography," *Modern Drama*, 5 (May 1962), 93–106. This good but dated bibliography has the advantage of a section on individual plays beginning with *All My Sons*. Thus the reader interested in a specific play can quickly find reviews and essays arranged conveniently for that purpose. The limitation of this work is, of course, that it can contain nothing beyond *A View from the Bridge* and no articles after 1962. Several other works published in the 1960s and early 1970s include selected bibliographies. Robert Hogan, *Arthur Miller* (Minneapolis: Univ. of Minnesota Press, 1964) has a brief "Selected Bibliography," pp. 46–48. Leonard Moss, *Arthur Miller* (New York: Twayne, 1967) contains a good "Selected Bibliography," pp. 135–53. Harold Clurman, ed., *The Portable Arthur Miller* (New York: Viking, 1971) has a short section on "Bibliography," pp. 563–66. In addition, Benjamin Nelson, *Arthur Miller: A Portrait of a Playwright* concludes with a six-page "Selected Bibliography," pp. 323–29.

A more thorough updating is Harriet Ungar, "The Writings of and about Arthur Miller: A Checklist 1936–1967," *Bulletin of the New York Public Library*, 74 (1970), 107–34. Two additional attempts at more comprehensive bibliographies were published in 1976. George H. Jensen, *Arthur Miller: A Bibliographic Checklist* (Columbia, S.C.: Faust, 1976) includes reproductions of title pages, the publishing history of Miller's books, and a full bibliography of the playwright's writings. That same year, Tetsumaro Hayashi issued a second edition, revising, updating, and enlarging his *Arthur Miller Criticism (1930–1967)* first published in 1969. Tetsumaro Hayashi, *An Index to Arthur Miller Criticism* 2nd ed. (Metuchen, N.J.: Scarecrow, 1976) is presently the most ambitious guide to scholarship on Miller. It contains a section on primary sources and a lengthy catalog of published and unpublished works about the dramatist including doctoral dissertations and master's theses. To Hayashi's list, the reader will have to add one 1972 dissertation, five for 1975, and one each for the years 1976 and 1977. The bulk of Hayashi's volume deals with periodical articles and reviews as well as newspaper articles, reviews, and reports. He concludes with a bibliography of bibliographies on Miller. Also useful to scholars is his appendix listing and locating unpublished manuscripts, letters, and postcards by the playwright.

The wise reader will also want to see the "Bibliography of Works (1936–1977) by Arthur Miller" supplied in *The Theater Essays of Arthur Miller*, ed. Robert A. Martin (New York: Viking, 1978), pp. 379–92. Professor Martin has done some of the most impressive work yet published on Miller, and his bibliographic entries here are listed chronologically by genre. This may be, in some ways and to many scholars, more convenient than Hayashi's traditional alphabetic listing. Martin also locates unpublished manuscripts, and identifies manuscript and typescript collections, principally at the University of Michigan, the New York Public Library, and the extensive holdings of the University of Texas, Austin. For this last, see Dwain E. Manske's dissertation, "A Study of the Changing Family Roles in the Early Published and Unpublished Works of Arthur Miller, to Which Is Appended a Catalogue of the Arthur Miller Collection at the University of Texas at Austin," University of Texas, 1970 (*DAI*, 32 (1972), 4008A). An excellent, and most recent, addition is John H. Ferres, *Arthur Miller: A Reference Guide* (Boston: G.K. Hall, 1979). This compilation is valuable for its updated comprehensiveness and its inclusion of intelligent summary abstracts of each item.

As well, cast lists and stage production details of Miller's plays are listed in Ronald Hayman, *Arthur Miller* (New York: Ungar, 1972), pp. 123–31, Sheila Huftel, *Arthur Miller: The Burning Glass* (New York: Citadel Press, 1965), pp. 237–51, and Martin, ed., pp. 364–78. Additional perspective on the reception of the plays might be gained from Jane F. Bonin, *Prize-Winning American Drama: A Bibliographical and Descriptive Guide* (Metuchen, N.J.: Scarecrow, 1973), pp. 94–97, 102–05, 125, 127–29, and the checklist of plays in the same author's *Major Themes in Prize Winning America Drama* (Scarecrow, 1975), pp. 172–73.

II. EDITIONS

There can be, of course, as yet no definitive edition of Arthur Miller's works. Those editions of individual plays available are listed conveniently in Martin, ed., and Hayashi, and Jensen.

In 1957, the Viking Press published *Arthur Miller's Collected Plays* (New York, 1957). While this volume includes only *All My Sons, Death of a Salesman, The Crucible, A Memory of Two Mondays*, and the expanded two-act version of *A View from the Bridge*, it also is prefaced by Miller's important "Introduction to the *Collected Plays*," pp. 3–55. This essay has rightly been called Miller's major theoretical contribution to the literature of his age. Incidentally, the reader interested in the one-act original version of *A View from the Bridge* will find it complete in *Theatre Arts* (September 1956), pp. 49–68. The same number of this magazine contains Miller's early comments on the play, "Viewing *A View from the Bridge*," pp. 31–32. Viking Press has also supplied a convenient paperback edition, Harold Clurman, ed., *The Portable Arthur Miller* (New York: Viking, 1971), which collects *Death of a Salesman, The Crucible, Incident at Vichy, The Price*, two versions of "The Misfits," two stories, an excerpt from *In Russia*, and a poem.

Miller's influential "Introduction to the *Collected Plays*" is reprinted in *The Theater Essays of Arthur Miller*, ed. Robert A. Martin (New York: Viking Press, 1978), pp. 113–70. This collection of Miller's essays reprints twenty-six prose pieces, including his most significant and controversial "Tragedy and the Common Man," pp. 3–7. When this essay appeared in *The New York Times*,

February 27, 1949, Sec. 2, pp. 1, 3, it opened a debate which still lingers for many critics and teachers of Miller's works, although some critics cannot understand the confusion Miller's theory has caused. To clarify his position, Miller followed this essay with "The Nature of Tragedy," *The New York Herald Tribune*, March 25, 1949, Sec. 5, pp. 1, 2, also reprinted in *Theatre Essays*, pp. 8–11.

While many of the essays in this collection have stirred critical controversy, what may have been overlooked by many is the brilliance of Arthur Miller's prose style. What makes Miller such an excellent essayist is not merely that he is so sound and perceptive—so rightheaded—for all that, after all, means is that this reader agrees with his vision and his values—but because Miller's thoughts are so accessible. His prose is clear and direct; he says what he thinks and though his prose is graceful, often poetic, it is never obscure, obstruent, or abstruse. Miller's essays are valuable because they reveal him to be a humanistic and humane human being concerned with the "community" of the theater and the world, and they express his vision *clearly*. Miller does not hide coyly behind the intricacies of prose as some writers do—writers who either do not know what they mean or lack the courage to say it. One thinks of Steinbeck's caution that communication is so difficult that only a fool would be willfully obscure. For above (and beneath) all, Miller is a courageous writer. The world has witnessed his demonstrations of personal and political courage. Miller's essays demonstrate his courage to the core: he knows what he means, and he says it—clearly. The reader does not have to search through rhetorical evasiveness and excesses or ponderous prose that might hide an indecision or indecisiveness. Miller is *there* in his essays—clear, intelligent, intelligible and, again and finally, accessible to the reader.

Martin's excellent collection of the essays aside, a good deal of scholarly work remains to be done in editions of Miller's works. The future must provide an edition of his letters, work should be done with his manuscripts, and most important, of course, a complete edition of his plays should be made available. Worthy of note, however, are critical editions of his two major plays. The Viking Critical Library series and Gerald Weales have given us Arthur Miller, *Death of a Salesman: Text and Criticism*, ed. Gerald Weales (New York: Viking, 1967), and Arthur Miller, *The Crucible: Text and Criticism*, ed. Gerald Weales, (New York: Viking, 1971), both worthwhile and serviceable editions.

III. BIOGRAPHY

If Miller's prose is doubly accessible the matter of biography is less than ideal. Because he is still alive, there can be as yet no definitive (or complete for that matter) biography. What the past has provided is a mixed blessing. Since Miller's second marriage, fortunately and unfortunately, was to one of the most celebrated women in the world, much of that period of his life is illuminated and shrouded in the popular biography of Marilyn Monroe. Finally, however, that must be seen as only one part of his life.

The best introduction to Miller, and the most thorough biographical study is Benjamin Nelson, *Arthur Miller: Portrait of a Playwright*, (New York:

McKay, 1970), a comprehensive study of the work and thought of the writer, set against the context of his life. Drawing upon biographical material, the book analyzes Miller's development as a writer up to and including *The Price*. An earlier and briefer treatment is Robert Hogan, *Arthur Miller* (Minneapolis: Univ. of Minnesota Press, 1964). This University of Minnesota Pamphlets on American Writers monograph is representative of the quality of the other volumes in the series. Also of special interest is Richard I. Evans, *Psychology and Arthur Miller* (New York: Dutton, 1969), a dialogue between Dr. Evans, a psychologist, and Miller. Dennis Welland, *Arthur Miller* (New York: Grove, 1961) attempts to separate the facts from the fiction before evaluating the dramas.

Chapter One of Leonard Moss, *Arthur Miller* (New York: Twayne, 1967) provides a chronology and a brief discussion of the man, as does Harold Clurman in his "Biographical Notes," pp. vii–x of *The Portable Arthur Miller*.

Miller has also been very generous in the matter of scholarly interviews. Of the forty-eight interviews, dialogues, and symposia listed by Hayashi (Martin, ed., selects a list of thirty-two, *Theater Essays*, pp. 388–90), perhaps a half dozen are worth special note. The first of three interesting interviews of Miller by Martin is Robert A Martin, "Arthur Miller and the Meaning of Tragedy," *Modern Drama*, 13, No. 1, pp. 34–39. As well, *Educational Theatre Journal* published Robert A. Martin, "The Creative Experience of Arthur Miller: An Interview," *ETJ*, 21 (1969), 310–17. A 1974 conversation between Miller and a class of students in American Drama at the University of Michigan has been published as Robert A. Martin and Richard D. Meyer, "Arthur Miller on Plays and Playwriting," *Modern Drama*, 19 (1976) 375–84.

Perhaps the longest interview was Miller's inclusion in "The Art of the Theater" Series in *The Paris Review:* Olga Carlisle and Rose Styron, "Arthur Miller: An Interview," *The Paris Review*, No. 38 (1966), 61–98. This 1966 interview is included as well in Martin, ed., *Theater Essays*, pp. 264–93. A year later, a collection of interviews with dramatists appeared, Walter Wager, ed., *The Playwrights Speak* (New York: Delacorte Press, 1967). Wager's initial interview, "Arthur Miller," pp. 1–24, tape-recorded on November 10, 1964, is interesting and informative. In addition, Ronald Hayman, *Arthur Miller* (New York: Frederick Unger, 1972) begins with an "Interview with Arthur Miller," pp. 3–21. Finally, it is worth noting that the most recent interview, recorded February 13, 1979, is included in the volume the reader now has before him.

All in all, time must pass, and scholarship must await definitive biographical study of the life of the playwright.

IV. CRITICISM

A. General Estimates

1. BOOKS

First to be considered of the books and monographs on Miller's work is Dennis Welland, *Arthur Miller* (New York: Grove, 1961). Robert Hogan,

Arthur Miller, Pamphlets on American Writers, No. 40, (Minneapolis: Univ. of Minnesota Press, 1964), briefly views the plays up to *Incident at Vichy*, and concludes that Miller's position in twentieth-century drama is both secure and high. Sheila Huftel, *Arthur Miller: The Burning Glass* (New York: Citadel, 1965), an interesting, if not altogether especially well written, book contains chapters on *Focus* and *The Man Who Had All the Luck* in addition to the standard fare. Perhaps most interesting is the inclusion of a transcript of Miller's 1956 appearance before the 84th Congress, House Committee on Un-American Activities, pp. 31–50. Two works were published in 1967: Edward Murray, *Arthur Miller, Dramatist* (New York: Ungar, 1967) and Leonard Moss, *Arthur Miller* (New York: Twayne, 1967), which focuses on the psychological processes of the characters in Miller's best plays that underpin his role as social dramatist. Moss believes that Miller has compromised his talent by attempting to enlarge the "interior psychological question" with "codes and ideas of social and ethical importance." While indicating weaknesses, Moss concludes with an appreciation of the playwright's exceptional achievement in world drama. In 1969, Prentice-Hall issued Robert W. Corrigan, ed., *Arthur Miller: A Collection of Critical Essays* (Englewood Cliffs, N.J.: Prentice-Hall, 1969). This Twentieth Century Views volume is a good collection of ten essays. Ronald Hayman, *Arthur Miller* (New York: Ungar, 1972), with individual chapters on the plays from *All My Sons* to *The Price*, centers on Miller's social commitment and his concern to analyze in terms of process, to ask how something came to be the way it is. Hayman focuses upon what he takes to be restrictions placed on Miller by his "by-and-large traditional form."

2. ARTICLES

Alan S. Downer, "Mr. Williams and Mr. Miller," *Furioso*, 4 (1949), 66–70, correctly seeing Miller and Williams as completely dissimilar (as men and as playwrights), points out that they are alike as serious artists who gave new promise to American drama. Another coupling of the two playwrights came five years after Downer's essay: Kenneth Tynan, "American Blues: The Plays of Arthur Miller and Tennessee Williams," *Encounter*, 2, No. 5 (1954), 13–19. In this fairly early evaluation, Tynan sees Miller and Williams as a younger generation replacing the older serious American playwrights, and this early on, bestows giant stature upon Miller and concludes that the pair have produced the most powerful body of dramatic prose in modern English.

An interesting essay published a year earlier is Alvin Whitley, "Arthur Miller: An Attempt at Modern Tragedy," *Transactions of the Wisconsin Academy of Sciences, Arts and Letters*, 42 (1953), 257–62. In pursuing the feasibility of Miller's theory of tragedy, Whitley stands *All My Sons* and *Death of a Salesman* against the playwright's view of tragedy and the Aristotelian tradition. Also of interest in the decade of the 1950s is John Gassner, "Modern Drama and Society," *World Theatre*, 14, No. 4 (1955), 34–35. Gassner's article is on social drama generally, and Miller's response in the same number, pp. 40–41, is interesting.

An important essay is Henry Popkin, "Arthur Miller: The Strange Encounter," *Sewanee Review*, 68, No. 1 (1960), 34–60, reprinted in *American Drama and Its Critics: A Collection of Critical Essays*, ed. Alan S. Downer (Chicago: Univ. of Chicago Press 1965), pp. 218–39. This article posits three of Miller's plays as parables or fables, which explains why the characters "cannot be individuals." As well, Popkin sees in Miller's works a consistent and emphatic, if implicit, indictment of sex as a wicked influence, and points out that illicit sexual activity is both the root and symptom of his heroes' disorders. Popkin concludes by suggesting that *Salesman*, *Crucible*, and *View* reflect the spirit of the time in which each was written and signify changes in the quality of the radical political climate in that the plays move "steadily inward."

Richard A. Cassell, "Arthur Miller's 'Rage of Conscience,' " *Ball State Teachers College Forum*, 1, No. 2 (1960–61), 31–36, examines Miller's first four major productions and the connection between them. An excellent essay is Emile G. McAnany, "The Tragic Commitment: Some Notes on Arthur Miller," *Modern Drama*, 5, No. 1, pp. 11–20. Actually two essays, in the first part, "1949–1957: The Development of a Critic," McAnany deals with two pieces of Miller's dramatic theory and critical comment, summarizing and quoting Miller heavily. This serves as a fair introduction to the playwright's critical writings. In the second section of the article, "Pattern and Reality: Willy Loman as Tragic Hero," McAnany reads the play and Willy quite differently than most critics. Reading Willy in his role as father, McAnany clearly points to the tension between two goals which drive Willy to tragic proportions. This is a richly suggestive article. Another discussion of Miller's theory of tragedy is John Prudhoe, "Arthur Miller and the Tradition of Tragedy," *English Studies*, 43, pp. 430–39, which then proceeds to Miller's dramatic technique, a search for the means by which the dramatist can stylistically express his hero's tragedy within the conventions of Realism. Prudhoe concludes that Miller is one of the most important dramatists of our time.

Arthur Ganz has written a pair of essays, "The Silence of Arthur Miller," *Drama Survey*, 3 (1963), 224–37, and "Arthur Miller: After the Silence," *Drama Survey*, 3 (1964), 520–30, the first evaluating Miller's canon up to the silence, and the second dealing with *After the Fall*, which Ganz suggests shows the writer entering a new area. Ganz, while conceding that Miller has written meaningful plays, sees his vision as too simple and too innocent, and with *After the Fall*, he sees the dramatist beginning to encompass greater complexities, and Ganz sees the promise of work of greater distinction. Also in 1964, Harold Clurman provides "Arthur Miller: Theme and Variations," *Theatre: The Annual of the Repertory Theatre of Lincoln Center*, 1 (1964), 13–22, an essay that Clurman expanded into his "Introduction" to *The Portable Arthur Miller*.

Another go at a familiar topic is Ralph W. Willett, "The Ideas of Miller and Williams," *Theatre Annual*, 22 (1965–66), 31–40, an evaluation of similar ideas and attitudes rather than a contrast of these two "delineators of post-war American life." Still another familiar subject is treated in Alan S. Stambusky, "Arthur Miller: Aristotelian Canons in the Twentieth Century Drama," in *Modern American Drama: Essays in Criticism*, ed. William E. Taylor (De

Land, Florida: Everett/Edwards, 1968), pp. 91–115, perhaps the most complete overview of Miller in relation to Aristotle. Stambusky attributes to Miller a misreading, in part at least, of Aristotle's concept of classical tragedy and then goes on to describe how Aristotelian canons are or are not represented in Miller's plays and how Miller's theory of tragedy is or is not exemplified in his own plays. The essayist applies Aristotle's, and Miller's, standards to *All My Sons*, *Salesman*, and *Crucible*. He then examines *A View from the Bridge*, *After the Fall*, and *Vichy*, which Stambusky suggests employ the trappings of the Aristotelian canons for high tragedy and are all lesser Miller. While finding the playwright short of the exalted heights of ancient tragedy, proposing the dramatist's major weakness to be his extreme intellectualism, Stambusky still concludes that Miller has come closer to the ancient tragedy than any of his contemporaries.

Two essays with very different approaches to the author were published in 1969. Raymond H. Reno, "Arthur Miller and the Death of God," *Texas Studies In Literature and Language*, 11 (1969), 1069–87, treats the plays as disclosing twenty years of dramatic activity as taking the shape of a vast work dealing with the death of God. Reno sees Miller's plays after *Salesman* as all postlapsarian, "subsequent to the fall of God." In a world emptied of theology, there is nothing left but a kind of sociology, the doctrine of man's responsibility for man. Each, the essayist sees, must be a Christ to his brother. It is sociology which is stressed in Paul Blumberg, "Sociology and Social Literature: Work Alienation in the Plays of Arthur Miller," *American Quarterly*, 21 (1969), 291–310, which sees the dramatist as sociologist par excellence, and literature as a rich form of social documentation. The author uses Miller's drama to illustrate ideas employed by sociologists, specifically Marx's concept of work alienation. The essay examines Miller's canon in this context with particular attention to *Salesman*, *The Misfits*, and *A Memory of Two Mondays*.

Allan Lewis, "Arthur Miller—Return to the Self," *American Plays and Playwrights of the Contemporary Theatre*, rev. ed. (New York: Crown, 1970), pp. 35–52, works backward from *After the Fall*. Examining earlier works in the light of this controversial play provides a fresh critical perspective. The particular focus of Edmond Schraepen, "Arthur Miller's Constancy: A Note on Miller as a Short Story Writer," *Revue des Langues Vivantes*, 36, pp. 62–71, is on "I Don't Need You Any More" and "The Prophecy," which Schraepen proposes give us a microcosm of Miller's favorite themes and preoccupations. Ronald Hayman, "Arthur Miller: Between Sartre and Society," *Encounter*, 37 (1971), 73–79 is a version, almost verbatim, of the author's "Conclusion" to his book *Arthur Miller*. Ruby Cohn, "The Articulate Victims of Arthur Miller," in *Dialogue In American Drama* (Bloomington: Indiana Univ. Press, 1971), pp. 68–96, looks at settings and symbol, but primarily examines idiom, syntax, and cliché—Willy Loman's linguistic poverty, the mannered rhetoric of *Crucible*, the free blank verse of *Memory*, the urban prose of *View*, the abstractions and images of Quentin in *Fall*, the dialogue in *Vichy*, and the divided brotherhood in *The Price*, illuminated by the fact that one cannot distinguish the brothers by their speech. Although Miller has been said to specialize in the inarticulate, Cohn sees all his victims as articulate.

The same year provides Morris Freedman, "The Jewishness of Arthur Miller," in *American Drama in Social Context* (Carbondale: Southern Illinois Univ. Press, 1971), pp. 43–58, which, acknowledging all Miller's plays deal with some aspect of guilt, points out that four set the matter in the specific context of a family with two sons: *All My Sons, Salesman, After the Fall,* and *The Price.* Freedman suggests that we may read these four plays as a kind of Galsworthian family tetralogy, an integrated saga in which there is a thematic progression. The development from play to play, Freedman indicates, records the changing values of American middle-class family life. As well, a major thrust of this essay is examining the "striking" ethnic anonymity of these plays. Finally, unlike most critics of *After the Fall,* Freedman finds the autobiographical import of the play to be found in "the very absence of truly significant autobiographical matter" (p. 51). This position gives Freedman a fresh and interesting approach to the play.

Helen McMahon, "Arthur Miller's Common Man: The Problem of the Realistic and the Mythic," *Drama and Theatre,* 10 (1972), 128–33, places Miller's plays in the Naturalist-Symbolist style while partaking of Realism, and McMahon centers on the efforts of the playwright to supply coherence between the mythic and the realistic. Quite another tack is taken by Irving Jacobson, "The Child as Guilty Witness," *Literature and Psychology,* 24, pp. 12–23 which proposes that "I Don't Need You Any More" is essential for an under- standing of family themes in Miller's works. Essentially, the bulk of the essay examines the short story in relation to the work of theoretical psychologists. Orm Överland, in "The Action and Its Significance: Arthur Miller's Struggle with Dramatic Form," *Modern Drama,* 18, No. 1 (1975), 1–14, sticks pretty much to form (dramatic form, that is) dealing with the presence or lack of narrators and matters of realism in covering eight Miller plays. Catharine Hughes, "Arthur Miller," in *American Playwrights 1945–75* (London: Pitman Publishing, 1976), pp. 32–43, provides a mostly negative, highly superficial run through Miller's canon which concludes that his standing as one of the leading American playwrights says more about the lack of great American drama than his performance.

B. Studies of Individual Works

1. BOOKS

There are four worthwhile collections on individual works, all published within a period of five years. The first two are The Viking Critical Library editions, edited by Gerald Weales. *Death of a Salesman: Text and Criticism* (New York: Viking, 1967) contains, in addition to the text, a three-page type- script facsimile, seven reviews, eight essays on *Salesman,* five general essays, and four analogous works by other writers. *The Crucible: Text and Criticism*

(New York: Viking, 1971), again edited by Weales, contains, in addition to the text, a note on the text, twelve reviews and comments, three essays, five essays on Miller, excerpts from historical documents, two "spin-offs," and excerpts from analogous works. Another collection on the same play is John H. Ferres, ed., *Twentieth Century Interpretations of The Crucible* (Englewood Cliffs: Prentice-Hall, 1972) which contains twenty articles and reviews. As well, sixteen essays and reviews are compiled by Walter J. Meserve in *Studies in Death of a Salesman* (Columbus, Ohio: Merrill, 1972). There are other volumes on individual works, Cliffs, Barron's, Monarch and other butterflies. Any other major monographs on Miller's individual plays are, as yet, still scrambled in some typesetter's font.

2. ARTICLES

The reader interested in the contemporary theatrical response to Miller's plays may, of course, find those reviews reprinted most conveniently in the *New York Theatre Critics' Reviews* (New York: Critics' Theatre Reviews, Inc., gathered yearly). These volumes are indexed 1940–1960, 1961–1972.

There is very little other than brief mention of Miller's first New York production, though Huftel devotes a chapter to it, "The Man Who Had All the Luck," pp. 76–83.

Miller's next play has drawn a bit more attention. A suggestive brief essay is Samuel A. York's, "Joe Keller and His Sons," *Western Humanities Review*, 13 (1959), 401–07, which sees Joe Keller's dilemma as being more cruel than Antigone's because he, like Miller, lives in more complex times in which moral law has lost much of its traditional force. As well, York sees the play as a realized internal conflict within Miller. On the other hand, Richard L. Loughlin, "Tradition and Tragedy in *All My Sons*," *English Record*, 14, No. 3 (1964), 23–27, discovers biblical parallels in *All My Sons*, and though a modern play, the author sees it as traditional in theme and other respects, relating the play to characters in the Old Testament, the ancient Greek epics, and medieval morality plays.

As expected, it is *Death of a Salesman* which has consumed the most typewriter ribbon. A near dozen will serve to illustrate. An early response is Sighle Kennedy, "Who Killed the Salesman?," *Catholic World*, 171 (1950), 110–16. In addressing much the same question of responsibility for Willy's fate as Kennedy, George R. Kernodle, "The Death of the Little Man," [Carleton] *Drama Review*, 1, No. 2 (1955–56), 56–60, rejects the purely psychiatric view of life and the purely sociological, and proposes that *Salesman* strikes a balance, looks at a dream from several angles, no one of them final. The essayist finds value in the play's not giving answers. In this conclusion of a longer essay, Kernodle turns to the play as an example of the dignity and importance of "the little man." Paul N. Siegel, "Willy Loman and King Lear," *College English*, 17 (1956), 341–45, sees the play as a successful tragedy and, comparing the drama of Loman and his sons to Shakespeare's play of a father and his daughters, finds fundamental similarities. A special item relating to the play is a gathering from the notebook kept by director Kazan. See Elia Kazan, "Excerpts from Kazan's Notebooks for *Death of a Salesman* (untitled)" in Kenneth Thorpe Rowe, *A Theater in Your Head* (New York: Funk and Wagnalls, 1960), pp. 44–61. Following the direction of many of its predecessors, Stephen A. Lawrence, "The Right Dream in Miller's *Death of a Salesman*," *College English*, 25 (1964), 547–49, treats the question of responsibilities for the corruption and values in Willy. A very different item is Ellen Douglass Leyburn, "Comedy and Tragedy Transposed," *Yale Review*, 53 (1964), 553–62, which uses Willy Loman as one of several characters to demonstrate the possibilities of the proposition that the genius of comedy is the same as that of tragedy. Barkley W. Bates, "The Lost Past in *Death of a Salesman*," *Modern Drama*, 11, No. 2 (1968), 164–72 is an adequate reading of the play, suggestive in places, elementary in places. Robert B. Heilman provides an interesting comparison of the play and Eudora Welty's "The Death of a Traveling Salesman" in "Salesmen's Death: Documentary and Myth," *Shenandoah*, 20, No. 3 (1969), 20–28. The same year, Lois Gordon, "Death of a Salesman: An Appreciation," appeared in Warren French, ed., *The Forties: Fiction, Poetry, Drama* (Deland, Florida: Everett/Edwards, 1969), pp. 273–83. As the title indicates, this is an appreciation of what the volume's editor calls the last great literary event of the decade. This is an interesting essay, especially on the use of symbols—the flute music, the car, the road—in the play. B. S. Field, Jr., "Death of a Salesman," *Twentieth Century Literature*, 18, No. 1 (1972), 19–24, claims that Willy Loman has castrated himself and made moral eunuchs of his sons, and that this is a crime for which Loman's miserable life and miserable death are deserved punishments. An original approach to the play is Joel Shatzky, "The 'Reactive Image' and Miller's *Death of a Salesman*," *Players*, 48, No. 3 (1973), 104–10. The purpose of this article is to analyze and explain what the author characterizes as the "narrowness" of contemporary American drama, using *Salesman* to illustrate. Shatzky reads a third of the play as hallucinations dramatizing an "unbalanced" Willy's "psychotic state."

Alan Thompson, "Professor's Debauch," *Theatre Arts*, 35, No. 3 (1951), 25–27, raises critical questions about Miller's handling of the text of *An Enemy of the People*.

Miller's own favorite play, *The Crucible*, has received a mixed response from scholars. Philip Walker, "Arthur Miller's *The Crucible:* Tragedy or Allegory?" *Western Speech*, 20 (1956), 222–24, views the play as a dramatic allegory concerning McCarthyism, but Walker proposes that the play is not fully achieved, either as a personal tragedy or a political allegory, but as falling between two stools. The author sees both the tragic and allegorical aspects of the play as lacking sufficient development. However, David M. Bergeron, "Arthur Miller's *The Crucible* and Nathaniel Hawthorne: Some Parallels," *English Journal*, 58, No.1 (1969), 47–55, discusses the play on its own merits, with the furor over the McCarthy hearings diminished, and no longer a *pièce d'occasion* combating McCarthyism. Contrary to Walker's position, Bergeron sees the play as high tragedy and contends that it captures themes in the work of Hawthorne. This paper is concerned with parallels in setting, characters, and themes, analogues rather than influence or indebtedness. The bulk of the essay compares *Crucible* and *The Scarlet Letter*, and points similarities between Proctor and Dimmesdale. Unlike Bergeron, Catharine R. Hughes, "The Crucible," *Plays, Politics, and Polemics* (New York: Drama Book Specialists Pub., 1973), pp. 15–25, relates *The Crucible* to the McCarthyism of the time of its composition as well as the ambience of its setting. As a sidelight to the play, Chadwick Hansen, "The Metamorphosis of Tituba, or Why American Intellectuals Can't Tell An Indian Witch From A Negro," *New England Quarterly*, 47, No. 1 (1974), 3–12, an interesting essay on the character of Tituba as presented in literature and history, concludes that "we live in a racist culture, and that we are all bound by it" (p. 12). Jeanne-Marie A. Miller, "Odets, Miller and Communism," *College Language Association Journal*, 19 (1974), 484–93, provides a brief look at *The Crucible* and *Till the Day I Die* (1935) by Clifford Odets, seeing both plays as a warning to the American people. Also of interest are John and Alice Griffin, "Arthur Miller Discusses *The Crucible*," *Theatre Arts*, 37 (1953), 33–34, and George Jean Nathan's comments on the play, "Henrik Miller," *Theatre Arts*, 37 (April 1953), 24–26.

Miller's *A View from the Bridge* has still not received the quantity of scholarly attention the play deserves. Richard Findlater, "No Time for Tragedy?" *Twentieth Century*, 161, No. 959 (1957), 56–62, is a mixed reaction to the play inspired by its London production. *Theatre Arts* provides two brief pieces, the anonymous "A View from the Bridge," *Theatre Arts*, 39 (1955), 18–19, and Margaret Webster's review in "A Look at the London Season," *Theatre Arts*, 41 (May 1957), 28–29. Also of interest are Pauline Kael's comments in her review of the film version of the play in "*The Innocents*, and What Passes for Experience," *Film Quarterly*, 15, No. 4 (1962), 27–29, and Wilfrid Sheed, "A View from the Bridge," *The Morning After: Selected Essays and Reviews* (New York: Farrar, Straus, and Giroux, 1971), pp. 168–71.

During the period of nine years between *View* and *After the Fall*, Miller would be divorced, married a second time, convicted for contempt of Congress, see the conviction reversed, provide a movie screenplay for *The Misfits*, and be again divorced and remarried. For details of this period of his life, see Nelson, pp. 176–98, 226–45. Also see John Edwards, "Arthur Miller: An Appraisal," *Time and Tide*, 42 (1961), 740–41.

Miller's first play in almost nine years,, which premiered on January 23, 1964, drew a storm of critical reaction. John Gassner, "Broadway In Review," *Educational Theatre Journal*, 16 (May 1964), 174–80, makes a survey of the plays in the opening of Lincoln Center, but the center of his essay is a moderate review of *After the Fall*; really, his is a voice calling for moderation in reviewing the play. He does not condemn Miller as many theatrical critics had, and while he does not find the play wholly satisfying, he is considerate of the playwright's effort. Readers interested in *After the Fall* will want to see Richard Schechner and Theodore Hoffman, "Look, There's The American

Theatre: An Interview with Elia Kazan," *Tulane Drama Review*, 9, No. 2 (1964), 61–83. As well, Nancy and Richard Meyer supply a pair of interesting items, "Setting the Stage for Lincoln Center," *Theatre Arts*, 48, No. 1 (1964), 12–16, 69, an essay on the first production of the play, and "*After the Fall*: A View from the Director's Notebook," *Theatre: The Annual of the Repertory Theater of Lincoln Center*, 2 (1965), 43–73, which draws heavily on Kazan's notebook for the play.

Scholarly reaction to the play has been no less divided. Allen J. Koppenhaver, "*The Fall* and After: Albert Camus and Arthur Miller," *Modern Drama*, 9, No. 2, pp. 206–09 points out the similarity to Camus' *The Fall* and evaluates Miller's play as a fine humanistic study as well as a masterpiece of theatrical expression. Leonard Moss, "Biographical and Literary Allusion in *After the Fall*," *Educational Theatre Journal*, 18, No. 1 (1966), 34–40, relates the play to Miller's earlier works by examining "autoplagiarism," a form of allusion less obvious than autobiography in the drama, then moves on to investigate allusion to two other literary sources, the Bible and, like Koppenhaver, Camus' version of the Adam story, *The Fall (La Chute)*, a novel published in 1956 and translated the following year. Edward Murray, "Point of View in *After the Fall*," *College Language Association Journal*, 10 (1966), 135–42, finds the serious defect in the play not to be the autobiographical aspects but a faulty and ill-chosen point of view that renders the play's structure static and repetitious. This point of view leads Miller, Murray proposes, into oversimplification and overconceptualization. An outstanding article is C. W. E. Bigsby, "The Fall and After—Arthur Miller's Confession," *Modern Drama*, 10, No. 2 (1967), 124–36 which sees Quentin as the achieved Willy Loman who would be forced, after his success, to truly face his values. John J. Stinson, "Structure in *After the Fall*: The Relevance of the Maggie Episodes to the Main Themes and the Christian Symbolism," *Modern Drama*, 10, No. 3 (1967), 233–40, while attempting all that its title promises, examines crucifixion and Christ symbols and notes the cleft struck between literary and dramatic critics by the play. Also of interest may be the brief review of the published version of the play in *Virginia Quarterly Review*, 40, No. 3 (1964), cxii, and an Arthur Miller interview by Oriana Fallaci, "A Propos of *After the Fall*," *World Theatre*, 14 (1965), 79, 81.

An essay which couples the two 1964 plays is Leslie Epstein, "The Unhappiness of Arthur Miller," *Triquarterly*, 1 (1965), 165–73. Responding to the *succès de scandale* aspects of the play, Epstein sees *After the Fall* as best where it is most personal. The author proposes that the weakness in the play is not in memory but in Miller's understanding. The event, the essayist states, is never allowed to speak for itself. Epstein compares Quentin with Hamlet, then roundly denounces *Incident at Vichy*, accusing Miller of a failure of understanding and a lack of courage. This is a virtuoso performance by a critic. Also of select interest to the audience of *Vichy* will be Harold Clurman, "Director's Notes: *Incident at Vichy*," *Tulane Drama Review*, 9, No. 4 (1965), 77–90.

While Miller has most often been commended as a writer of social plays,

Ralph Willett, "A Note on Arthur Miller's *The Price,*" *Journal of American Studies,* 5, No. 3, pp. 307–10, sees in his major works, *Vichy* excepted, an emphasis on individual behavior in a family context. The author of the essay looks at *The Price* in this light, suggesting finally that the dramatist embraced romantic individualism. Gerald Weales, "All About Talk: Arthur Miller's *The Price,*" *Ohio Review,* 13, No. 2 (1972), 74–84, suggests that in this play, Miller is using and questioning the dramatic, social, and therapeutic uses of talk. Weales is fascinated by the way the major theme emerges in a play in which talk is both tool and subject. Finally, it should be noted that Miller's 1974 play, *The Creation of the World and Other Business,* has yet to receive major scholarly attention.

V. CONCLUSION

Before concluding, a brief word on some of the essays in this volume may be appropriate. It has been the intention of the editor to include the best possible selection of articles and reviews available. Qualitative consideration was always primary. But there were other concerns. This volume presents, for the most part and where possible given the qualitative standard, essays that had previously never been reprinted. Then, each section of the work attempts to be representative. For example, John Simon's blistering review of *After the Fall* that centers upon the autobiographical elements in the play is characteristic of much of the negative general reaction to it, allowing for Simon's special rhetorical gifts. On the other hand, Frederick Morgan's scathing one paragraph denunciation of *Death of a Salesman* and Miller is included to suggest that there was negative initial reaction to what is now considered one of America's great plays. It should be noted, however, that the New York critics were overwhelming in their praise for the play at its premiere. Brooks Atkinson's review is the most representative, while Morgan's reaction suggests, as a contrast, that the approbation was not without exception. As well, the shape of the book was dictated by an attempt to provide a special balance—that is, the major plays draw a greater proportion of the weight of the volume. Put simply, more pages are devoted to the dramas of wider interest, and the space devoted to each work in relation to the others is, hopefully, proportionate to, and representative of, the ink that has flowed evaluating each play. As well, the essays were selected in an attempt to be representative of the reaction to Miller's separate dramas, which is often a tricky matter.

In conclusion, it should be pointed out that this volume does not pretend to be comprehensive. Miller is still hard at work, on a musical and a new drama, and one must wait for complete bibliographies, editions, and a definitive biography. Perhaps only years from now will criticism and scholarship be able to see him with eyes unclouded by bias or controversy. Despite being a private man, Miller has been such a public personality that one simply cannot catalog every time he appears in the news. There are, for example, over 950 items in the present editor's working bibliography. Whenever the playwright speaks, whether it be on the theater, society, television, culture, whatever, he seems to turn up in the *New York Times* or on the *Today* show. Miller has been a controversial subject, first because of his dramatic theories, then because of his political commitment in the 1930s and its echo in the 1950s. Evaluation of three of his major works has been complicated by controversial elements. *Salesman* was seen against the controversy over Miller's theory of tragedy. *The Crucible* was seen initially in the perspective of the 1950s and McCarthyism. Perhaps, as well, too strong an emphasis by critics on biographical elements in *After the Fall* has obscured the real merit and meaning of that play. His very celebrity has often been a detriment to calm, objective evaluation of his work. However, he remains one of the most respected, and produced, of American playwrights abroad, from Sweden to Latin America.

Perhaps only a generation from now—with a completed canon, adequate editions of his plays and prose (for he is a brilliant essayist and theorist as well as dramatist), and a completed, definitive biography will American literature finally be able to evaluate the presence and power of Arthur Miller. We can make an informed guess, however, that Miller is one of the most important dramatists of this century. Only O'Neill and Williams among Americans are mentioned as peers as serious playwrights. Few would argue with Clinton Trowbridge's estimate of Arthur Miller as our most important and our most serious playwright.

Works of this sort inevitably engender great pleasures as well as significant debts. This volume afforded its editor the opportunity of meeting its subject, and this was a pleasure. I am indebted to Miller for his taking time to give, and later edit, the interview which appears here. As well, it was a pleasure to correspond with most of the writers represented here. One has to be pleased with the generosity and courtesy of Tom Porter, John Simon, and Walter Kerr, to name but a few. Many thanks to the authors and publishers represented here.

Special thanks go to Paula Reed, graduate student at the University of Minnesota, who spent a good part of a semester doing the difficult task of compiling a preliminary bibliography. John Holmes helped with last minute details and double checking. As well, thanks to colleagues and friends Dan Brislane and Boyd Litzinger, Joseph S. Tedesco for his cooperation, Brennan Fitzgerald, O.F.M., the staff of the Pattee Library of The Pennsylvania State University, and the St. Bonaventure University Council on Research. And, finally, a particular thank you to the Drs. Nagel, the best there are.

JAMES J. MARTINE

St. Bonaventure University

The Man Who Had All The Luck

The Philosophy of Work Against Chance Makes Up *The Man Who Had All The Luck*

Lewis Nichols°

There can be no doubt that as an evening in the theatre "The Man Who Had All The Luck" contains a certain amount of merit. There are some good performances and careful staging and one or two effective moments. The fact that they have not been multiplied is the new play's misfortune, for the author and director—Arthur Miller and Joseph Fields—at least have been trying to do something away from the theatre's usual stencils. But in the Forrest's current tenant they have not edited out the confusion of the script nor its somewhat jumbled philosophies, nor have they kept it from running over into the ridiculous now and then. "The Man Who Had All The Luck" can be set down as a play which tried, but which did not come off—through luck or whatever.

The discussion of "The Man Who Had All The Luck" is whether success springs from fortune or work, from divine plan about which it is useless to work, or from care. Mr. Miller takes as a central character an automobile mechanic. He wins his wife when her father, who hated him, is killed; he branches out in business when another mechanic happens along to show him how to fix a car he cannot repair. He gets a farm, he wants children and has one, he starts a mink farm and that is successful also. His friends and others all suffer disasters, and he thinks his luck presently will change, too. That it does not, Mr. Miller concludes finally, is due to the fact that all the things which seemed to be luck were only just rewards for work and care.

The confusion of the play lies in the fact that Mr. Miller has been working on all sides of his argument, setting them forth and not going on to give proof. The man who had all the luck ends by deserving his success through the care he had taken, yet his brother, who had taken much more, fails. Luck, or good work, you get your choice. Added to the fact that the play sometimes is impossible to follow is the additional one that some of its situations are corny to the extreme. Mr. Miller has written some good dialogue in spots, but he also has not been innocent of the obvious. It also is possible the author has been reading

°Reprinted from *The New York Times*, November 24, 1944. Copyright © 1944 by The New York Times Company. Reprinted by permission.

Saroyan now and again, a few of the characters and situations being of that school, with Mr. Saroyan handling them better.

Karl Swenson is the man with the luck, and for the most part plays him very well. Until the end of the drama, when the philosophies begin whirling, he is quiet and at ease; that he finally whirls, also, probably is not his fault. Herbert Berghof has the role of a refugee mechanic and friend; he is a sort of mild Jacobowsky who introduces the philosophy of American freedom—which hasn't much bearing on the play. Dudley Sadler is the brother who has spent his life trying to be a big-league baseball pitcher, Jack Sheehan is excellent as the father, Eugenia Rawls is the bride. Mr. Fields has directed the play carefully, and such minor roles as that of Lawrence Fletcher, as a baseball scout, are nicely done. For one of the scenes Frederick Fox has designed a garage, complete with automobile.

"The Man Who Had All The Luck" lacks either the final care or the luck to make it a good play. But it has tried, and that is something.

The Man Who Had
All The Luck
A Good Try,
But is Out of Luck

John Chapman[*]

"THE MAN WHO HAD ALL THE LUCK" is about a fellow who tries a lot of things and they all click, but he keeps thinking that sooner or later something will flop because it stands to reason he's got to pay up in the end. Arthur Miller, the newcomer who wrote the play has done all his paying-up right off the bat. His first offering tries a lot of things—too many by far—and most of them flop.

And now I hope Mr. Miller will go right back to work writing another piece, for he has a sense of theatre and a real if undeveloped way of making stage characters talk and act human.

There isn't much use in trying to detail what went on at the Forrest Theatre last night, for it would involve explaining about repairing a Marmon 8, about an embittered war veteran, about a goofy baseball pitcher, about the filling station business, about the hazards of raising mink and about a few other things, including the hazards of begetting a baby and delivering same.

Almost all these elements have something of interest in them—but they won't stick together and make a whole play. Mr. Miller would have been much happier today had he taken just one part of his plot—the part about the ballplayer—and made three acts of it.

For here is something true and touching—a little story about a big hunk of a kid whose father has trained him from babyhood to be a pitcher, and when the chance comes to get into the big leagues he fails because he is just a dumb lug who can throw a ball accurately. The doting father had never figured that brains as well as ball-throwing ability might be needed on the mound and had never trained his boy to think.

The role of the ballplayer is acted by another newcomer, Dudley Sadler, and Mr. Sadler is no less than splendid. Working nicely with him as the father is Jack Sheehan. But these two are only secondary characters, and all the others who appear upon the stage have a rather mixed-up time of it.

[*]Reprinted from *New York Daily News*, November 24, 1944. Copyright 1944 by the New York News Inc. Reprinted by permission.

3

Karl Swenson acts "the man who had all the luck" with all the sincerity he can muster, but things get too much for him. Herbert Berghof is similarly floored in the role of an Austrian who comes to this country seeking freedom—but here we go again with some more plot. Less plot would have made "The Man Who Had All The Luck" more play.

All My Sons

The Living and The Dead
in *All My Sons*

Arvin R. Wells°

Looked at superficially, Arthur Miller's *All My Sons* may appear to be simply a social thesis play. Such classification—a valid one if severely qualified—is suggested both by the timeliness of the story and by the presence of considerable overt social criticism. The story itself is obviously calculated to engage the so-called social conscience. Joe Keller, a small manufacturer, is forced to accept individual social responsibility and, consequently, to accept his personal guilt for having sold, on one occasion during World War II, fatally defective airplane parts to the government.

However, while this bare-bone synopsis is essentially accurate, it does, in fact, do violence to the actual complexity of the play. In his well-known essay "Tragedy and the Common Man,"[1] Miller comments,

> ... Our lack of tragedy may be partially accounted for by the turn which modern literature has taken toward the purely psychiatric, or purely sociological. ... From neither of these views can tragedy derive, simply because neither represents a balanced concept of life.

What is reflected here is Miller's own careful avoidance of the "purely" this or that. And it might similarly be said that no satisfactory understanding of Miller's *All My Sons* may be derived from a criticism which commits itself to a "purely" or even predominantly sociological or psychiatric view. The sociological view is particularly limiting in that it carries with it the temptation to approach the dramatic action from the level of broad sociocultural generalizations and, consequently, to oversimplify character and action and, stumbling among subtleties of characterization, to accuse the playwright of a confusion of values which belongs appropriately to the characters in their situations.[2]

Actually, like most of Miller's plays, *All My Sons* demands of the reader an awareness of the deviousness of human motivation, an understanding of the way in which a man's best qualities may be involved in his worst actions and cheapest ideas, and, in general, a peculiarly fine perception of cause and effect. Nowhere is it suggested that the social realities and attitudes that are bought within the critical focus of the play can be honestly considered outside of some such context of human aspirations and weaknesses as is provided by the play;

°Reprinted from *Modern Drama*, 7, No. 1 (1964), 46-51, by permission of the journal.

and nowhere is it suggested that the characters are or can be judged strictly on the basis of some simple social ethic or ideal that might be deduced from the action. The characters do not simply reflect the values and attitudes of a particular society; they use those values and attitudes in their attempt to realize themselves. And it is these characteristics that give *All My Sons*, and other Miller plays, a density of texture so much greater than that of the typical social thesis play, which seeks not only to direct but to facilitate ethical judgments upon matters of topical importance.[3]

For most of us there is no difficulty in assenting to the abstract proposition which Chris puts to his mother at the end of the play:

> You can be better! Once and for all you can know now that the whole earth comes through those fences; there's a universe outside and you're responsible to it.

And there is no problem either in giving general intellectual assent to the morality of brotherhood for which Chris speaks. There is, however, considerable difficulty in assenting to the actual situation at the end of the play, in accepting it as a simple triumph of right over wrong. For the play in its entirety makes clear that Joe Keller has committed his crimes not out of cowardice, callousness, or pure self-interest, but out of a too-exclusive regard for real though limited values, and that Chris, the idealist, is far from acting disinterestedly as he harrows his father to repentance.

Joe Keller is a successful small manufacturer, but he is also "a man whose judgment must be dredged out of experience and a peasant-like common sense." Like many uneducated, self-made men, he has no capacity for abstract considerations; whatever is not personal or at least immediate has no reality for him. He had the peasant's insular loyalty to family which excludes more generalized responsibility to society at large or to mankind in general. At the moment of decision, when his business seemed threatened, the question for him was not basically one of profit and loss; what concerned him was a conflict of responsibilities—his responsibility to his family, particularly his sons to whom the business was to be a legacy of security and joy, versus his responsibility to the unknown men, engaged in the social action of war, who might as a remote consequence suffer for his dishonesty. For such a man as Joe Keller such a conflict could scarcely exist and, given its existence, could have only one probable resolution.

When the worst imaginable consequence follows—twenty-two pilots killed in Australia—Keller is nonetheless able to presume upon his innocence as established before the law. For in his ethical insularity—an insularity stressed in the play by the hedged-in backyard setting—he is safe from any serious assault of conscience so long as he can believe that the family is the most important thing and that what is done in the name of the family has its own justification. Yet, he is not perfectly secure within his sanctuary. His apparently thick skin has its sensitive spots: in his unwillingness to oppose his wife's unhealthy refusal to accept her son Larry's death, in his protest against Ann Deever's rejection of her father, in his insistence that he does not believe in "crucifying a man," and in his insistence that Chris should use what he, the father, has earned, "with joy . . . without shame . . . with joy," he betrays a deep-seated fear. His appeal on behalf of Herb Deever (Act I) is in fact, partly a covert appeal on his own behalf, an appeal for merciful understanding called forth by the shocked realization that some considerations may override and even destroy the ties of family upon which his own security rests.

It is Chris Keller who, in reaching out for love and a life of his own, first undermines and then destroys this security altogether. Chris has brought out of the war an idealistic morality of brotherhood based on what he has seen of mutual self-sacrifice among the men whom he commanded. But he has not survived the war unwounded; he bears a still festering psychological wound, a sense of inadequacy and guilt. He has survived to enjoy the fruits of a wartime economy, and he fears that in enjoying them he becomes unworthy, condemned by his own idealism. Even his love for Ann Deever, the sweetheart of his dead brother, has seemed to him a guilty desire to take advantage of the dead to whom he somehow owes his life.

As the play opens, however, he had decided to assert himself, to claim the things in life and the position in life which he feels should rightfully be his, and as the initial step he has invited Ann to his family home. His decision brings him into immediate conflict with his mother, Kate Keller, who looks upon the possible marriage between Chris and Ann as a public confirmation of Larry's death. At first Joe Keller seems only peripherally involved in this conflict; his attempt to evade Chris's demand that Kate be forced to accept Larry's death carries only ambiguous suggestions of insecurity. However, at the end of Act II, Kate, emotionally exhausted by the fruitless effort to use George Deever's accusations as a means of driving out Ann, and opposed for the first time by the declared disbelief of both husband and son, breaks down and reveals the actual basis of her refusal: if Chris lets Larry go, then he must let his father go as well. What is revealed here is that Kate is fundamentally like her husband, only what is personal or immediate is real for her. If Larry is alive, then, in a sense, the war has no reality, and Joe's crimes do not mean anything; their consequences are merely distant echoes in an unreal world. But if Larry is dead, then the war is real, and Joe is guilty of murder, even, by an act of association, guilty of murdering his own son. Her own desperate need to reject Larry's death against all odds and upon whatever flimsy scrap of hope has been the reflex of her need to defend her relation to her husband against whatever in herself might be outraged by the truth about him. Actually, however, Kate has "an overwhelming capacity for love" and an ultimate commitment to the living which makes it possible for her to "let Larry go" and rise again to the defense of her husband at the end. It is Larry living not Larry dead that she clings to, and she does this because to admit his death would make both life and love more difficult. Moreover, as is generally true of Miller's important women, Kate's final loyalty is to her husband; to him as a living, substantial being, she, like Linda in *Death of a Salesman*, has made an irrevocable commitment in love and sympathy which no knowledge about him can destroy.

Chris, on the other hand, is incapable of any such surrender of the letter of morality in the name of love or mercy; he cannot, as his father would have him, "see it human." At the rise of the curtain in Act II, Chris is seen dragging away the remains of Larry's memorial tree. The action is clearly symbolic; Chris, because of his own needs, has determined to free the family of the shadow of self-deception and guilt cast over it by the memory of Larry, to let in the light of truth. Yet, when the light comes, he is less able to bear it than the others. Ann, in the hope of love and marriage, rejects the seeds of hatred and remorse which her brother, George, offers her, and Kate sacrifices the dead son to the living father. But Chris has too much at stake; his life must vindicate the deaths of those who died in the war, which means that he must maintain an ideal image of himself or else be overwhelmed by his own sense of guilt. Because he is closely identified with his father, his necessary sense of personal dignity and worthiness depends upon his belief in the ideal image of his father; consequently, he can only accept the father's exposure as a personal defeat.

It becomes clear in the exchange between Chris and George Deever (Act II) that Chris has suspected his father but has suppressed his suspicions because he could not face the consequences—the condemnation of the father, whom he loves, and the condemnation of himself as polluted by sharing in the illicit spoils of war. Yet, this is precisely what the exposure of Joe Keller forces upon him, and Joe's arguments in self-defense—that he had expected the defective parts to be rejected, that what he did was done for the family, that business is business and none of it is "clean"—all shatter upon the hard shell of Chris's idealism not simply because they are, in fact, evasions and irrelevant half-truths, but because they cannot satisfy Chris's conscience. Consequently, even after Larry's suicide letter has finally brought to Joe a realization of his personal responsibility, Chris must go on to insist upon a public act of penance. The father becomes, indeed, a kind of scapegoat for the son; that is, if Joe expiates his crimes through the acceptance of a just punishment, then Chris will be relieved of his own burden of paralyzing guilt. His love of his father and his complicity with his father will then no longer imply his own unworthiness. In insisting that Joe must go to prison, Chris is, in effect, asking Joe to give him back his self-respect, so that he may be free to marry Ann and assume the life which is rightfully his. But Chris's inability to accept his father "as a man" leads Joe to believe that not only have his defenses crumbled but that the whole basis of his life is gone, and he kills himself.

Because it forces upon the reader an awareness of the intricacies of human motivation and of human relationships, *All My Sons* leaves a dual impression: the action affirms the theme of the individual's responsibility to humanity, but, at the same time, it suggests that the standpoint of even so fine an ideal is not an altogether adequate one from which to evaluate human beings, and that a rigid idealism operating in the actual world of men entails suffering and waste, especially when the idealist is hagridden by his own ideals. There is no simple opposition here between those "who know" and those who "must learn," between those who possess the truth and those who have failed to grasp it, between the spiritually well and the spiritually sick.[4] Moreover, the corruption and destruction of a man like Joe Keller, who is struggling to preserve what he conceives to be a just evaluation of himself in the eyes of his son, implies, in the context of the play, a deficiency not only in Keller's character but in the social environment in which he exists. Keller's appeal to the general ethics of the business community—

> If my money's dirty there ain't a clean nickel in the United States. Who worked for nothin' in that war? . . . Did they ship a gun or a truck outa Detroit before they got their price? . . . It's dollars and cents, nickels and dimes; war and peace, it's nickels and dimes, what's clean?

—is irrelevant to his personal defense; yet, it is an indictment of that community nonetheless. For it indicates that the business community failed to provide any substantial values which might have supplemented and counter-balanced Keller's own limited, family-based ethics. From the business community came only the impulse to which Chris also responds when he feels prompted to express his love for Ann by saying, "I'm going to make a fortune for you!"

Furthermore, there is a sense in which Kate's words, "We were all struck by the same lightning," are true; the lightning was the experience of the second World War—a massive social action in which they were all, willy-nilly, involved. It was the war that made it possible for some to profit by the suffering and death of others and that created the special occasion of Joe Keller's temptation, which led in turn to his son Larry's suicide and his wife's morbid obsession. Chris Keller and George Deever brought something positive out of the war—an ideal of brotherhood and a firmer, more broadly based ethic—but George, as he appears in the play, is paying in remorse for the principles that led him to reject his father, and Chris's idealism is poisoned at the source by shame and guilt, which are also products of his war experience and which make it impossible for him to temper justice with mercy either for himself or anyone else.

Notes

1. Arthur Miller, "Tragedy and the Common Man," *Theater Arts*, XXXV (March, 1951). Often reprinted.

2. See Samuel A. York, "Joe Keller and His Sons," *Western Humanities Review*, XIII (1959), pp. 401–407.

3. Cf. W. Arthur Boggs, "*Oedipus* and *All My Sons*," *Personalist*, XLII (1961), pp. 555–60. Treating the play as if it were a "tragedy of recognition" in the classical sense, Mr. Boggs declares *All My Sons* a failure because it does not have the bold sweep, the precise emphasis, and the simple focus of *Oedipus Rex*.

4. For the development of another point of view, one which this study implicitly rejects, see William Wiegand, "Arthur Miller and the Man Who Knows," *The Western Review*, XXI (1957), pp. 85–102.

All My Sons and
the Larger Context

Barry Gross°

Arthur Miller has always maintained that his plays have not been immediately understood, that *After the Fall* was not about Marilyn Monroe and *Incident at Vichy* was not about anti-Semitism, that *A View from the Bridge* was not about longshoremen and *The Crucible* was not about McCarthyism, that *Death of a Salesman* was not about the business world and *All My Sons* was not about war-profiteering. What, then, twenty-five years later, is *All My Sons* about?

In 1947 the generation gap was not the cliché it has since become and *All My Sons* is certainly, on one level, about that. Joe Keller is almost twice his son Chris' age. He is an "uneducated man for whom there is still wonder in many commonly known things," for instance, that new books are published every week or that a man can earn "a living out of . . . old dictionaries." He is the product of a vanished America, of a time when "either you were a lawyer, or a doctor, or you worked in a shop," a time of limited possibilities for someone "put . . . out at ten" to "earn his keep," for someone who learned English in "one year of night-school" and still does not know what "roué" means or that it is French, still says "brooch" when he means "broach."

We can only guess at Joe Keller's history because the kind of play Miller had in mind would, of necessity, exclude it. *All My Sons* was to be a "jurisprudence," and, as Miller says in the introduction to *Collected Plays,*

> when a criminal is arraigned . . . it is the prosecutor's job to symbolize his behavior for the jury so that the man's entire life can be characterized in one way and not in another. The prosecutor does not mention the accused as a dog lover, a good husband and father, a sufferer from eczema, or a man with a habit of chewing tobacco on the left and not the right side of his mouth.[1]

Well and good: Miller is entitled to establish the design for his own work and to be judged according to the terms he proposes. But the jury is also entitled to hear the defense, indeed must hear it if it is to reach a fair verdict, and Joe Keller's unrevealed history is his defense. "Where do you live, where do you come from?" Chris asks him, "Don't you have a country? Don't you live in the world? What the hell are you?" The answers lie buried in Joe Keller's past.

°Reprinted from *Modern Drama*, 18, No. 1 (1975), 15–27, by permission of the journal.

Is he an immigrant? The son of an immigrant? If he had to learn English in night-school, does that mean he grew up speaking German? Yiddish? These are not irrelevant questions if Joe Keller's crime is to be understood in human, rather than aberrational, terms, and it is clearly an important part of Miller's design that Keller's crime be seen as a profoundly human one. There are logical answers to Chris' questions; that Chris cannot imagine them is both result and proof of the generation gap that inevitably separates father and son. The gap can be defined by their differing perceptions of and attitudes toward the idea and the reality of community. Joe Keller is guilty of an anti-social crime not out of intent but out of ignorance; his is a crime of omission, not of commission. For him there is no society, and there never has been one. It is not simply that Joe's "mind can see" only "as far as . . . the business" or that for Joe "the business" is "the world." Actually, he does not see as far as that and for him the world is smaller. Where does he live? He lives at home. Does he live in the world? No. Does he have a country? No. What the hell is he? Provider, breadwinner, husband and father. His world is bounded by the picket fence that encloses the suburban back yard in which the play takes place, his commitments and alle-giances do not extend beyond its boundaries. He is an engaged man, but not to man or to men, only to his family, more precisely to his sons, not all the sons of the title but the two sons he has fathered.

"In my day," Joe Keller says wistfully, "when you had a son it was an honor." What else "did [he] work for"? That is not an excuse but it is an explanation. It is not that Joe Keller cannot distinguish between right and wrong, it is that his understanding of what is right and what is wrong has been ineluctably determined by the only reality he has ever known. When he advises Ann not to hate her father he begs her to "see it human," and if we fail to see Joe Keller human then we relegate him to that dark other-world where only mon-sters dwell, safely removed from the world in which we think we live so we do not have to identify with it or admit our own compliance in it. What is right in Joe Keller's ethos—and it is an ethos—is the familial obligation, the father's duty to create something for his son. He is not proud of being a self-made man or of his material success, he is proud that he has made something for his son. There is no zealot like a convert and there is probably no more devoted parent than a neglected or an abandoned child. We know that Willy Loman was abandoned by his father when he was an infant, and that goes far to explain his passionate involvement in his sons' lives. If Joe's father turned him out at age ten, it is not surprising that his first article of faith should be "a father is a father and a son is a son." Impossible as it may be for Chris to understand or appreciate the fact, Joe was keeping that faith when he shipped out the faulty plane parts: "I did it for you, it was a chance and I took it for you. I'm sixty-one years old, when would I have another chance to make something for you? . . . For you, a business for you!" Misguided, yes; malevolent, no, no more so, in intent, than Willy Loman's suicide, Willy's refusal to die empty-handed, Willy's commit-ment to the paternal obligation as he understands it, Willy's need to express his love for his son in the only way he knows how. Joe "didn't want [the money] that way" any more than Willy wanted it the way he chose, but he had "a family" and for Joe "nothin' is bigger . . . than the family": "There's nothin' he could do that I wouldn't forgive. Because he's my son. Because I'm his father and he's my son. . . . Nothin's bigger than that. . . . I'm his father and he's my son." There is literally no other frame of reference. It is not only that "a man can't be a Jesus in this world," it is that, to Joe, Jesus is irrelevant. Jesus was never a father.

As a change of heart and a change of mind the denouement is, thus, unconvincing. Joe promises to "put a bullet in [his] head . . . if there's something bigger" than family, he reads Larry's letter, agrees that "they were . . . all [his] sons," and shoots himself. Joe Keller has not overthrown sixty years of thinking and feeling in a minute. Like Willy Loman, he goes to his death deluded, dies in the name of his delusion, dies a believer. He knows only that his sons think there is something bigger than family, that he has shamed them, one to the point of suicide, that his sons for whom he has lived consider him an animal and do not want to live in the same world with him. Joe's suicide is less a moral judgment than an act of love. In effect, Joe kills himself so that Chris need not kill himself—Chris: "What must I do?"—and because Chris tells him to—Chris: "Now you tell me what you must do." Joe commits his second anti-social crime in the name of the same love that motivated the first.

For Joe Keller there is no conflict beyond the fact that time has passed and values have, at least according to his sons, changed. The conflict in the play is Chris Keller's, not so much between him and his father, or between his generation's and his father's, but within his own generation, within himself. Chris' is the conflict between who and what he is and who and what he wants to be, or thinks he ought to be. He wants to be, or thinks he ought to be, different from his father. Watching his comrades die for each other and for him, he has become aware of "a kind of—responsibility, man to man." Upon returning from the war, he had thought "to bring that on to the earth again like some kind of monument and everyone would feel it standing there, behind him, and it would make a difference to him." He knows that if he is alive at all "to open the bankbook, to drive the new car, to see the new refrigerator," it is because "of the love a man can have for a man." Yet when Chris returns home he finds "no meaning in it here," finds that "nobody . . . changed at all."

So Chris knows things his father cannot know, and yet he remains his father's son. He will spend his life in a business that "doesn't inspire" him for more than "an hour a day," he will "grub for money all day long," if it can be "beautiful" when he comes home in the evening. The only monument he can think to build is precisely the one his father has constructed: "I want a family, I want some kids, I want to build something I can give myself to. . . . Oh, Annie, Annie, I'm going to make a fortune for you!" In this light, it is not fair for Chris to make other people feel guilty for their "compromises" or for their inability or unwillingness "to be better than it's possible to be." Chris makes no visible efforts to be better than it is possible to be, or even to be as good as it is possible to be. Sue's branding of Chris as hypocrite—"if Chris wants people to put on the hair-shirt let him take off his broadcloth"—is valid. His shame and guilt are meaningless because they do not lead to action. Society's case against Chris

Keller is stronger than its case against Joe Keller because Chris knows better. His tendency is to embroider what he obviously thinks of as an unacceptable reality—Ann: "As soon as you get to know somebody you find a distinction for them"—rather than to attempt to transform that reality into something different, something better.

Chris's self-proclaimed love for his parents is also suspect. "You're the only one I know who loves his parents," Ann exclaims, to which he replies with some self-congratulation, "I know. It went out of style, didn't it?" He thinks his father is "a great guy," he promises his mother he will "protect" them against George's attacks—but Chris' devotion to his father is based on his assumption that "the man is innocent." He could not love a guilty father, not out of moral fastidiousness but out of self-love. If, as George says, Chris has lied to himself about his father's guilt, it is more to deny what he himself is than what his father is. When Biff Loman stumbles and weeps when he discovers at age seventeen that his father is not the god he thought him, we understand that an adolescent has made a painful but inevitable discovery. When Chris Keller, who has been "a killer" in the war, does the same thing at thirty-two, we must conclude that he is responding to some private drama unwinding inside him rather than to the revelation of his father's guilt. Even his mother is surprised that it is "such a shock" to him; she "always had a feeling that in the back of his head . . . Chris almost knew." Jim insists that Chris could not have known because he "would never know how to live with a thing like that," but Jim idolizes Chris, though we never see why, and his testimony is not reliable. Chris has not allowed himself to admit what he knew because he would not know how to live with it. Chris will come back, Jim tells Kate, he will make the necessary compromise; he has gone off so he can "be alone to watch . . . the star of [his] honesty . . . go out." The star Chris has gone out to watch flicker and die is not the star of his honesty but the star of his image of himself as honest, not the fact of his innocence but the lie of his innocence which he has persisted in believing. It is not that he will compromise himself, it is that he has compromised himself, and now he can no longer deny it.

When Chris returns from his vigil he admits that he "suspected his father and . . . did nothing about it," less in the name of love of father, we suspect, than of love of self. Like his brother Larry, Chris could not imagine himself such a man's son, he would not be able to "face anybody" or himself. Joe Keller's sin, it would seem, is not so much that he profited from the war or sold faulty plane parts to the government or indirectly caused the death of twenty-one men, but that, in revealing himself to be no better "than most men," he "broke his son's heart." For Chris "thought" he was "better," that distinction he must assign those he knows: "I never saw you as a man. I saw you as my father. I can't look at you this way. I can't look at myself!" An unwittingly illuminating admission: he cannot look at his father as no better than most *because* he cannot look at himself as no better than most, he has never seen his father as a man because he has not wanted to see himself as one. In Act One Sue makes a remark about how uncomfortable it is living next door to the Holy Family and now we know what she means: as long as Joe (Jehovah?) is The Father, Chris (Christ?) is surely the son, by definition. What Chris cannot forgive Joe for is that, by his crime, the father has robbed the son of his "distinction." Chris laments that he is "like everyone else now," meaning he is "practical now" like "the cats in the alley" and "the bums who ran away when we were fighting," meaning he is not "human any more." But the converse is true: he is now and finally human *because* he must admit he is like everybody else. If "only the dead ones weren't practical" Chris has always been practical but has never admitted it. Quentin reaches the same conclusion in *After the Fall:* no one who did not die in the concentration camps, he says, can ever be innocent again. As a survivor, Chris will have to learn to live with his "practicality," which is his loss of innocence, which is his humanity.

We do not see this happen. Chris is allowed to have Miller's final words and to point the moral of the play: "It's not enough . . . to be sorry. . . . You can be better! Once and for all you can know there's a universe of people outside and you're responsible to it." Fine words, but their validity is undercut by our knowledge that Chris no more lives in that world outside than his father does, and his father has, at least, always known where he has lived. Similarly, Chris' criticism of America—"This is the land of the great big dogs, you don't love a man here, you eat him. That's the principle; the only one we live by. . . . This is a zoo, a zoo!"—is compromised by his own inability to put the great principle he presumably learned in the war into practice and his own inability to love. However narrowly his values are circumscribed by the family circle, Joe does love, Joe does live by another and better principle, one he is even willing to die for. The gunshot with which Joe ends his life casts Chris' fine words into a silent void because we know that, behind them, Chris is incapable of the commitment and love his father's suicide represents. Not only is Chris incapable of fulfilling his responsibility to the universe of people out there, he is even incapable of assuming his responsibility for the few people in here, in the enclosed back yard: his last words in the play are "Mother, I didn't mean to—." But he did, and that, too, Chris will have to learn to live with.

The Arthur Miller who wrote *All My Sons*, Miller told Josh Greenfield in a 1972 interview for the *New York Times Sunday Magazine*, thought of "writing as legislating, as though the world was to be ordered by the implications in [his] work."[2] He thought then, he says in the introduction to *Collected Plays*, of each member of his audience as "carrying about with him what he thinks is an anxiety, or a hope, or a preoccupation which is his alone and isolates him from mankind," and of the play as the antidote to that condition, as "an experience which widens his awareness of connection," which reveals "him to himself so that he may touch others by virtue of the revelation of his mutuality with them."[3] He thought all serious plays had that function, but especially *All My Sons*, in which he meant to lay "siege" to the specific "fortress of unrelatedness," in which he meant to arraign a particularly heinous anti-social crime, Joe Keller's failure to acknowledge "any viable connection with his world, his universe, or his society."[4] His ultimate goal in the play was to suggest a new order, "the right way to live so that the world is a home and not a battleground or a fog in which disembodied spirits pass each other in an endless twilight."[5]

But it is precisely in Miller's own terms, it is precisely as legislation, that *All My Sons* fails, fails where, oddly enough, *Death of a Salesman*, a far less obviously "legislative" work, succeeds. The similarities between *All My Sons* and *Death of a Salesman* are sufficiently obvious to render their elucidation unnecessary, but something should be said about the basic difference between them. *Death of a Salesman*, Miller says in the *Collected Plays* introduction, grew from "simple" but specific "images":

> From a little frame house on a street of little frame houses, which had once been loud with the noise of growing boys, and then was empty and silent and finally occupied by strangers. Strangers who could not know with what conquistadorial joy Willy and his boys once re-shingled the roof. Now it was quiet in the house, and the wrong people in the beds.
>
> It grew from images of futility—the cavernous Sunday afternoons polishing the car. Where is that car now? And the chamois cloths carefully washed and put up to dry, where are the chamois cloths?
>
> And the endless, convoluted discussions, wonderments, arguments, belittlements, encouragements, fiery resolutions, abdications, returns, partings, voyages out and voyages back, tremendous opportunities and small, squeaking denouements—and all in the kitchen now occupied by strangers who cannot hear what the walls are saying.
>
> The image of aging and so many of your friends already gone and strangers in the seats of the mighty who do not know you or your triumphs or your incredible value.
>
> The image of the son's hard, public eye upon you, no longer swept by your myth, no longer rousable from his separateness, no longer knowing you have lived for him and have wept for him.
>
> The image of ferocity when love has turned to something else and yet is there, is somewhere in the room if one could only find it.
>
> The image of people turning into strangers who only evaluate one another.
>
> Above all, the image of a need greater than hunger or sex or thirst, a need to leave a thumbprint somewhere on the world.[6]

In short, *Death of a Salesman* is dominated and conditioned by the father's point of view, and *All My Sons* is one of those plays Miller derides in "The Shadow of the Gods" as being dominated by "the viewpoint of the adolescent," one of those predictable plays "in which a young person, usually male, usually sensitive, is driven either to self-destructive revolt or impotency by the insensitivity of his parents, usually the father."[7] As such, *All My Sons* bears less of a resemblance to *Death of a Salesman* than it does to *Cat on a Hot Tin Roof*, or, rather, to Miller's reading of Williams' play:

> Essentially it is . . . seen from the viewpoint of the son. He is a lonely young man sensitized to injustice. And his is a world whose human figures partake in various ways of grossness. . . . In contrast, Brick conceives of his friendship with his dead friend as an idealistic, even gallant and valorous and somehow elevated one. . . . He clings to this image as to a banner of purity to flaunt against the world.[8]

For Brick, read Chris; for Brick's dead friend, read Chris' dead comrades-in-arms. But Miller insists that *Cat on a Hot Tin Roof* ultimately fails, not because of the adolescent viewpoint, which "is precious because it is revolutionary and insists upon justice," but because Williams fails "to open up ultimate causes," because the father should have been "forced to the wall in justification of his world" and the son should have been "forced to his wall in justification of his condemning that world," because the father should not have been portrayed as "the source of injustice" but as "its deputy," not as "the final authority" but as "the shadow of the gods."[9] As he told the *Paris Review* interviewers, Williams, in emphasizing "the mendacity of human relations. . . . bypasses the issue which the play seems . . . to raise, namely the mendacity in social relations."[10] No play that ignores social relations, Miller argues in "The Family in Modern Drama," can achieve what he considers to be the goal and justification of drama, an "ultimate relevancy to the survival of the race," because, as he insists must be "obvious to any intelligence, . . . the fate of mankind is social."[11]

It is useful to keep Miller's criticisms of *Cat on a Hot Tin Roof* in mind as we turn to a consideration of the failures of *All My Sons*. Most notable is what might be termed its failure in mode, a serious flaw in methodology: simply and baldly stated, the play is too insistently "realistic"—which is, of course, what Miller meant it to be—to accommodate Chris' fine speeches or to give any weight or resonance to their words. In the narrow and pedestrian setting of the Keller back yard they announce themselves as speeches, in this mundane place the words ring loud and hollow. Miller himself provides the best analysis of this conflict of modes in "The Family in Modern Drama," in which he argues that "the force or pressure that makes for Realism, that even requires it, is the magnetic force of the family relation within the play, and the pressure which evolves in a genuine, unforced way the unrealistic modes is the social relation within the play."[12] The realistic mode is adequate to *All My Sons* as long as the play is dominated by the family relation; it is not adequate to the social relation Miller requires the play to represent, nor does Miller attempt to express that social relation in another, less realistic mode. The problem is clearly illustrated in the case of appropriate stage speech:

> When one is speaking to one's family one uses a certain level of speech, a certain plain diction perhaps, a tone of voice, an inflection, suited to the intimacy of the occasion. But when one faces an audience . . . it seems right and proper for him to reach for the well-turned phrase, even the poetic word, the aphorism, the metaphor.[13]

Chris' speeches fall flat because they violate our sense of suitability, our sense of context. They are made at the wrong time in the wrong place to the wrong people.

What Miller might have done is suggested by his discussion of how other playwrights have handled similar problems. Ibsen solved them by bursting "out of the realistic frame" altogether when he came to write *Peer Gynt*, leaving behind not only "the living room" but "the family context" as well, to allow Peer Gynt to confront "non-familial, openly social relations and forces."[14] *All My Sons* does not burst out of the living room, or, more precisely, the back yard, and yet Miller insists that his characters confront nonfamilial, openly social relations and forces which exist only beyond it. The result is that same tension Miller feels in *The Cocktail Party*, that "sense of . . . being drawn in two opposite directions."[15] In Eliot's play, Miller argues, the tension is created by the language, or, rather, by "the natural unwillingness of our minds to give to the husband-wife relation—a family relation—the prerogatives of the poetic mode," whereas no such problem existed in Eliot's more successful *Murder in the Cathedral* which "had the unquestioned right to the poetic" because its situation was "social, the conflict of a human being with the world."[16] It is, of course, Miller's thematic and philosophic intention to draw us in two opposite directions in *All My Sons*, to dramatize the polar conflict between the familial and the social. But he fails to counter the natural unwillingness of our minds to give to the social relation the prerogatives of the prosaic mode. We grant *All My Sons* the unquestioned right to the prosaic as long as its situation is familial, but if the situation is also to be social, then Miller must extend his play to the poetic, not just in language but also in concept, as, he argues, Thornton Wilder does in *Our Town:*

> The preoccupation of the entire play is . . . the town, the society, and not primarily this particular family—and every stylistic means used is to the end that the family foreground be kept in its place, merely as a foreground for the larger context behind and around it. . . . This larger context . . . is the bridge to the poetic for this play. Cut out the town and you will cut out the poetry.[17]

Miller's preoccupation in *All My Sons* is no less social than Wilder's, but the society never becomes the larger context it is in *Our Town*. In Miller's play the foreground the Keller family occupies looms too large, so large as to obliterate any other context which might or should be behind or around it.

The absence of the larger context does not represent a failure in technique alone—it also represents, and more unaccountably, a failure in content. Miller says in the introduction to *Collected Plays* that *All My Sons* is usually criticized for lack of subtlety, for being too insistently "moral" and too aggressively "straightforward,"[18] but I want to argue that, for its stated intentions, the play is not straightforward enough. During an interesting interview with Philip Gelb, published under the title of "Morality and Modern Drama," Miller recalls "a book by Thomas Mann about Moses in which . . . he portrays Moses as being a man bedevilled by the barbaric backwardness of a stubborn people and trying to improve them and raise up their sights," the Ten Commandments being Moses' "way of putting into capsule form what probably the most sensitive parts of the society were wishing would be stated," Moses' attempt to "pinpoint . . . things that were otherwise amorphous and without form."[19] That is no less, Miller would certainly agree, the writer's presumption and his function. In *All My Sons* Miller is not guilty of presuming to teach, or even of presuming to preach, but of not doing it with sufficient force and directness, of not pinpointing with sufficient sharpness Chris' amorphous and formless sentiments. That the world should be reordered is not at issue: *how* it should is.

"Where the son stands," Miller says in "The Shadow of the Gods," "is where the world should begin,"[20] but this does not happen in *All My Sons* anymore than it does in the "adolescent" plays Miller criticizes. It is undeniably true that "the struggle for mastery—for the freedom of manhood . . . as opposed to the servility of childhood—is the struggle not only to overthrow authority but to reconstitute it anew,"[21] but by this token Chris has achieved neither mastery nor manhood by the play's end. It might be argued that it is only after the play ends that Chris is equipped to make the world begin, to reconstitute authority anew, that is, only after he learns that his brother killed himself and watches his father do the same thing. If so, that is a high price in human life—to Miller, perhaps because he is not Christian, the highest price imaginable—to rouse Chris Keller to action. And, judging from Chris' past record, one cannot be sure that these two deaths will have that effect. The deaths of his comrades presented him with that opportunity before the play began and he has done nothing to reconstitute authority in their name. If we are to take Chris' stated sentiments about the men who died so that he might live seriously, then he is in the position at the beginning of *All My Sons* that Miller (in the *Sunday Times Magazine* article "Our Guilt for the World's Evil") sees the Jewish psychiatrist in at the end of *Incident at Vichy*: his is "the guilt of surviving his benefactors" and whether he is "a 'good' man for accepting his life in this way, or a 'bad' one, will depend on what he makes of his guilt, of his having survived."[22] By that criterion, Chris Keller is a bad man when *All My Sons* begins and he is no better when the play ends.

Am I arraigning Miller unfairly? Am I asking more of his play than it need do or is supposed to do? Is not Miller entitled to exclude Chris Keller's vision of the future as well as Joe Keller's past in order to pinpoint the particular crime Joe is being prosecuted for? I think not. Our full awareness of that crime and our willingness to convict him of it is based on our belief that a better world is not only preferable but possible, that it not only should be made but could be made. Joe Keller's failure to find a connection with the world is a crime only if there is a world to connect with and only if there is a way to connect with it. Chris' case would be strengthened if, for instance, he expressed himself in the terms in which Miller defines the meaningful rebellions of the sixties generation in "The War Between Young and Old":

> When a man has spent the best years of his life punishing himself with work he hates, telling himself that in his sacrifice lie honor and decency, it is infuriating to confront young people who think it is stupid to waste a life doing hateful work. It is maddening to hear that work ought to be a pleasure, a creative thing rather than a punishment, and that there is no virtue in submission to the waste of one's precious life.[23]

These are, essentially, the terms, if not the immediate causes, of Biff Loman's rebellion. But Chris Keller does not have or propound a theory of work different from his father's: he will waste his precious life doing hateful work as long as he can have it beautiful in the evening when he comes home to wife and kids. As Miller admits in the introduction to *Collected Plays*, Chris does not "propose to liquidate the business built in part on soldiers' blood; he will run it himself, but cleanly."[24] Perhaps; the only line in the play that allows for even this modest hope is Joe's remark that Chris gets upset about a two-cent overcharge.

Chris should not be at such a loss to know how to reconstitute authority anew. If, as he complains, nothing changed at home, and if, as he says, it is a moral imperative for those who have survived to return home to change things, he should know what kind of changes should be made and how they might be accomplished. Chris is, after all, a contemporary of Miller's: he grew up in the depression thirties, he is a member of the generation Miller describes in "The Bored and the Violent," a generation "contemptuous of the given order" which translated its contempt into social action—"joining demonstrations of the un-employed, pouring onto campuses to scream of some injustice by college ad-ministrations, and adopting to one degree or another a Socialist ideology."[25] It might be argued that the post-war forties was a different time altogether, that the Socialist ideology was not as attractive as it had been in the thirties. But Miller is his own best argument against such contentions: he certainly did not hesitate to involve himself in causes and programs which promised to alleviate social injustice. As he told the House Committee on Un-American Activities, he was not "a dupe" or "a child" but "an adult . . . looking for the world that would be perfect,"[26] an honorable and, to Miller's way of thinking, necessary search. As a child of the thirties he knew where to look—to that "old illusion" Miller pays tribute to in *In Russia*

> which the great October Revolution raised before the world—that a government of and by the insulted and injured had finally risen on the earth, a society which had somehow abolished the motivations for immorality, the incarnation at long last of the human community.[27]

Miller translated the Russian idea into American terms in his radio play *That They May Win*, a modest playlet which achieves in fifteen minutes the larger context two hours of *All My Sons* fails to approximate and which suggests the direction *All My Sons* might have—and should have—taken. A soldier returns from the war to find his wife and child living in a slum and prices out of control. Like Chris, he was a killer in the war, he is "proud" that he "killed twenty-eight of the lowest dogs in the world," but unlike Chris he has learned from his experience: he has learned the efficacy of united action, and he is appalled by his wife's apparent apathy toward and helplessness before unfair conditions:

> What's the matter with you? They knock you down; they walk all over you; you get up, brush yourself off and say it's workin' out great. What do you pay taxes for; what do you vote for? . . . What do you do, just go around and let them take the money out of your pocket? Doesn't anybody say anything? What're they all, dumb? . . . Write to Congress . . . stand on the street corner . . . go to the Mayor . . . talk!

True, we are still in the back yard, the living room, the kitchen. But Miller even tackles and even solves that problem in this play, a contrived borrowing from Pirandello, but a solution nevertheless: a member of the audience begins to argue with the actors, others argue with him, and finally one man emerges as spokesman and makes the speech that the actors conceded would have ended the "play" had they been allowed to continue, a speech much more acceptable coming from him than if "husband" had made it to "wife":

> You got to *keep* fighting. The people can work it out. . . . You don't seem to realize the power we got. . . . Enough people together can do anything! . . . Don't it stand to reason in a democracy? The big guys have organized to lobby for laws *they* want in

Washington. What about the people waking up and doing the same thing? . . . We the people gotta go into politics. . . . You have to go to those Senators and Congressmen you elected and say, "Listen here, Mister! We're your boss and you have to work for us!"

Idealistic, to be sure, maybe even an illusion. But an ideal and an illusion worthy of and necessary to anyone—Chris or Miller—who believes in the even older ideal, the even greater illusion, that the world can be saved and that the individual can do something about saving it.

Notes

1. "Introduction," *Arthur Miller's Collected Plays*, New York, 1957, p. 6.

2. Josh Greenfield, "Writing Plays is Absolutely Senseless, Arthur Miller Says, 'But I Love It. I Just Love It,'" *New York Times Magazine*, February 13, 1972, p. 38.

3. *Collected Plays*, p. 11.

4. Ibid., p. 19.

5. Ibid., p. 32.

6. Ibid., p. 29.

7. Arthur Miller, "The Shadow of the Gods," *American Playwrights on Drama*, ed. Horst Frenz, New York, 1965, p. 144.

8. Ibid., p. 148.

9. Ibid., p. 150.

10. *Writers at Work, Third Series*, ed. George Plimpton, New York, 1969, p. 207.

11. Arthur Miller, "The Family in Modern Drama," *Modern Drama: Essays in Criticism*, ed. Travis Bogard and William I. Oliver, New York, 1965, p. 230.

12. Ibid., p. 221.

13. Ibid., p. 225.

14. Ibid., pp. 221-222.

15. Ibid., p. 226.

16. Ibid., P. 226.

17. Ibid., pp. 227-228.

18. *Collected Plays*, p. 22.

19. Arthur Miller, as interviewed by Philip Gelb, "Morality and Modern Drama," *Educational Theatre Journal*, 10, October 1958, p. 191.

20. "The Shadow of the Gods," p. 151.

21. Ibid., p. 151.

22. Arthur Miller, "Our Guilt for the World's Evil," *New York Times Magazine*, January 3, 1965, p. 11.

23. Arthur Miller, "The War between Young and Old," *McCalls*, July 1970, p. 12.

24. *Collected Plays*, p. 37.

25. Arthur Miller, "The Bored and the Violent," *Harpers*, November 1962, p. 52.

26. *Thirty years of Treason*, ed. Eric Bentley, New York, 1971, p. 824.

27. Arthur Miller, "In Russia," *Harpers*, September 1969, p. 45.

Death Of A Salesman

Death of a Salesman, A New Drama by Arthur Miller, Has Premiere at the Morosco

Brooks Atkinson°

Arthur Miller has written a superb drama. From every point of view "Death of a Salesman," which was acted at the Morosco last evening, is rich and memorable drama. It is so simple in style and so inevitable in theme that it scarcely seems like a thing that has been written and acted. For Mr. Miller has looked with compassion into the hearts of some ordinary Americans and quietly transferred their hope and anguish to the theatre. Under Elia Kazan's masterly direction, Lee J. Cobb gives a heroic performance, and every member of the cast plays like a person inspired.

Two seasons ago Mr. Miller's "All My Sons" looked like the work of an honest and able playwright. In comparison with the new drama, that seems like a contrived play now. For "Death of a Salesman" has the flow and spontaneity of a suburban epic that may not be intended as poetry but becomes poetry in spite of itself because Mr. Miller has drawn it out of so many intangible sources.

It is the story of an aging salesman who has reached the end of his usefulness on the road. There has always been something unsubstantial about his work. But suddenly the unsubstantial aspects of it overwhelm him completely. When he was young, he looked dashing; he enjoyed the comradeship of other people—the humor, the kidding, the business.

In his early sixties he knows his business as well as he ever did. But the unsubstantial things have become decisive; the spring has gone from his step, the smile from his face and the heartiness from his personality. He is through. The phantom of his life has caught up with him. As literally as Mr. Miller can say it, dust returns to dust. Suddenly there is nothing.

This is only a little of what Mr. Miller is saying. For he conveys this elusive tragedy in terms of simple things—the loyalty and understanding of his wife, the careless selfishness of his two sons, the sympathetic devotion of a neighbor, the coldness of his former boss' son—the bills, the car, the tinkering around the house. And most of all: the illusions by which he has lived—opportunities

21

missed, wrong formulas for success, fatal misconceptions about his place in the scheme of things.

Writing like a man who understands people, Mr. Miller has no moral precepts to offer and no solutions of the salesman's problems. He is full of pity, but he brings no piety to it. Chronicler of one frowsy corner of the American scene, he evokes a wraithlike tragedy out of it that spins through the many scenes of his play and gradually envelops the audience.

As theatre, "Death of a Salesman" is no less original than it is as literature. Jo Mielziner, always equal to an occasion, has designed a skeletonized set that captures the mood of the play and serves the actors brilliantly. Although Mr. Miller's text may be diffuse in form, Mr. Kazan has pulled it together into a deeply moving performance.

Mr. Cobb's tragic portrait of the defeated salesman is acting of the first rank. Although it is familiar and folksy in the details, it has something of the grand manner in the big size and the deep tone. Mildred Dunnock gives the performance of her career as the wife and mother—plain of speech but indomitable in spirit. The parts of the thoughtless sons are extremely well played by Arthur Kennedy and Cameron Mitchell, who are all youth, brag and bewilderment.

Other parts are well played by Howard Smith, Thomas Chalmers, Don Keefer, Alan Hewitt and Tom Pedi. If there were time, this report would gratefully include all the actors and fabricators of illusion. For they all realize that for once in their lives they are participating in a rare event in the theatre. Mr. Miller's elegy of a Brooklyn sidestreet is superb.

Review of
Death of a Salesman

Frederick Morgan*

Arthur Miller's *Death of a Salesman* has received, this year, most of the prizes, plaudits and acclamations that inevitably attend the doings on Broadway. It is, not surprisingly, a miserable affair; and it would be unfair to single it out here from among the many Broadway productions which are completely devoid of merit, were it not for just this excessive publicity which it has received. The action outlines the mental and moral collapse, leading to suicide, of an aging traveling salesman, who comes to realize that he had based his life on false ideals. Miller had the makings of some sort of play; but he was unfortunately unable to bring a single spark of dramatic intelligence to bear on his material. The terms in which he conceived of his theme are so trite and clumsy as to invalidate the entire play and render offensive its continual demand for the sympathy and indulgence of the audience. It proceeds, with unrelieved vulgarity, from cliche to stereotype. The language is entirely undistinguished (the personages are continually grunting, groaning and vehemently repeating the tritest colloquialisms); the tone of the play can best be described as a sustained snivel. With Tennessee Williams, one can at least maintain that he was "cut out to be" a playwright rather than a poet. But one would be justified in suspecting that the author of *Death of a Salesman* would have attained the same level of untalented and conscientious dullness if he had decided to write an epic poem or a novel instead of a play. On the basis of certain of his newspaper articles I presume that Miller considers his new play to be the Tragedy of a Common Man. It is not a tragedy; nor is it, rightly speaking, about any man, common or uncommon. It is, however, pure Broadway, Broadway in a self-pitying mood; and this no doubt accounts for its success, and for the esteem in which it is held by the newspaper reviewers.

*Reprinted from "Notes on the Theatre," by Frederick Morgan, *The Hudson Review*, 2 (1949), 272–73. Copyright © 1949 by The Hudson Review, Inc. Reprinted by permission.

Acres of Diamonds:
Death of a Salesman

Thomas E. Porter°

The most salient quality of Arthur Miller's tragedy of the common man *Death of a Salesman* is its Americanism. This quality in the play is demonstrated by the contrasting reactions of American and English reviewers. The English took the hero at face value and found little of interest in his person or his plight:

> There is almost nothing to be said for Loman who lies to himself as to others, has no creed or philosophy of life beyond that of making money by making buddies, and cannot even be faithful to his helpful and long-suffering wife.[1]

Brooks Atkinson, on the other hand, thought Willy "a good man who represents the homely, decent, kindly virtues of a middle-class society."[2] The Englishman treats Willy without regard for his American context, the New York reviewer sees him as the representative of a large segment of American society. When the literary critics measure the play against Greek and Elizabethan drama, they agree with the English evaluation; the hero seems inadequate. His lack of stature, his narrow view of reality, his obvious character defects diminish the scope of action and the possibilities of universal application.[3] Against a large historical perspective and without the American context, the salesman is a "small man" who fails to cope with his environment. But for better or worse, Miller's hero is not simply an individual who has determined on an objective and who strives desperately to attain it; he is also representative of an American type, the Salesman, who has accepted an ideal shaped for him and pressed on him by forces in his culture. This ideal is the matrix from which Willy emerges and by which his destiny is determined. It is peculiarly American in origin and development—seed, flower and fruit. For Arthur Miller's salesman is a personification of the success myth; he is committed to its objectives and defined by its characteristics. *Salesman* deals with the Horatio Alger ideal, the rags-to-riches romance of the American dream.

The success myth is not concealed beneath the facade of the action; it is used consciously by the playwright in depicting the plot-situation, in drawing

°Reprinted from Thomas E. Porter, *Myth and Modern American Drama* (Detroit: Wayne State Univ. Press, 1969), pp. 127–52, by permission of the Wayne State University Press and the author. Copyright © 1969 by Wayne State University Press.

24

the hero, in arranging the events of the action. Thoughtful American reviewers and critics got the point:

> Success is a requirement Americans make of life. Because it seems magical, and inexplicable, as it is to Willy, it can be considered the due of every free citizen, even those with no notable or measurable talents. . . . The citizen may justly and perhaps even logically ask—if Edison, Goodrich, and Red Grange can make it, why not me, why not Willy Loman?[4]

Willy's quest for the secret of success is central to the drama. By choosing this focus for his play, Miller is drawing on the popular mind and a popular formula from which he shapes his dramatic form.

The attitudes which the myth expresses have a long history in American culture. The success myth, as Max Weber has demonstrated, has roots in seventeenth-century bourgeois England; it came to this continent with the founding fathers and was later popularized by the efforts of Ben Franklin, its outstanding exemplar. The "land of opportunity" offered enough verification of the basic tenets of the doctrine to assure its triumph in the popular mind. Virgin land, undeveloped resources, the possibility of industrial progress, all allowed scope for enterprise and imagination. No man lacked an enterprise to turn his hand to. The successful man became the idol of the public; the road to success was pointed out from the pulpit, in the marketplace, by the family fireside. From Franklin through the nineteenth century and well into the twentieth, the success myth, and all the possible variations on it, did not lack prophets and interpreters.

The success ideology developed a basic outline in the early Colonial period and its essential shape has not changed appreciably since. The Franklin image of the hard-working, early-rising, self-disciplined, ambitious adventurer engaged the public imagination in 1758 when *Poor Richard* included Father Abraham Weatherwise's monologue on "The Way to Wealth."[5] The proverbs from the 1758 *Poor Richard* passed into the texture of the American language: "Early to bed . . . Never leave till tomorrow that which you can do today." Emerson's doctrine of self-reliance fitted neatly into this pattern; the great lecturer subscribed to the theory that the thirst for wealth and the drive to power were essential to the growth of civilization.[6] . . . It suffices to recall that material success was taken to be the tangible sign of God's blessing and the reward of virtue.

In the latter half of the nineteenth century the alliance between religion and business took a curious turn. Business no longer received the benediction of religion, rather religion was described in terms of business. The servant became the master in that strange cultural reversal that has been described by Will Herberg. "Organized" religion passed into the hands of the corporation; the culture began to control the religious concepts. Clergymen found no disparity between the acquisition of riches and Christianity; indeed, they were delighted to find they went hand in hand. Russell H. Conwell, a Baptist preacher and the founder of Temple University in Philadelphia, traveled over the country, preaching this gospel. His celebrated lecture *Acres of Diamonds* was delivered in large cities and at whistle-stops 5,124 times between 1870 and 1915. The central illustration in *Acres* is the story of the Arab who journeyed the world over in search of diamonds, while his successor on the farm found acres of diamonds in his own backyard. The industrious, the honest, the determined man can mine diamonds at home, in the city, wherever he is; this is Conwell's message.

> The men and women sitting here, who found it difficult perhaps to buy a ticket to this lecture or gathering to-night, have within their reach "acres of diamonds," opportunities to get largely wealthy. Never in the history of the world did a poor man without capital have such an opportunity to get rich quickly and honestly as he has now in our city.[7]

Conwell is content to show that religion and business are not opposed, that religion encourages men to get rich. Ten years later Bruce Barton reduced this kind of argument to an absurdity in his life of Jesus, *The Man Nobody Knows*. The Savior, Barton proclaimed, is an epitome of success, the greatest corporate leader and the most successful advertising man the world has ever seen. He is a man of great personal magnetism, possessed of all the qualities that mark the successful executive. The wheel comes full circle when Jesus becomes a Nazarene Carnegie, and Christianity is defined in terms of United States Steel.

Today, the author whose name is most closely linked with the dream of success is Horatio Alger, another clergyman, who embodied the myth in his novels. Alger caught the quintessence of the dream and developed a formula in which to express it. The ragged urchin, bootblack or newspaper boy of humble origin capitalizes on his opportunities and, by "pluck and luck," rises to the top of the economic heap. Alger made this formula an American byword.

> Like many simple formulations which nevertheless convey a heavy intellectual and emotional charge to vast numbers of people, the Alger hero represents a triumphant combination—and reduction to the lowest common demoninator—of the most widely accepted concepts in nineteenth-century American society. The belief in the potential greatness of the common man, the glorification of individual effort and accomplishment, the equation of the pursuit of money with the pursuit of happiness and of business success with spiritual grace: simply to mention these concepts is to comprehend the brilliance of Alger's synthesis.[8]

Alger converted the attitude that canonized the successful businessman into a popular literary formula, the rags-to riches romance. His heroes, often with a boost from Fortune in their background (Tom the bootblack is really the disinherited son of a successful businessman), rise to the top by seizing opportunity by the forelock, by being industrious, thrifty, devout (but not pious), commonsensical. They are likeable chaps with a ready quip and a vigorous sense of humor. They have little trouble getting employment and, once in the shop, there is no stopping them. "Ragged Dick" and "Tom the Bootblack" have that aura around them; success is natural to personalities of their stripe. In Alger as for preachers like Conwell, the key to success is not genius or gentle breeding, but "character."

At best, successful methods were merely by-products of successful character. The businessman who had the right personal qualities would have little difficulty in developing the necessary managerial skills, but the possession of no amount of skill could compensate for lack of character or other essential personal traits.[9]

All success literature, of which Alger's was the fictional apotheosis, assumed that the individual could pull himself up by his bootstraps. "The Creator made man a success-machine . . . and failure is as abnormal to him as discord to harmony."[10] The Alger hero had character; luck and pluck brought him inevitably from rags to riches.

Between 1868 and 1929 Alger's books sold ten million copies, and the people who did not read the books could hardly have been able to escape the aura of the name. With the boom of the 1920s authors like Babson and Marsden and Bruce Barton kept the success doctrine before the eyes of the public. Whether they advocated success as the reward of virtue or as the result of strength or as the consequent of personality, their position was essentially the same. The secret lies inside the individual character. The emphasis can shift from one personal quality to another, but there is never any doubt where the quality is found. Moreover, if Christianity can be defined by business concepts, "virtue" can easily be reduced to "personality." The "miracles" of Jesus, according to Barton, reside in his personal magnetism. Thus, before the god Opportunity, all are equal. Those mysterious internal qualities of character—"virtue," "personality,"—become the charismatic gifts that are prayed for by the true believer and, when found, are acknowledged as the work of the Spirit. This myth, deep-seated in the American consciousness, provides the raw material for *Death of a Salesman.*

The success myth, in the hands of the playwright, becomes the model for the events of the plot, the situation and the character of the hero, but Miller uses this model in order to subvert it. His play is an anti-myth, the rags-to-riches formula in reverse so that it becomes the story of a failure in terms of success, or better, the story of the failure of the success myth. The events of the play are a mirror-image of the hero's progress. Willy Loman's history begins at the end of the line; instead of the young, determined bootblack an exhausted salesman enters, carrying, along with his sample cases, sixty years of uphill struggle. The subsequent events show him failing to overcome each obstacle, just as he has failed to achieve the phantom success he has pursued his life long. He returns from a trip without making a single sale, he braces the boss for a New York job and a salary raise (like the Alger hero) and is fired for his pains; his "boys," now well out of boyhood, make the big play for high stakes according to their father's teaching and fail. Willy finishes by facing the harsh fact that his whole life has been a lie. The triumphal ascent of the Alger hero is reversed in every particular. The rags-to-riches dream never materializes, and the salesman never escapes his rags. The race with the junkyard finds Willy an also-ran. In the collapse of the salesman, Miller attempts to illustrate the collapse of the myth.

Death of a Salesman encompasses two dimensions—the dream-world of the success myth with its merging of past triumphs, indications of glory to come, glimmering possibilities and the actual world of the small, brick-enclosed house in Brooklyn. To achieve this merger, Miller uses an èxpressionistic setting, a skeletonized house which symbolizes the encroachment of urban economics on the family. The "one-dimensional" roof is surrounded on all sides by a "solid vault of apartment houses." The walls of the Loman home are cut away to permit free passage to the personae in dream and reminiscence sequences. This device, along with changes in lighting, allows for a condensation of time so that the life of the family can be encompassed by the action. "An air of the dream clings to the place, a dream rising out of reality."[11] The expressionistic technique—the use of typical personae, a symbolic setting, mobility in time— follows on the mythic focus of the playwright's vision. Miller himself is conscious of the possibilities of this technique and its significance; he defines expressionism: "The stage is stripped of knickknacks; instead it reveals symbolic *designs* which function as overt pointers toward the moral to be drawn from the action."[12] The freedom which this technique supplies allows the playwright to express the salesman's dream and his experiences in the context of the dream. The flashbacks in the course of the action can be considered hallucinatory, and the salesman can be played as mentally unbalanced, but such an interpretation takes actuality as the norm and loses sight of the mythical dimension.[13] Any attempt to decide which elements of the play are "real" and which "unreal" is as futile as trying to sort out the "historical" elements in any myth. The mythical attitude and Willy's experiences form one texture; they are the warp and woof of the salesman's world.

The typical characteristics of the Willy Loman persona establish him in the tradition of the mythical hero, or in *Salesman,* in the tradition of the anti-hero. The name is descriptive; Willy is "low man" on the economic and social totem-pole. Linda, his wife, who sees him clearly and sympathetically, calls him "a small man." He is a white-collar worker who works on salary and/or commission for a company, his economic future at the mercy of his employer. He does not show any marked intellectual capacity or training, and his wisdom, expressed in platitudes, is garnered from common-sense authorities. When he is away from home, his moral life functions according to the "traveling salesman" tradition, not excluding the clandestine affair or the blue joke. He does not, however, consider himself dissolute; according to his lights, he is honest enough. For better or worse, the salesman is intended to represent the average lower-middle-class American.

The antecedents of the salesman are also typical. For a man who resides in Brooklyn, the family background which Miller gives his hero stretches the imagination. In a sequence with Ben, Willy remembers his father, a man with a big beard who played the flute. His father, too, was a traveling salesman:

> Ben. Father was a very great and very wild-hearted man. We would start in Boston, and he'd toss the whole family into the wagon and then he'd drive the team right across the country; through Ohio and Indiana, Michigan, Illinois and all the Western states. And we'd stop in the towns and sell the flutes that he'd made on the

way. Great inventor, Father. With one gadget he made more than a man like you could make in a lifetime. (SALESMAN, p. 49.)

The father disappeared one day when Willy was a baby, following the Yukon gold-strike. He lived many years in Alaska, and Willy had a yearning to join him there. (SALESMAN, p. 85.) This is the stock from which Willy and his boys are sprung, American stock with a penchant for traveling and selling. This background fits an idealized model rather than any plausible or realistic family-tree.[14] As typical character, the salesman has a typical background; he envisions his origin in terms of the American experience. It is one version of the idealized experience of the race.

Willy's status in society, his family background are typical; even more of a type is Willy's identity as Salesman. He is a product of a producer-consumer society in which the go-between is a pivotal figure. Society has labeled him, and Willy has accepted the label; society has offered Willy a set of values and an objective, and Willy has committed himself to those values and that objective. In so accepting, Willy becomes THE Salesman. He cannot define himself in any other terms. So he insists in his debate with Charley that "he has a job," that he is the "New England man," even after he has been fired. His adherence to the cult of personality, of being "well liked," is a reflection of his identity; before he can sell anything and if he can sell nothing else, he must sell himself, his own personality. He has been shaped by a society that believed steadily and op-timistically in the myth of success, and he has become the agent and the representative of that society.

This image of the Salesman includes the image of an older, freer America. Before the frontier closed down and the apartments closed in, before business became an impersonal, corporate endeavor, opportunity knocked incessantly. For Willy (and for the audience), the achievement possible in this earlier society is typified by Uncle Ben, the shadowy figure who appears out of no-where, to the accompaniment of flute music, on his way to new capitalistic triumphs. Whether Ben is a projection of Willy's imagination or a real figure out of the family history is irrelevant; his function in the action does not depend on his "reality." He comes from an idealized past; he is the robber baron, the captain of industry. Ben carries with him the aura of success, and when he visits, it is only for a few minutes between expeditions. There are diamond mines in Africa, timberlands in Alaska, and mysterious appointments in Ketchikan which demand his attention. Ben's methods are illustrated in a sparring match with Biff. He is physically strong—Biff can hit him in the stomach with im-punity. He is ruthless—the sparring ends abruptly when Ben suddenly trips the boy and poises the point of his umbrella over Biff's eye. "Never fight fair with a stranger, boy. You'll never get out of the jungle that way." (SALESMAN, p. 49.) This is the code of the self-made man.

Ben possesses the precious secret to success. It is summarized in his ritual chant, the formula which sums up his accomplishment: "When I was seventeen I walked into the jungle and when I was twenty-one I walked out. And by God I was rich." (SALESMAN, p. 48.) What happened in the jungle is never explained. It is the mystery of success, the Eleusinian rite known only to initiates. Uncle Ben is the older version of the Salesman, the ruthless capitalist whose adventurous strength ripped riches from the frontier. To Willy, Uncle Ben is the palpable proof of his doctrine.

While the shadowy figure of Ben establishes the general truth that any man can succeed, Willy does not accept (or perhaps has no chance to accept) Ben's method. Ben represents the robber baron who travels out to unknown frontiers and ruthlessly carves out an empire. As Ben's method has faded with the passing of the empire builders and with the advent of the big corporations, Willy decides to rely on personality:

> It's not what you do, Ben. It's who you know and the smile on your face! It's contacts, Ben, contacts! The whole wealth of Alaska passes over the lunch table at the Commodore Hotel, and that's the wonder, the wonder of this country, that a man can end with diamonds here on the basis of being well-liked. (SALESMAN, p. 86.)

This quality cannot be held in the hand like Ben's timber, but on the other hand, Ben's own formula—his inner strength and ruthlessness—is also mysterious. Willy accepts the Dale Carnegie approach to success; winning friends and influencing people become his pick and shovel to dig diamonds as industriously as Ben ever did. But Willy does not go off to Africa or Alaska, nor is his confidence in a transcendentally virtuous life. His faith in personality conceals the secret in an imponderable and makes that faith untestable by any pragmatic standard. The dream of success, in the eyes of the playwright, is the more destructive because, though indemonstrable, it has a myth-like capacity for inspiring a transcendent belief.

There are, however, certain tangible signs which characterize the personality likely to succeed. Willy discovers them in his sons. The boys are physically strong, well-built, attractive. Biff is a football hero, the captain of the high school team; Happy, if not gifted with Biff's athletic ability, has a pleasant personality and basks in Biff's reflected glory. Against this picture of the glowing athlete and the hail fellow, Bernard, the neighbor's boy, wears glasses, studies hard, and is not well liked. If physical prowess and a moderate anti-intellectualism seemed to have little to do with success, the propagators of the success ideology saw an intimate connection:

> Statistics show that executives are physically stronger and larger of stature than their subordinates. For example, college presidents, as a class, are taller and heavier than the college professors. Bank presidents are physically stronger than the clerks. Railway presidents are larger and physically stronger than the employees . . . Physical welfare is the second qualification for winning the race of making good.[15]

Biff does not have to work hard at his studies; books are not necessary for advancement. Bernard, whose scholastic efforts are the object of mild derision, supplies Biff with answers and this is only right, the homage due the personable and popular. When, in spite of Bernard's help, Biff fails in math, Willy blames the teacher. Willy shows a typical ambivalence toward education. On the one hand, attendance at college confers prestige, especially when coupled with an athletic career; on the other, education does not really make an appreciable difference in the struggle to succeed. Some self-help advocates maintained that college was actually harmful to a young man's chances. It undermined those rugged personal qualities demanded by a career by an overemphasis on the development of the mind, it fostered an interest in impractical humanistic matters, it devoured the best years of a man's life.[16] The salesman finds in his sons those qualities which point toward success. As high-school boys, they are leaders, popular with the crowd, athletic and handsome. Their present status as philandering clerk and wandering farmhand cannot erase the glory of their past potential as Willy experienced it. "A star like that, magnificent, can never really fade away." (SALESMAN, p. 68).

Willy's commitment to the success ideology directed the education of his sons. Even if success passes him by, he can still look forward to a vindication of his life in them. They have been instructed in the cliches of both the "virtue" and the "personality" school. Industry is important: whatever else can be said about Biff, he is a "hard worker." One of Willy's fondest reminiscences is the high sheen the boys kept on the red Chevvy. If Biff "gets tired" hanging around, he can paint a new ceiling in the living room. Willy's aphorisms emphasize the importance of industry and perseverance: "Never leave a job till you're finished." "The world is an oyster, but you don't crack it open on a mattress." But personality has its privileges and Willy can wink at the boys' faults in the name of personality. Biff has been a thief from his high-school days; he steals a football from the locker-room and lumber from a local construction job. Willy laughs at both thefts because they reveal the power of personality and a fearless competitiveness like Ben's. "Coach will probably congratulate you on your initiative . . . That's because he likes you. If somebody else took the ball there'd be an uproar." (SALESMAN, p. 30.) When Charley warns Willy that the watchman will catch the boys at their thieving, Willy avers that, though he gave them hell, the boys are "a couple of fearless characters." When Charley responds that the jails are full of fearless characters, Ben adds that the Stock Exchange is also. The boys have been brought up to respect the success ideology; their success will be the salesman's vindication.

In the chronological present of the play Willy's fortunes are at low ebb. His faith in the myth is tested by harsh realities which he alternately faces and flees. He fights to hold on to his identity. This means holding on to his faith, and, in the name of faith, Willy lies constantly: about the gross sales he has made, about the reaction of businessmen to his personality, about his boys' success and importance, about his own prospects. These lies echo, not the drab reality about him, but the shining hope he has. From the observer's point of view established in the play through Charley and Linda, they are pathetic efforts to protect his identity. Willy is unfaithful to his long-suffering wife, but this infidelity is an assuagement of his loneliness on the road, a restorative to his flagging spirits, and a provision against the rebuffs of the day. When he momentarily faces reality—his inability to drive to Boston, the mounting bills and the dwindling income—he has to flee to the past and to project the future. The salesman cannot abandon the myth without reducing himself to zero. Thus he must hope.

Perpetual optimism, then, is not so much a piece of transparent self-deception as it is a necessary quality of his personality. It can be associated with the kind of wishful hoping that underlies the entire American business operation, an indefatigable spirit of the-impossible-takes-a-little-longer.

> Basically this optimism represents no precise philosophical position at all, but rather a studiously cultivated sense of euphoria. It is an emotional attitude marked by a tendency to emphasize the brighter side of things. . . . It is an effusive and expansive attitude. In the business world one of its typical manifestations is the conviction that there is no assignable limit to business opportunities, that markets need not remain static but are constantly open to further development, even with territory geographically limited. It is somewhat beside the point to ask if Americans believe in this optimism. It is not a thing you believe in. It is in the air. It is felt. It has its effect, whether you elect to believe in it or not.[17]

Miller has not left this optimism hanging in the air; he weaves it into his hero's personality. Happy's diagnosis is accurate: "Dad is never so happy as when he's looking forward to something!" (SALESMAN, p. 105.) When Willy is lost, disturbed, hanging on the ropes, he demands that this hope be fed: "The gist of it is I haven't got a story [*read:* 'lie'] left in my head, Biff. So don't give me a lecture about facts and aspects. I am not interested. Now what've you got to say?" (SALESMAN, p. 107.) Willy must have hope because it sustains him; when identity is at stake, there are matters more important than facts and aspects.

The plot structure of *Salesman* dramatizes the failure of the myth by depicting the past and present failures of the salesman. Events in the chronological present are germinations of seeds sown in the past; both present and past are inextricably bound together in Willy's consciousness:

> *Linda.* And Willy—if it's warm Sunday we'll drive in the country. And we'll open the windshield and take lunch.
> *Willy.* No, the windshields don't open on the new cars.
> *Linda.* But you opened it today.
> *Willy.* Me? I didn't. (He stops.) Now isn't that peculiar! Isn't that a remarkable—(He breaks off in amazement and fright as the flute is heard distantly.) . . . I was thinking of the Chevvy. (Slight pause.) Nineteen twenty-eight . . . when I had that red Chevvy—(Breaks off.) That funny? I coulda sworn I was driving that Chevvy today. (SALESMAN, p. 19.)

Miller builds up a sense of fate in his drama by showing the impingement of the unalterable past upon the present. Willy's whole life has been shaped by his commitment to the success ideology, his dream based on the Alger myth; his present plight is shown to be the inevitable consequence of this commitment.

> What is perhaps less frequently stressed is the bearing of the past-present relationship on the metaphysical content of tragedy. It is probably true to say that the greater proportion of the 'past' that is allowed to impinge upon, or to modify, the present, the easier it is to give the impression of a rigid or semi-rigid structure enclosing the action, and the larger the apparent content of determinism.[18]

Just as the hero's commitment comes to him as a heritage of the American past, so his sorry situation at sixty comes of his early life. Except for the deceptive expanse of time, there is no real difference in the salesman's life then and now.

The events of the first act—past and present—contrapose optimism and harsh reality. In the chronological present Willy is a tired drummer and his boys are mediocre also-rans, a clerk and a farmhand, both over thirty. Biff and Happy are lost and confused by their failure to get ahead, and Willy is at the end of his rope because he can't even drive a car any more. Willy's return home after the abortive trip is contrasted with his return in the "good old days." Then he came home to the security of his boys' adulation, bringing with him the glamor of the traveler and his own ebullient interpretation of the trip. He is proud of his boys and their potential sustains him.

> *Willy*. Bernard can get the best marks in school, y'understand, but when he gets out in the business world, y'understand, you are going to be five times ahead of him. That's why I thank Almighty God you're both built like Adonises. Because the man who makes an appearance in the business world, the man who creates personal interest, is the man who gets ahead. Be liked and you will never want. (SALESMAN, p. 33.)

Willy "knocked 'em cold in Providence, slaughtered 'em in Boston." The patois of the rugged sportsman, of the prize ring, flavors Willy's speech and plants the image of the ideal career in his sons. It is reflected in the chronological present by Happy's wildly impractical scheme to recoup the Loman fortune. On the basis of the idea, they lay "big plans":

> *Happy*. Wait a minute! I got an idea. I got a feasible idea. Come here, Biff, let's talk this over now, let's talk some sense here. . . . You and I, Biff—we have a line, the Loman line. We train a couple of weeks, and put on a couple of exhibitions, see? . . . We play each other. It's a million dollars' worth of publicity. Two brothers, see? The Loman Brothers. Displays in the Royal Palms—all the hotels. And banners over the ring and the basketball court: "Loman Brothers." Baby, we could sell sporting goods!
> *Willy*. That is a one-million-dollar idea! (SALESMAN, p. 63.)

This scheme is generated out of the heart of the myth. "Loman Brothers" has, for Willy and the boys, the ring of personality and solidarity and achievement. It would not entail entering the impersonal arena of the office; the "boys" would be "out playin' ball again." With no regular hours to cramp their freedom and no fierce outside competition, there would be "the old honor and comradeship." Sportsmanship, clean living, economic freedom would blend in a million-dollar enterprise, the ideal life crowned with financial achievement. Only the glowing pair who ran to carry their father's valises and to listen to his prideful predictions would consider such a scheme "talking sense." It is significant that Happy makes the proposal; he is Willy's double without Willy's excuse, a liar and a philanderer. The flashback sequence explains the optimism the "big plan" generates.

Willy's reminiscences also cast another shadow over the present prospect. His version of the sales trip to young Biff and Hap is contrasted with the version he gives Linda. Bills have piled up and if business "don't pick up I don't know what I'm gonna do!" Willy confesses to his wife that people laugh at him, that he is not noticed, that he talks too much and laughs too loudly so that people don't respect him. (SALESMAN, pp. 36–37.) On the road, alone and assailed with doubts, without his wife and his sons to bolster his ego, he turns to the Woman. She picked Willy out, she likes him, he makes her laugh. Willy's problems are no different in the present, except that the financial crisis looms larger and the philandering has passed over to Happy. But in the first act all difficulties, past and present, are smoothed over by a pervading optimism.

Under the spell of the dream, Biff determines to see Bill Oliver, a former employer, and ask for financial backing. Family legend has refined his theft of basketballs from the firm out of existence and converted his position from shipping clerk into salesman. This prospect raises Willy's hopes; the dream can convert the possibility into triumphant actuality. "I see great things for you kids, I think your troubles are over." Given this incentive, the salesman determines to ask for a place in New York for himself, for an office job that would take him off the road. Personality yet may carry the day.

At the outset of the second act the hopes of the evening carry over to the following morning. The boys have departed "nice and early"; "early to rise" and "the early bird" are good omens. As he considers the actual burdens of the moment, however, Willy's spirits begin to slide. His description of the consumer's fate has a symbolic reference to his own life.

> Whoever heard of a Hastings refrigerator? Once in my life I would like to own something outright before it's broken! I'm always in a race with the junkyard! I just finished paying for the car and it's on its last legs. The refrigerator consumes belts like a goddam maniac. They time those things. They time them so when you've finally paid for them, they're used up. (SALESMAN, p. 73.)

Earlier, it was made clear that Willy bought this brand because the company displayed the largest ads and, from the day of installation, the box chewed up belts. The battle of the Hastings (with Willy on the Anglo-Saxon side) was lost from the start. This discussion is a forecast of Willy's fate in the coming interview. The morning hope is somewhat revived when Linda gives him something to look forward to: the boys are going to "blow him to a big dinner." In anticipation of a victory celebration, the salesman goes off to his job-interview with renewed confidence.

The interview incidents are central to the movement of the second act. They contrast with the typical interview of the Alger formula. For the Alger hero, this is the first rung on the ladder of success. The young bootblack or newsboy immediately engages the prospective employer's attention and impresses him with his intelligence, sensible adjustment to circumstances, industry, self-confidence, and honesty. Willy and Biff fail to impress on all points. Willy's employer, some years the salesman's junior—"I named him Howard"—has not the time to listen to Willy's reminiscences. He is preoccupied with industry's newest gadget, a wire recorder. The impersonal business world no longer has any room for personality among the machines. In a reversal of the Alger formula, the salesman's rambling convinces Howard that the company has no more use for him. He has outlived his limited usefulness, and the upshot is that Willy is summarily fired. Biff's interview is even more disastrous. He cannot even get inside the office, and far from demonstrating his honesty, he steals Oliver's fountain pen for no reason he can fathom. In terms of structure, the interview episodes, one witnessed and the other reported, are dramatizations of the failure of the myth as Willy understood it and preached it to his sons.

Their respective experiences produce different reactions in father and son. It is the pressure of past experience that is invoked to explain the difference. Willy cannot understand his defeat even when Charley, the good neighbor, spells it out for him:

> When're you gonna realize that them things don't mean anything? You named him Howard, but you can't sell that. The only thing you got in this world is what you can sell. And the funny thing is that you're a salesman, and you don't know that. (SALESMAN, p. 97.)

At this late date, there is no chance that the salesman will be able to distinguish the marketable from the mythical. Moreover, he still preserves the hope of Biff's success and the prospect of the big dinner. To a man a little less the salesman than Willy, his chance meeting with Bernard, Charley's son and the high-school follower, would raise a rash of doubts. But Willy can only, in desperation, ask Bernard, who is off to try a case before the Supreme Court, about the secret of success. The lawyer does not volunteer any advice except not to worry about it. "Sometimes, Willy, it's better for a man just to walk away." (SALESMAN, p. 95.) Willy cannot walk away; he affirms his faith in his sons.

The meeting in the restaurant is an ironic reversal of the "victory" banquet. Biff's experience, as he relates it to Happy, has convinced him that his whole life has been "a ridiculous lie." He is determined to get the facts out in the open, but habit is not so easily broken. The salesman refuses to listen to "facts and aspects"; he will have a celebration of the glorious future. When it becomes clear that Biff will not cooperate in the lie and that Willy cannot face the truth, the Loman boys react according to the pattern. They run away from the failure their father has become and from their own failure. They leave the old man babbling in the rest room and go off with two prostitutes. Happy is responding to his training when he denies his father before one of the floozies:

> *Letta.* Don't you want to tell your father—
> *Happy.* No, that's not my father. He's just a guy. Come on, we'll catch Biff, and,
> honey, we're going to paint this town. (SALESMAN, pp. 115–16.)

Happy cannot hear the cock crow; this unhappy wandering old man is not *his* father. Willy's own teaching and example flow back on his own head.

Bracketed within the restaurant sequence are two crucial past events, also the fruit of teaching and example. Biff's failure with Oliver is related to his

failure in math and his flight to Boston. Relying on personality, Biff had mim-
icked the effeminate instructor to his face and had cut the class for football
practice. In spite of Bernard's help on the exam, he lacked four points of
passing, and the instructor refuses to make a concession. When the boy runs to
seek his father's help, he finds the Woman in Willy's hotel room. His idol
crumbles; his father is "a phoney little fake." The traveling-salesman joke
becomes a traumatic experience for the boy, driving his disillusion deep and
preparing him for his present insight. Biff sees the affair as a betrayal of Linda,
the family and the home. The image of the husband and father is broken when
Willy gives the Woman "Mama's Stockings." But Willy does not understand
Biff's reaction; what he does on the road has no connection with his home-life.
Thus all he feels is the weight of his son's disapproval. Biff has ruined his life
"for spite." Willy's firing, Biff's panic at Oliver's, are linked with Biff's high-
school failure and Willy's inability to cope with his boy's disillusion in the
Boston hotel room.

The climactic scene in the second act is the confrontation of father and son.
Because he suspects the truth, Willy is unwilling to face Biff or Linda. But this
time Biff is not to be put off: "The man don't know who we are! The man is
gonna know! (To Willy) We never told the truth for ten minutes in this house."
Willy is no longer Salesman, no longer Father; Willy is "the man." The identity
supplied by economic and familial society is stripped away and the issue is
joined at rock bottom.

> I am not a leader of men, Willy, and neither are you. You were never anything but a
> hard-working drummer who landed in the ash can like all the rest of them. I'm one
> dollar an hour, Willy! . . . Do you gather my meaning? I'm not bringing home any
> prizes any more, and you're going to stop waiting for me to bring them home.
> (SALESMAN, p. 132.)

But facts fall before faith and the salesman cannot admit such heresy. Willy
knows who he is: "I am not a dime a dozen. I am Willy Loman, and you are Biff
Loman." He simply cannot comprehend and, when Biff breaks down and sobs
on his father's shoulder, Biff's emotional rapport destroys his point. There is the
sudden revelation that Biff likes him; this the salesman can understand. The
removal of Biff's disapproval rekindles the salesman's optimism—"that boy—
that boy is going to be magnificent." In spite of all the explanations and because
of the sudden emotional reunion, the myth endures. Whatever his failures on
the road and in the office, Willy turns out to be "well-liked" by his alienated
son.

With this realization and the resurgence of the myth, Brother Ben reap-
pears. Ben's advice is now *ad hoc* and in the tradition of *Acres of Diamonds*: "It
does take a great kind of man to crack the jungle . . . . The jungle is dark but full
of diamonds . . . . One must go in to fetch a diamond out." (SALESMAN, pp.
133–134.) Ben's promise is the promise of all the self-help prophets of the
nineteenth century. The salesman wanted to find his success in Brooklyn. Ben
offers him his chance. There are "acres of diamonds" in his backyard. To

achieve that success which thus far eluded him, Willy drives his car into the wall. In terms of the myth, his motivation is no different now than it was when he drove off to New England. His boy likes him and deserves the twenty thousand insurance money, the capital which will finally put him on the road to success. The success ideology is stronger than the reality, and he goes to his death with his goal sparkling before him.

The "success" structure in the play, as the critic immediately recognizes, is not the whole *Salesman* story. As the English critic sees Willy as a detestable little man, the American sees him as a pathetic figure who suffers deeply. The pathetic quality is produced by the playwright's emphasis on the culture that shaped the salesman's personality.[19] The pressures of economic growth in urban society created the salesman mystique and these same forces punish the unsuccessful inexorably. The 1929 crash impressed Miller greatly:

> The hidden laws of fate lurked not only in the characters of people, but equally if not more imperiously in the world beyond the family parlor. Out there were the big gods, the ones whose disfavor could turn a proud and prosperous and dignified man into a frightened shell of a man whatever he thought of himself, and whatever he decided or didn't decide to do.[20]

These powers were economic crisis and political imperatives at whose mercy man found himself. The myth holds them at bay, overcomes them, puts the successful man out of their reach. As anti-hero, the salesman (and his family) is at their mercy. Time-installment buying, the enclosure of the house by apartments, the impersonal attitude of the executive illustrate these external forces. If these "hidden gods" decide to doom a generation, they can grind exceeding small. When the stock market crashed, once safe and happy millionaires left by the window. The common man does not control such a phenomenon, and the success myth does not take such catastrophes into account. Willy's faith in the myth leaves him vulnerable to the big gods.[21] No version of the success myth really equips anyone to deal with these forces.

One solution to coping with this impersonal culture is a concomitant impersonality in dealing with it. Miller dramatizes this reaction in his depiction of the good neighbors, Charley and Bernard. Charley is a successful businessman in a minor way; Bernard, the bespectacled tag-along, is a successful lawyer. Out of the goodness of his heart, Charley supports Willy and Linda by "loaning" the salesman fifty dollars a week. He drops by to play cards with Willy and generally tolerates his blustering irritability. He offers Willy a steady job. He is the lone unrelated mourner at the funeral. Out of the salesman's own mouth, the bitter truth is that Charley is the only friend he has. The good neighbor has no theory about success, no magic formula but unconcern: "My salvation is that I never took any interest in anything." (SALESMAN, p. 96.) He never preached at his son or exhibited any interest in success or money. Without preaching, Charles goes about doing good. It is not clear where all the virtue this good neighbor displays springs from. He is the good Samaritan for whose conduct no explanation need be given. More significantly, though Charley makes no concessions to the cult of success in his actions or his manner, he knows the rules: "The only thing you got in this world is what you can sell."

Bernard is the opposite number to Biff and Happy. He, too, is a good neighbor. Though his boyhood relations with the Lomans kept him a subordinate, he holds no grudge, is still sincerely interested in Biff and respectful with Willy. Bernard has followed his father's example, if not his counsel.

> *Bernard.* Goodby, Willy, and don't worry about it. You know, "If at first you don't succeed . . . ."
> *Willy.* Yes, I believe in that.
> *Bernard.* But sometimes, Willy, it's better for a man just to walk away. (SALESMAN, p. 95.)

The successful lawyer has no other word for Willy, except perhaps a footnote to the success formula; he points out that Biff never prepared himself for anything. Charley and Bernard really have no alternate faith to offer Willy. They show a distrust of the big gods and treat them gingerly. Otherwise, they are good people who sympathize with the Lomans' plight, who understand their aspirations without emulating them, who put friendship above the law. They bear witness to the vacuity of success worship, but provide no faith with which to replace it.

This is not to say that Miller suggests no alternative. On the one hand, he suggests a family solidarity centering around the wife and mother; on the other hand, he tentatively offers a retreat from the competitive business world to an agrarian, manual-labor society. Linda is the heart of the family. She is wise, warm, sympathetic. She knows her husband's faults and her sons' characters. For all her frank appraisals, she loves them. She is contrasted with the promiscuous sex symbolized by the Woman and the prostitutes. They operate in the world outside as part of the impersonal forces that corrupt. Happy equates his promiscuity with taking manufacturers' bribes, and Willy's Boston woman can "put him right through to the buyers." Linda holds the family together—she keeps the accounts, encourages her husband, tries to protect him from heartbreak. She becomes the personification of Family, that social unity in which the individual has a real identity.

> The concepts of Father and Mother and so on were received by us unawares before the time we were conscious of ourselves as selves. In contrast, the concepts of Friend, Teacher, Employee, Boss, Colleague, Supervisor, and the many other social relations come to us long after we have gained consciousness of ourselves, and are therefore outside ourselves. They are thus in an objective rather than a subjective category. In any case what we feel is always more "real" to us than what we know, and we feel the family relationship while we only know the social one.[22]

If Willy is not totally unsympathetic (and he is not), much of the goodness in him is demonstrated in his devotion to his wife, according to his lights. Though he is often masterful and curt, he is still deeply concerned about her: "I was fired, and I'm looking for a little good news to tell your mother, because the woman has waited and the woman has suffered." (SALESMAN, p. 125.) Biff is attached to his mother, and Happy's hopelessness is most graphic in his failure to be honest with, or concerned about, his family. The family's devotion to one another, even though misguided, represents a recognizable American ideal.

Linda, for all her warmth and goodness, goes along with her husband and sons in the best success-manual tradition. She tries to protect them from the forces outside and fails. The memory of her suffering and her fidelity does not keep Willy and Happy from sex or Biff from wandering. Miller's irony goes still deeper. While Linda is a mirror of goodness and the source of the family's sense of identity, she is no protection—by her silence and her support, she unwittingly cooperates with the destructive myth. Linda follows the rules laid down by the self-help advocates. She is a good home manager, she understands and encourages her husband, she keeps her house neat and is a good mother. Babson recommends a good wife as a major factor in working toward success: "A good wife and well-kept house and some healthy children are of the utmost importance in enabling one to develop the six 'I's' of success and to live the normal, wholesome, upright life."[23] Linda stays in her place, never questioning out loud her husband's objectives and doing her part to help him achieve them.

As another possible alternative to the success myth, Miller proposes a return to a non-competitive occupation in an agrarian or trade-oriented society. In the context of *Death of a Salesman* he makes this offer, not explicitly as a universal panacea, but in terms of the Lomans' problem. The good days of hope and promise in the play are connected with a warm sun and clusters of trees in the neighborhood, fresh air and gardening. The reminiscence sequences are marked by this scenic change: "The apartment houses are fading out and the entire house and surroundings become covered with leaves." (SALESMAN, p. 27.) The neighborhood once bloomed with lilac, wisteria, peonies and daffodils, but now it is "bricks and windows, windows and bricks," and overpopulation. Willy is a talented workman; he has practically rebuilt the house: "All the cement, the lumber, the reconstruction I put in this house! There ain't a crack to be found in it any more." (SALESMAN, p. 74.) Biff, who understands this strength in his father, has actually escaped to the West. His ambition to succeed conflicts with the satisfaction he finds on the farm:

> This farm I work on, it's spring there now, see? And they've got about fifteen new colts. There's nothing more inspiring or—beautiful than the sight of a mare and a new colt. And it's cool there now, see? Texas is cool now and it's spring. (SALESMAN, p. 22.)

Biff suspects that perhaps the Lomans have been miscast in their salesman role:

> They've laughed at Dad for years, and you know why? Because we don't belong in this nuthouse of a city! We should be mixing cement on some open plain, or—or carpenters. A carpenter is allowed to whistle! (SALESMAN, p. 61.)

So when Biff comes to realize who he is, his insight flashes out of the contrast between the office and the open sky. The things he loves in the world are "the work and the food and time to sit and smoke." And his obituary for his father is a memorial to the good days when Willy was working on the house: "There's more of him in that front stoop than in all the sales he ever made." (SALES-MAN, p. 138.) Charley agrees that Willy was "a happy man with a bunch of cement." In a freer, older society, the doomed salesman might have been a happy man.

The pathos of this situation—the square peg in a round hole—is drama-tized in the garden scene. After the ordeal in the office and the restaurant, Willy feels the impulse to plant as an imperative; "I've got to get some seeds, right away . . . . I don't have a thing in the ground." (SALESMAN, p. 122.) He then begins to plant his garden in the barren patch beside the house by flashlight. All the contradictions in the salesman's life come into focus. His instinct to plant, to put something that will grow in the ground, is ineffectual—he must work by artificial light, surrounded by apartment houses, in the hard-packed dirt. The seeds will not grow; Willy, who was going to mine diamonds in Brooklyn, reverts to hoeing and planting, but the urbanization of his world has already defeated him. As he plants, he talks "business" with Ben. His suicide will bring twenty thousand "on the barrelhead." This insurance money is the diamond he sees shining in the dark. (SALESMAN, p. 126.) All the forces that conspired to make—and break—Willy Loman are gathered here. His instinct to produce from the earth, the happy farmer he might have been, is frustrated by the society that has boxed him in. The dream of diamonds and his idealization of Ben have "rung up a zero"; the only way he can make his life pay off is by self-destruction.

Taken at the level of parable, the play presents the failure of the success myth by destroying the Horatio Alger image of the Rags-to-riches triumph of the common man. This view of the play considers Willy as Salesman, Linda as Family, Ben as Success, and the moral of the play is the fall of the Golden Calf.[24] But Miller has not written a morality plan in *Salesman,* nor does he make the mistake of preaching. The audience says, "That's the way middle-class America lives and thinks"; it also says: "I know a man just like that." The Willy Lomans who see the play do not recognize themselves and respond to Willy's collapse with the now legendary remark: "That New England territory was no damned good!" Wrapped in the trappings of instruction is the deep personal anguish of a contemporary American that audiences can recognize.

Willy the Salesman represents all those Americans caught in the mesh of the myth and the moral pressures it generates. As a type, he is a product of social and economic forces outside himself. But in his struggle with those forces, Willy is also a suffering human being. He battles to retain his faith, is shaken by doubts about his ability to live according to his belief, humiliates himself to discover the secret that lies at its heart. His blind commitment to his ideal is whole-hearted, and if Willy the Salesman is necessarily destroyed by that commit-ment, the audience feels that Willy the person is worth saving.

Thus, when he goes to his death without knowing why he has lived or why he is dying, he fulfills the destiny of the type, but as an individual who has suffered, he remains unfulfilled. The Salesman can neither suffer nor be converted (he would then cease to be Salesman), but the family man—the husband and father and friend—does suffer and, by virtue of it, can change. If Willy were only an abstract set of stereotyped characteristics, a figure in a Morality play, there would be little sympathy for his plight. In the "Requiem" epilogue, the various aspects of Willy's character come in for comment. Biff's epitaph considers what Willy might have been, the happy carpenter, the outdoorsman. Charley, on the other hand, reads the apologia for the Salesman:

> Nobody dast blame this man. You don't understand: Willy was a salesman. And for the salesman, there is no rock bottom to life. He don't put a bolt to a nut, he don't tell you the law or give you medicine. He's a man way out there in the blue, riding on a smile and a shoeshine. And when they start not smiling back—that's an earthquake. And then you get yourself a couple of spots on your hat, and you're finished. Nobody dast blame this man. A salesman is got to dream, boy. It comes with the territory. (SALESMAN, p. 138.)

This speech defends Willy in the context of myth and moral, but as a justification of his uncomprehending self-destruction, it fails to consider the individual who suffered through his life and rang up a zero at the end. Linda, the long-suffering, says the last word for the husband and the father:

> Willy, dear, I can't cry, Why did you do it? I search and I search and I search, and I can't understand it, Willy. I made the last payment on the house today. Today, dear. And there'll be nobody home .... We're free and clear .... We're free. (SALESMAN, p. 139.)

Linda cannot understand the mystery as Willy could not understand it. Suffering and sacrifice, for the family, have led to the "freedom" of an empty house and the grave.

Miller, who set out to write the tragedy of the common man, is finally trapped both by the myth he is denouncing and by the dramatic form he has chosen. The salesman's version of the success myth—the cult of personality—is shown to be a tissue of false values that lead only to frustration. Miller dramatizes the problem of guilt and the reality of Willy's suffering because of his values, but, try as he may, he can neither bring Willy to an insight by which he understands his failure nor find a societal strategy that can absolve him of it. The traditional tragic pattern of action demands an epiphany, a purgation and a renewal that does not cancel the suffering of the protagonist, but that does make sense of it. Miller recognizes this demand of the form and struggles to fulfill it; in the end the myth defeats him.

At the level of dianoia, the conscious treatment of values, Miller tries to find a replacement for the success myth and fails:

> This confusion [about "true" and "false" values] is abetted by the greater clarity of the rejected values which are embodied in the dream of success. The false dream is fully and vividly sketched; positive values seem rather dim and conventional.[25]

The false values, tightly woven into Willy's personality, are clearly destructive. But when Biff, the man who "knows who he is," advocates a return to the farm, it becomes clear how meager are the resources of the culture for coping with Willy's problem. The return to a pre-Alger agrarian way of life is an example of nostalgia for the garden; turning back the clock is no solution for a million city-dwelling Willy Lomans who left the farm to seek their fortunes. Charley's detachment from the myth does not supply a positive answer either. For Charley, whether he cares about it or not, *is* a success; he owns his small business and supports Willy. If the successful must protect the failures, then Willy's values are not altogether false, and the common man who cannot get along with the myth cannot get along without it either.

Society cannot absolve Willy; it can only understand and sympathize. Understanding and sympathy are not enough; Willy still goes to his "freedom" in the grave uncomprehending. At the level of dramatic action, there is no epiphany in which suffering leads to insight, that moment of revelation when the hero sees himself and his situation clearly, understands what he has lost, and finds the path to regeneration. Willy has suffered, but, because he is the Salesman, his suffering does not bring him to understanding. Miller recognizes this difficulty also and tries to circumvent it by promoting Biff to hero, by giving him the insight of which Willy was incapable. Nonetheless, it is Willy's fate that concerns us. He must go to his death hapless and deluded, but his end leaves the play without that final stage which the conventional tragic structure demands. Like the detective-hero, the salesman cannot acknowledge his mistake without also destroying his identity.

In *Death of a Salesman* Miller taps a popular formula for the structure of his drama. Although the Dale Carnegie approach, the cult of personality, is on the wane in the present generation, the drive for success is very much alive. Willy's plight, grounded in the excesses of a previous generation but fostered by attitudes still shared by the present generation, draws from the audience both recognition of the illusion and sympathy for the visionary. Willy's suffering is real and deep. America cannot accept the success myth—"Horatio Alger" is now a term of derision—but there is no real substitute for it. Because Miller has built his play around an American dream, he strikes deep into the consciousness of the audience. The contemporary American, because he cannot solve the dilemma either, becomes involved in the sufferings of Willy the person as he watches the death of Willy the Salesman.

Notes

1. Ivor Brown, "As London Sees Willy Loman," New York *Times* (August 28, 1949), Book Section, p. 59.

2. "Death of a Salesman," New York *Times* (February 11, 1949), p. 27.

3. See Sewall, *The Vision of Tragedy*, pp. 130, 167; H. J. Mueller, *The Spirit of Tragedy* (New York, 1956), pp. 316–17; T. R. Henn, *The Harvest of Tragedy* (London, 1956), p. 268.

4. Henry Popkin, "The Strange Encounter," *Sewanee Review*, LXVIII (Winter, 1960), 53.

5. The enormous success of this tract and its perennial appeal are attested by its frequent republication. In 1826 Simon Ide republished the essay along with Franklin's "Advice to Young Tradesman." Much later, in 1921, Roger Babson's *Making Good in Business* reiterated the major points of Franklin's essay as part of Babson's advice to the success-seeker.

6. Ralph Waldo Emerson, *The Conduct of Life* (Boston, 1904), p. 95.

7. *Acres of Diamonds* (New York, 1915), p. 18.

8. Kenneth S. Lynn, *The Dream of Success* (Boston, 1955), pp. 6–7.

9. Irwin G. Wyllie, *The Self-Made Man in America* (New Brunswick, N.J., 1954), p. 27.

10. Orison Marsden, *Entering Business* (New York, 1903), p. 27.

11. Arthur Miller, *Death of a Salesman* (New York, 1949), p. 11. Subsequent references to this edition are marked SALESMAN.

12. Arthur Miller, "The Family in Modern Drama," *Atlantic Monthly*, CXCVII (April, 1956), 37.

13. See John Gassner, *Form and Idea in Modern Theatre* (New York, 1956), p. 13.

14. There have been attempts to give Willy a specific ethnic heritage. After seeing Thomas Mitchell do Willy, Miller himself commented that he did not realize he had written a play about an Irish family. (Popkin, "Stranger Encounter," *Sewanee Review*, LXVIII, 35.) George Ross reviewed a Yiddish production, pointing out underlying Jewish elements in the play. He felt that Miller had "censored out" the specifically Jewish in favor of an anonymous Americanism. ("*Death of a Salesman* in the Original," *Commentary*, XI [1951], 184–86.) This controversy underscores the point—relating the Lomans to any ethnic background destroys Miller's perspective.

15. Roger Babson, *Making Good in Business* (New York, 1921), pp. 98–9.

16. Wyllie, *Self-Made Man in America*, p. 107.

17. W. J. Ong, *Frontiers in American Catholicism* (New York, 1957), p. 31.

18. Henn, *Harvest of Tragedy*, p. 29.

19. "Pathetic" is used here, not in the sentimental, nice-doggy sense, but in the root meaning. Willy is acted upon by outside forces, he suffers the incursion of societal pressures. As he is shaped by these forces, he is "pathetic."

20. "Shadows of the Gods," *Harper's Magazine*, CCXVII (August, 1958), 36.

21. Willy has an unhappy penchant for falling into their hands. He owns and operates a Hastings refrigerator and a Studebaker car.

22. Miller, "The Family in Modern Drama," *Atlantic Monthly*, CXCVII, 39–40.

23. *Making Good in Business*, p. 73.

24. Miller emphasizes this view. He is convinced that drama can instruct, that its power to move an audience can be reformatory: "There lies in the dramatic form the ultimate possibility of raising the truth-consciousness of mankind to a level of intensity as to transform those who observe it." ("The Family in Modern Drama," *Atlantic Monthly*, CXCVII, 41.)

25. Popkin, "Strange Encounter," *Sewanee Review*, LXIII, 55.

Family Dreams in
Death of a Salesman

Irving Jacobson*

One critic, perhaps facetiously, has called *Death of a Salesman*[1] a "tragedy for extroverts."[2] This differentiates Willy Loman from a dramatic tradition of introspective figures who, like Shakespeare's Hamlet or Milton's Samson, confront their situations in a profound social and metaphysical solitude. By contrast, a protagonist who cannot be alone, who cannot summon the intelligence and strength to scrutinize his condition and come to some understanding of it—whatever agony it may cost him—seems disqualified for the tragic stature literature can bestow. With reference to Aristotelian standards, Sheila Huftel has remarked that Loman fell only from "an imagined height."[3] Indeed, to an extent his drama represents merely the collapse of a Philistine. Yet if one does not look upon Loman with a scowl of condemnation for his adherence to values he barely understands, for his anti-intellectualism, his contradictions, his insensitivities and petty cruelties, he does not because the fall from a height only imagined is nevertheless a fall. Loman is not, as critics have too facilely stated, a modern Everyman but an anomaly, a bourgeois romantic, an odd synthesis of Joe and Chris Keller, or of Everyman and Faust. He moves one not with his mediocrity and failure but with the frustrated energies of his outreach beyond mediocrity and failure toward a relationship to society constantly denied him.

Loman wants success, but the meaning of that need extends beyond the accumulation of wealth, security, goods, and status. As Arthur Miller said in an interview, "The trouble with Willy Loman is that he has tremendously powerful ideas."[4] But he yearns toward them more than he lives by them. What Loman wants, and what success means in *Death of a Salesman*, is intimately related to his own, and the playwright's, sense of the family. Family dreams extend backward in time to interpret the past, reach forward in time to project images of the future, and pressure reality in the present to conform to memory and imagination. These "ideals," these dreams, can be examined in terms of four variables: transformation, prominence, synthesis, and unity.

*Reprinted from *American Literature*, 47, (1975), 247-58 by permission of Duke University Press and the author.

I

Robert Hogan has noted that much of Miller's work developed from the image of man "struggling to be at one with society."[5] Miller elucidates the nature of this struggle in "The Family in Modern Drama," where he finds all great drama to be concerned with some aspect of a single problem: "How may a man make of the outside world a home?" What does he need to do, to change within himself or in the external world, if he is to find "the safety, the surroundings of love, the ease of soul, the sense of identity and honor which, evidently, all men have connected in their memories with the idea of family?"[6] This concern remains a constant in Miller's work. He is quoted in *Psychology and Arthur Miller* by Richard I. Evans as observing that his own sense of drama resides in the emotional tension within a person drawn to the past in order to orient himself to the present. His characters feel displaced from what they should be, even from what they "really" are.[7] Although Miller does not make explicit reference here to childhood and the family, the sense of radical loss and the passionate need to reattain some previous and necessary state seem fundamentally the same as in "The Family in Modern Drama."

With the success of *All My Sons*, wrote Miller, "It suddenly seemed that the audience was a mass of blood relations and I sensed a warmth in the world that was not there before."[8] He attributed success to the power to transform a relatively impersonal social world into a home that offered familial warmth. His next play, probably the most stunning portrayal of failure in the American theatre, dramatized a man's inability to achieve this transformation. Nothing Loman says or does can evoke that "warmth in the world." Instead, society responds to him with an indifference that can only seem cruel in juxtaposition to the hopes he carries with him even to the point of death.

Loman articulates his need in appealing to his employer with an image of the past, a Golden Age: "In those days there was personality in it, Howard. There was respect, and comradeship, and gratitude in it. Today it's all cut and dried, and there's no chance for bringing friendship to bear—or personality" (pp. 180-181). Earlier Miller characters found these values outside the business world: Gus in the Merchant Marine, in *The Story of Gus*;[9] Chris Keller in the Army, in *All My Sons*.[10] Loman once found them in having coffee with the mayor of Providence, in being recognized in places like Slattery's, Filene's, and the Hub, and by enjoying such good standing with New England policemen that he could park his car anywhere he liked without getting a ticket. His sense of self-value, then, depended upon the response of others. Such gestures of recognition provided signals that society, for a period in his life, was a home for him, one where he might hope to make his sons as happily at ease as he.

Prominence, whether gained through wealth, business associations, or public esteem, appeared to be the major catalyst in turning the world's indifference into warmth and admiration. Loman expressed awe at the prominence of Thomas Edison, B.F. Goodrich, and Frank Wagner, but the most compelling images of success were Ben, Dave Singleman, and Biff. The entrepreneur, the renowned salesman, and the star high school athlete represented possibilities in life to which Loman could not attain. They were surrounded men. At school, Biff was surrounded by admiring classmates and, at the Ebbets Field game, by cheering crowds and brilliant sunlight. At the peak of his career and at the end of his life, Singleman was surrounded by the affection of customers and fellow salesmen.

Ben, however, was surrounded by the mystery and power of his enterprising audacity. He represented a way of being at home in the world that differed from Miller's statement about the public response to *All My Sons* and from the attainments of other successful characters in *Death of a Salesman*. The world was a home for Ben not by the affection he won from it but by the command of his wealth, power, and mobility. In the world of finance he was as much a pioneer, a "great and wild-hearted man," as his father. His imagination and life extended as easily to Alaska, South Dakota, and Africa as to New York. Apparently indifferent to social relationships, he needed neither the human warmth of the family nor society's positive response. His sphere of action related to things and quantities rather than people; even his seven sons seemed more like commodities than members of a family. Thereby the play implies, not without irony, Ben was more capable of becoming at ease in the world than Willy Loman, whose refusal to join with his brother, a choice rooted in an ethic oriented to the family and to society, signaled his financial, social and family failure.

The world became a home for Dave Singleman in an opposite fashion. Like Ben, he enjoyed wealth, power and mobility; but these were more entirely enmeshed within social relationships. The nature and extent of his prominence was succinctly illustrated in his ability to sit in a hotel room and make his living by phone, comfortably attired in the luxury of green velvet slippers. This image has had a decisive power in Loman's life:

> And when I saw that, I realized that selling was the greatest career a man could want. 'Cause what could be more satisfying than to be able to go, at the age of eighty-four, into twenty or thirty different cities, and pick up a phone, and be remembered and loved and helped by so many different people? (p. 180)

Unlike Ben, Singleman achieved a success that presented him with a world of loyalty, aid, and love. His scope of action was spatially more limited in being national rather than international; but response to him was more personal. For Loman, the surest indication of public love for Singleman is that when he died the "death of a salesman" in the smoking car of a train on the way to Boston, people travelled from all over the country to attend his funeral. In juxtaposition to Loman's funeral in the "Requiem" of the play, this reveals the extent to which Singleman's prominence granted him a home in society that Loman cannot achieve. Singleman mastered his society not through the demonic qualities one perceives in Ben but through a synthesis of man's social and economic impulses.

The world became a home for Biff Loman when, as an athlete, he evoked affection and admiration from the people around him. His life seemed full of promise, with a choice of three college scholarships to signify the abundance of future success life can offer the already successful. When he became captain of the football team, a crowd of girls surrounded him after classes, and girls paid for him on dates. His friends waited for him after school, not knowing how to occupy themselves until he arrived to organize them into sweeping out the furnace and hanging up his mother's laundry. As contrasted with his friend Bernard, who was only "liked," Biff was "well-liked," which seemed to grant him, in Loman's view, certain allowances that could not be bestowed upon those who received less fervent popular esteem. At the all-star Ebbets Field game he was the tallest player, dressed in gold with the sun all around him while the crowd shouted "Loman, Loman, Loman!" (p. 171), so that his father sensed him raised beyond the level of the merely human by the extent of his prominence among others.

Prominence for Ben, Singleman, and Biff has an impersonal quality that contradicts Loman's repeated insistence upon the value of personality and what he calls "personal attractiveness." His heroes tend to stand among yet above other people. He remarks that at the Ebbets Field game Biff seemed like "Hercules—something like that" (p. 171), and his accounts of Ben's being "success incarnate" have more the tone of hagiography than family anecdote. For Loman these figures exist less as individuals with actual characters, talents, and problems than as mythological projections of his own needs and his society's values. This has two kinds of consequences for his life. For one, the means for achieving success remain a mystery to him. Although he perceives Ben as a sign that "The greatest things can happen!" he can never discover how those things happen. When he asks Ben how to succeed he receives not an answer but an incantatory formula: "When I was seventeen I walked into the jungle, and when I was twenty-one I walked out. And by God I was rich" (p. 157). Ben proves willing to use violence when it is necessary or useful, and he boasts of his mnemonic powers; but these cannot lead Loman to understand how Ben became wealthy, much less how anyone else might. Another consequence of Loman's mythological projection is that characters without strikingly luminous qualities, such as Charlie or Linda, cannot move Loman deeply enough to help him. Charlie's aid and friendship represent the only instance where someone in society does form something like a family tie with him. Yet Charlie can offer only help, not promise; realistic advice, not transformation. He has succeeded in business, but no aura of magic power surrounds him or his advice.

The consequences of failing to attain prominence and to transform society into a home are loneliness, frustration, and ultimately despair. Because Loman needs gratification to take a social form, his life is crushed by indifference, criticism, rejection, and abandonment. In his scene with Howard Wagner he appeals to quasifamilial ties in the past—"I was with the firm when your father used to carry you in here in his arms" (p. 179)—but the reality that "business is business" and not a family makes his appeal irrelevant. At the same time that Wagner's act corresponds, figuratively, to rejection by a son, it also records a final loss of hope that family ties can exist on a social level. But, still unable to accept failure in his struggle to be at one with society, Loman prefers death with the illusion of transformation to life without it.

II

The assumption that prominence brings affection and privilege frequently has led the Lomans to boast or lie about themselves. Signs of prominence, what Loman and Happy refer to as "the old humor, the old confidence" (p. 137), can be used as a facade. Loman returns from a business trip exclaiming, "I'm tellin', you, I was sellin', thousands and thousands, but I had to come home" (p. 147). His fabrications create so extreme a polarization with his incapacities that an acceptance of failure—his own or Biff's—becomes impossible. Happy proves more calculating in the scene at Frank's Chop House, where he presents himself and his brother with false, glossy images for the sake of seducing women.

Happy's need to command attention comprises a persistent if minor note throughout the play. He admires and envies the merchandise manager— "when he walks into the store the waves part in front of him. That's fifty-two thousand dollars a year coming through the revolving door . . . " (p. 140). The distorted reference to the Moses myth signifies the extent to which monetary values have absorbed religious emotions. When he asserts that he can become "number one man," Happy has the merchandise manager in mind; and this represents a decayed ideal, one of mere wealth and power, with neither Ben's daring nor Singleman's social prominence. Happy's need to be "number one" has another significance also, for he has never been the sole focus of his father's attention, always a poor second to Biff. He seems always to be merely present in the Loman household, an adjunct. At several points he makes an open bid for his father's attention, asking whether Loman has noticed how much weight he has lost; but his father never answers. As an adult, Happy envies the positions of those above him while achieving an underhanded sort of prominence by taking bribes and seducing "gorgeous creatures," including the fiancées of company executives. Although he describes himself as having "an overdeveloped sense of competition," he cannot compete on an appropriate level but instead does so sexually, or takes refuge in an athletic past, claiming he can outbox anyone in the office. He claims not really to want these forms of pseudo-prominence; but as much as his brother, though in a different form, Happy becomes a thief, stealing women for transient pleasure and stealing the illusion of prominence with lies.

Unlike his father and brother, Biff does not emulate the images of prominent men but rejects the years he has spent riding subways, keeping stock, buying and selling, feeling it ridiculous to spend a year in suffering for the sake of a two-week vacation. He surrenders his opportunities for a prominent adulthood by refusing to repeat a mathematics course after he has found his father with a woman in a Boston hotel room. Yet his need for the illusion of prominence continues with his repeated acts of petty theft—repetitions, in essence, of behavior his father once applauded as "initiative." As an adult he has the same problem as the young David Frieber in *The Man Who Had All the Luck*:[11] "I don't know what the future is. I don't know—what I'm supposed to want" (p. 138). However gratifying his life of simple physicality on ranches in the West, he has thought himself less than mature—"I'm like a boy" (p. 139)—and has found himself periodically returning home with a sense of incompletion and waste. Only the intense pressure applied by his father, and his experience of failure and theft in Bill Oliver's office, reconciles him in a final sense to his life of simple work, food, and leisure without expectations of prominence.

Insisting that it is not a matter of what you do but "who you know and the smile on your face!" Loman optimistically locates the secret of success in "contacts" and "personal attractiveness," expectant that "a man can end with diamonds here on the basis of being liked!" (p. 184). Yet even the means of becoming "liked" evade him, as in his contradictory advice to Biff:

> Be quiet, fine, and serious. Everybody likes a kidder, but nobody lends him money. (p. 168).

> Walk in with a big laugh. Don't look worried. Start off with a couple of your good stories to liven things up. (p. 169).

The inconspicuous diligence of a youth like Bernard is dismissed as "anemic." Instead of reconciling himself to failure in business skills, Loman blames the responses of others: people do not "take" to him, they pass him by, find him too fat, poorly dressed, foolish, a "walrus" (p. 149). Under stress, his needs demand vicarious gratification through the success of his sons. This becomes evident in his response to an insult from his brother:

> Ben: Great inventor, Father. With one gadget he made more in a week than a man like you could make in a lifetime.
> Willy: That's just the way I'm bringing them up, Ben—rugged, well-liked, all around. (p. 157)

Because he habitually deflects consciousness of his own failure by focusing attention on his sons, Loman cannot accept Biff's way of life in the West on its own terms but tries to reabsorb him into a business-oriented culture. Unable to accomplish this, he perceives his life as an empty, infertile waste. "Nothing's planted. I don't have a thing in the ground" (p. 209).

III

Blurring distinctions, Loman tends to view prominence and transformation as identical, and this habit of mind prevents him from enjoying the skills he has and appreciating the supportive elements within his own family. Loman neglects the distinctions between different people, values and methods, attempting through sheer force of hope to reconcile the disparate. His decision not to join Ben in business is rooted in his assertion that the values of Ben can be synthesized with those of Dave Singleman, and this ignores the contrast Ben points out between social gestures and tangible commodities. He also ignores the differences between criminality and initiative, encouraging his sons to steal, so that the front stoop of the Loman house, which Biff claims to contain "more of him" than his career as a salesman, is built with stolen materials.

Happy and Biff formulate schemes to synthesize values, hoping to attain prominence and to reunite as brothers. Their short-lived dream of a Loman ranch in the West attempts to synthesize sports and commercialism, the pastoral and the urban, playfulness and seriousness, youth and adulthood. They imagine that their partnership will regain them the public attention they enjoyed in high school. Biff's pastoral values reflect his father, who bewails the loss of open air and space, the overcrowded conditions of city life, and the absence of flowers almost as often as he condemns his son for becoming a farmhand. On a Loman ranch, Biff could not only do the kind of work he liked but also "be something." Yet a brief but revealing bit of dialogue exposes the rapid death of this dream:

> Biff: Hap, the trouble is we weren't brought up to grub for money. I don't know how to do it.
> Happy: Neither can I!
> Biff: Then let's go!
> Happy: The only thing is—what can you make out there? (p. 140)

The synthesis they try to create collapses under the weight of a single question. Happy's later plan for a Loman line of sporting goods would also give them an opportunity to work together. "And the beauty of it is, Biff, it wouldn't be like a business," Happy exclaims, "We'd be out playin' ball again" (p. 168). But this dream of synthesis, like that of a Loman ranch, founders upon the need for money.

The ultimate attempt at synthesis in the play is Loman's suicide. Leonard Moss has noted that he chooses death "not simply as an escape from shame but as a last attempt to re-establish his own self-confidence and his family's integrity."[12] The insurance money makes it seem possible to synthesize the values of Ben and Singleman. For by entering the dark, unknown "jungle" of death Loman might bring out tangible wealth, "like diamonds," thus becoming as much an adventurer as Ben but within the skyscraper world of New York. He imagines himself then having a funeral as massive as Singleman's, one that would leave Biff "thunderstruck." Thus in a single act Loman hopes to achieve transformation, prominence, synthesis, and his lost unity with Biff.

IV

Scattered images of family unity in *Death of a Salesman* evoke the sense of loss: "All I remember is a man with a big beard, and I was in Mama's lap, sitting around a fire, and some kind of high music" (p. 157). Loman's very early family life remains the vaguest of memories, symbolized by the high-pitched sound of the flute which, as Edward Murray has noted, acts as an "auditory binder" in the play.[13] It juxtaposes Loman's pastoral longings for the past with the overbearing actualities of the city towering around him. Also, Loman's image contrasts the quiet repose of the past with restlessness that characterizes the rest of his life. Another passage evoking an image of lost family unity captures his relationship with the young Biff, when life was "so full of light, and comradeship" (p. 213).

Loman wants to feel a unity of generations linking his father and Ben with him and his sons. He appeals to Ben: "You're just what I need, Ben, because I—I have a fine position here, but I—well, Dad left when I was such a baby, and I never had a chance to talk to him and I still feel—kind of temporary about myself" (p. 159). Yet the need for family unity is juxtaposed against the reality of family disintegration. Loman's father abandons his family, and Ben leaves soon afterward. Loman violates the unity of his family with the woman in Boston, not only by sexual infidelity but by giving her the stockings that should go to Linda. Biff leaves home because of his discovery, and Happy leaves to set up his own apartment and enjoy his women. Sex proves a powerfully divisive force among the Lomans, separating parents from each other and parents from sons. Happy abandons his father in another way, by merely sending him away to Florida when Loman's emotional breakdown becomes embarrassingly visible. He cannot respond sympathetically to his father's problems. "No, that's not my father," he dismissively remarks in the restaurant scene, "He's just a guy" (p. 205).

Linda remained loyal, but her constancy cannot help Loman. She can play no significant role in her husband's dreams; and although she proves occasionally capable of dramatic outbursts, she lacks the imagination and strength to hold her family together or to help Loman define a new life without grandiose hopes for Biff. Critics have attacked her as "profoundly unsatisfactory" as a character,[14] "not in the least sexually interesting,"[15] and a symbol of the "cash-payment fixation."[16] But given Loman's inability to accept disagreement from his sons or Charley, it is hard to suppose that he would tolerate a less acquiescent wife. He calls her "my foundation and my support," but her stability cannot prevent his collapse.

In "The Family as a Psychosocial Organization," Robert D. Hess and Gerald Handel have noted that "The family's life together is an endless process of movement in and around consensual understanding, from attachment to conflict and withdrawal—and over again. Separateness and connectedness are the underlying conditions of a family's life, and its common task is to give form to both."[17] In *Death of a Salesman*, beginning the process "over again" becomes impossible. The present action of the play forces an explosive reunion, bringing members of the family together in order to make their separateness explicit and irrevocable. This pattern typifies Arthur Miller's work; it occurs in *All My Sons*; it characterizes *After the Fall*;[18] and it encompasses most of *The Price*.[19] Attempts to recreate family unity—like Ben's offer of partnership, Biff's return home, or the brothers' schemes to go into business together—have the dual effect of illuminating areas of conflict and forever sealing family members off from one another. The peripatetic big dinner scene toward the end of the play, then, presents a cacophony of dissonant motives; and the centripetal forces of their separate lives prove stronger than the need for unity that brought the Lomans together. Torn between Happy's callous ability to let him continue living in illusion and Biff's cruel but necessary demand for honesty, Loman yields to a hope forged in despair: that Biff might finally recant and become "magnificent" with the insurance money. But his death changes nothing; it implies instead that a man's frenetic attempt to make the world a home can defeat the viability of his private home, even cost him his life.

Notes

1. Arthur Miller, *Death of a Salesman: Certain Private Conversations in Two Acts and a Requiem*, in *Arthur Miller's Collected Plays* (New York, 1957), pp. 130-222. Further references to this edition will be noted in the text by page number.

2. Richard Watts, "A Matter of Hopelessness in *Death of a Salesman*," *Tulane Drama Review*, II (May, 1958), 64.

3. Sheila Huftel, *Arthur Miller: The Burning Glass* (New York, 1965), p. 114.

4. Arthur Miller, "Morality and Modern Drama: Interview with Philip Gelb," *Educational Theatre Journal*, X (Oct., 1958), rpt. in *Arthur Miller, Death of a Salesman: Text and Criticism*, ed. Gerald Weales (New York, 1967), p. 175.

5. Robert Hogan, *Arthur Miller* (Minneapolis, 1964), p. 8.

6. Arthur Miller, "The Family in Modern Drama," *Atlantic Monthly*, CXCVII (April, 1956), 36-37.

7. Richard I. Evans, *Psychology and Arthur Miller* (New York, 1969), p. 56.

8. Arthur Miller, "Introduction to the Collected Plays," p. 22.

9. Arthur Miller, *The Story of Gus*, in *Radio's Best Plays*, ed. Joseph Liss (New York, 1947), pp. 307-319.

10. Arthur Miller, *All My Sons*, in *Arthur Miller's Collected Plays*, pp. 58-127.

11. Arthur Miller, *The Man Who Had All the Luck*, in *Cross-Section: A Collection of New American Writing*, ed. Edwin Seaver (New York: 1944), pp. 486-552.

12. Leonard Moss, *Arthur Miller* (New Haven, 1967), p. 45.

13. Edward Murray, *Arthur Miller, Dramatist* (New York, 1967), p. 34.

14. C. W. E. Bigsby, *Confrontations and Commitment: A Study of Contemporary American Drama 1959-66* (London, 1967) p. 35.

15. Henry Popkin, "Arthur Miller: The Strange Encounter," *Sewanee Review*, LXVII (Winter, 1960), 56.

16. G. Bliquez, "Linda's Role in *Death of a Salesman*," *Modern Drama*, X (Feb., 1968), 383.

17. Robert D. Hess and Gerald Handel, "The Family as a Psychosocial Organization," in *The Psychosocial Interior of the Family*, ed. George Handel (Chicago, 1967), p. 10.

18. Arthur Miller, *After the Fall* (New York, 1964).

19. Arthur Miller, *The Price* (New York, 1969).

An Enemy Of The People

Frederic March in
An Enemy of the People,
Adapted by Arthur Miller

Brooks Atkinson[*]

Papa Ibsen has had a shot in the arm. Taking a literal translation of "An Enemy of the People" as the source material, Arthur Miller has made a new adaptation, which was put on at the Broadhurst last evening. Next to "King Lear," it is the bitterest play in town, and it is also a vast improvement over the lugubrious Archer translation that for years has represented Ibsen to us in English.

Without a knowledge of the original Norwegian, no one can tell how much of the surface of the drama is Ibsen or Miller. But the theme of the honest man standing for his convictions against the mob is pure Ibsen, angry and defiant. It is Ibsen speaking a good word for the truth of the individual and shaking his fist at society. Since it falls into none of the current political categories, it is a stirring thing to hear in the theatre and a good deal fresher than most of the political thought of today.

By dispensing with the previous English translation, Mr. Miller has released the anger and scorn of the father of realism. But don't overlook the passion that the current performance contributes. For Robert Lewis has directed it with the fury of moral melodrama, and Frederic March plays it with a breadth and volume that are overwhelming. You may find the impact too stunning, since it calls attention to itself. Sometimes it makes you uncomfortably aware of the mechanics of the acting and the arbitrariness of the playwriting. But no doubt that is a matter of personal taste. For you can hardly escape the power and excitement of a bold drama audaciously let loose in the theatre by actors and stage people who are not afraid of their strength.

Ibsen was mad all the way through when he wrote "An Enemy of the People." Having just written "Ghosts," he was regarded as an enemy of the people himself. Instead of being frightened by the attacks, he was provoked to vengeance. "An Enemy of the People" is the horrifying story of a man who is persecuted by his townspeople for telling them the truth. Dr. Stockmann has proved that the water supply in his town is polluted. Instead of hailing him as an industrious public servant, the whole town turns against him, stones his house, abuses his family and boycotts him from society.

Reasonable people may complain that Ibsen was overwrought, and fastidious craftsmen may regard his play as contrived. It is a polemic no less than a drama. But, again, those objections are beside the main point. Ibsen had a savage case against society, and he stated it furiously. It is a case that cuts across party lines and hurts everyone. Ibsen stood alone against mankind when he wrote this trenchant drama.

There is none of the sweetness of pure reason in the acting. Mr. Lewis' direction pits the black against the white, and makes a fight out of them. As the embattled Dr. Stockmann, Mr. March gives an enormously rousing performance in a part that he probably respects. The brushstrokes are sweeping, but the moral integrity stands back of them. Florence Eldridge plays the less ferocious part of the wife with a pleasant womanliness that acquires conviction as the play develops. For the character of Mrs. Stockmann sharpens with the experience of the play, and Miss Eldridge's acting sharpens with it.

The impact of Mr. March's acting is dramatically balanced by the rich, forceful and accomplished acting of Morris Carnovsky as the cynical mayor of the town. Art Smith gives an amusingly flavorsome performance as Dr. Stockmann's crafty father-in-law, and knows how to put the heat on the drama when the proper moment comes in the last act. There are excellent performances also by Fred Stewart, Ralph Dunn, Martin Brooks and Anna Minot.

Living in a more prodigal era of the theatre Ibsen required quite a lot of scenery. Aline Berstein has provided both the scenery and the costumes with the purity and lucidity that inform all her work. Those are about the only things in "An Enemy of The People" that are not dark and stormy. For Papa Ibsen was discharging thunderbolts in all directions. Mr. Miller has abetted him ably.

An Enemy of the People:
A Key to Arthur Miller's
Art and Ethics

David Bronson[*]

Arthur Miller has been generous in acknowledging his debt to his avowed master, Henrik Ibsen. It is the Ibsen of the middle period with whom he identifies, the author of *The Pillars of Society, A Doll's House, Ghosts*, and *An Enemy of the People*. These are Ibsen's realistic social dramas, all of them examples of the so-called well-made play in which the central character is observed in his relationship to society. In all but the first of these, a protagonist who is preoccupied with justice commits himself to an ideal which he refuses to relinquish, although his own life would be made easier if he accepted the alternative proffered him.

By taking it upon himself to adapt the Norwegian playwright's *An Enemy of the People,* Miller was in effect saying that his basic concerns approximate those of Ibsen. By and large he is not wrong in his assumption, insofar as it pertains to the period in Ibsen's career which saw the creation of the dramas mentioned. On the other hand, although Miller was attracted to *Enemy* by what he looked upon as its message and by certain affinities he felt he shared with Ibsen, the fact of the matter is that his adaptation of the play is marked by a decidedly different bias. By comparing the work of the master with that of the disciple who is handling the same characters, plot material, and construction, the measure of the latter as a playwright will be taken.

I

The present study should be instructive in other ways. It will test, if only indirectly, the fault-finding of a number of critics who look upon Ibsen's *Enemy* as a second-rate work.[1] In most instances, such commentators can arrive at their conclusions only by overlooking the complex ambivalence of the play. They insist on its straightforwardness, on its portrayal of a righteous hero at loggerheads with a corrupt mob. In reality, however, it is a dubious and egotistical "hero" who stands accused by a "sensible" and hypocritical assembly of citizens. *Enemy* is a study in ambiguity in which the lines between good and evil are less clearly drawn than these critics would have us believe.

[*]Reprinted from *Comparative Drama*, 2 (1968–69) 229–247, by permission of the journal.

Most of the detractors of *Enemy* see the play as an aggressive apologia written in response to the abuse heaped upon the author as a result of *Ghosts*, its controversial predecessor.[2] According to this line of reasoning, *Enemy* is a weak play because the author uses Dr. Stockmann as his mouthpiece to express his contumely and exasperation. Ibsen himself, to be sure, commented on certain similarities between his make-up and that of Dr. Stockmann.[3] But he overdrew some of these similarities to the point of self-mockery. The excessive wrath and resentment of Dr. Stockmann, to the extent that they reflect Ibsen's rancor over the reception of *Ghosts*, are transmuted into a satire Ibsen directs at himself for being carried away into the equivalent of the overly emotional harangues of the fourth act.

Ibsen as the author of *Ghosts* played the role of doctor in diagnosing a societal malady and was himself accused of spreading illness. In *Enemy* he dramatizes the situation of a doctor who discovers the source of infection in the community and is rewarded by being denounced as "an enemy of the people." But contrary to what these facts seem to suggest, *Enemy* does not constitute a clearcut attempt on the part of the dramatist at self-vindication. The Dr. Stockmann that Ibsen has drawn and who is so eager to criticize is for his own part very much open to criticism. There is a leavening of comedy expressing itself in the form of irony and satire in *Enemy*, and that this was conscious is borne out by a letter the author wrote his publisher on completion of the play: "I am still a little uncertain whether to call it a comedy or simply a play; it has much of the character of a comedy, but there is also a serious basic theme" (Meyer 203). Stockmann's temperament and character open the door to the discrepancy between his idealistic self-image and the reality of his behavior. Ibsen has made the Doctor a muddled hothead. This fact gives the play a consistent strain of the irrational, which sometimes, as in the fourth act, takes on the aspect of the grotesque, and marks the ambivalence of Ibsen's attitude towards his less-than-perfect hero.

Miller, in his effort to achieve economy and concentration, has shortened the length of the original by one-third, in several instances to the play's advantage, often to its detriment. He has reduced Ibsen's five acts to three by changing acts I and II of the original into scenes one and two of act I. Similarly, acts III and IV become scenes one and two of act II. And Ibsen's act V becomes Miller's act III. What does this actually amount to? Miller's "improvement" in the structure looks more impressive on the printed page than it does on stage. The play has five major divisions and four scene changes in both versions, a structure which does not really bear improving upon. It is indicative that Kenneth Burke has singled out *Enemy* as an exemplary instance of what he calls the "scene-act ratio," i.e. settings and action are developed in consistent correlation to one another.[4]

In Miller's version, the conclusion of each scene does undergo a degree of dramatic heightening. In the original Dr. Stockmann has the last word only at the end of the first act. After that it is Petra, the Mayor, Billing and again Petra who respectively conclude each act with remarks which amount to no more than trivial exclamations. In his adaptation Miller gives the curtain speech to Dr. Stockmann at the end of each of the five scenes.

In general, Miller tends to be more careful of details and credibility than Ibsen. In Miller's scene at the newspaper office the manner in which the Mayor obtains his brother's manuscript—his attention is called to it when Aslaksen attempts to hide it—is more dramatically appropriate than the equivalent stage action in the original, in which Aslaksen simply announces that he has it. Also, one is left rather incredulous by the passage in the final act of the original, in which Dr. Stockmann learns from the Mayor that his father-in-law is bequeathing a considerable fortune to his children. It is asking too much of the audience to believe that the Mayor would have been aware of this information while his brother, who is directly affected, would have had no inkling of it. The adaptation handles this more effectively. Instead of bringing up the matter of the inheritance, the Mayor mentions only that Kiil is buying up stock in the springs at half its usual value. Miller lets the Doctor suspect there will be an inheritance in store for him, which Kiil himself then confirms.

Miller "advances" Aslaksen from printer to publisher, which more adequately justifies the influence he claims for himself over the townspeople. After Stockmann's break with the local citizenry Ibsen overlooks the obvious—that the alternatives open to the Doctor are not limited simply to staying on or going to America. He could carry on his attack from the vantage point of another Norwegian town. The adaptation has the Mayor understandably threatening his brother with a subpoena if he does just that.

II

As suggested, Miller has achieved economy, and with an eye for detail, has tidied up a number of rough spots in the stage action of the original. To a certain extent, however, these emendations could have been carried out by a director or a copy editor, since they require more the work of a technician than that of a masterly craftsman.

In his preface Miller explains that he had a translator render a literal word-for-word translation of the original, which he then recast into colloquial American English. It was no doubt the ring of Victorianism in William Archer's translation which put him off, although those of Eva Le Gallienne, Michael Meyer, Peter Watt and R. Farquharson Sharp, while less racy than Miller's, are all of satisfactory literary quality. There is no question, however, that Miller's dialogue is vivid and spans a broad range from playfulness to asperity. But in clothing this play in the American idiom, he has also thoroughly Americanized it, making Dr. Stockmann into a "good guy" with all that that implies. The following description serves to introduce the Doctor:

> DR. STOCKMANN is laughing and talking outside. He is in the prime of his life. He might be called the eternal amateur—a lover of things, of people, of sheer living, a man for whom the days are too short, and the future fabulous with discoverable joys.

> And for all this most people will not like him—he will not compromise for less than
> God's own share of the world while they have settled for less than Man's.[5]

In general, the effect of the authentic colloquial tone which Miller has gained in the dialogue is vitiated for the reader by the gaucherie of his character introductions, as exemplified by the embarrassing lines which describe Captain Horster (Miller 113). When Miller is not moralizing in his character descriptions, he is likely to be delivering himself of a tongue-clucking warning. Miller has Kiil appear in the first scene as a curmudgeon who fills his pockets with apples and tobacco taken from Dr. Stockmann's table when no one is looking. As if that were not suggestive enough, Miller insists on being more explicit in a subsequent character description:

> He is the archetype of the little twinkle-eyed man who sneaks into so much of Ibsen's
> work. He will chuckle you right over the precipice. He is the dealer, the man with the
> rat's finely tuned brain. But he is sometimes likable because he is without morals and
> announces the fact by laughing. (Miller, pp. 121-2)

Similarly, of Petra Miller has the following to say:

> She is Ibsen's clear-eyed hope for the future—and probably ours. She is forthright,
> determined, and knows the meaning of work, which to her is the creation of good on
> earth. (Miller, p. 114)

The author takes recourse to such explanatory interpolations with regard to both major and minor characters. In these instantaneous character delineations the *dramatis personae* are reduced to one or two salient traits which inadvertently verge on caricature. This idiosyncrasy, which is so foreign to the nature of drama, is one of long standing with Miller, and one which he apparently finds difficult to surrender.

By pointing out what he admires in Ibsen, Miller has put his finger unerringly on some of his own weaknesses: "We could do with more of [Ibsen's] basic intention, which was to assert nothing he had not proved. . . ."[6] Another of his statements regarding Ibsen, equally instructive, reads like a personal indictment: "I . . . saw . . . his ability to forge a play upon a factual bedrock. A situation in his plays is never stated but revealed in terms of hard actions, irrevocable deeds; and sentiment is never confused with the action it conceals" (*Collected Plays*, p. 19). Miller also gives himself away in his preface to *Enemy*, where he observes:

> There is one quality in Ibsen that no serious writer can afford to overlook. It lies at the
> very center of his force, and I found in it—as I hope others will—a profound source of
> strength. It is his insistence, his utter conviction, that he is going to say what he has to
> say, and that the audience, by God, is going to listen. . . . Every Ibsen play begins with
> the unwritten words: "Now listen here!"

In his own eagerness to be heard and understood, Miller is apparently so fearful that his public will miss the point that he is driven to oversimplification and overstatement. Like an immoderately solicitous parent, he either allows his brain children too little chance to act on their own or he insists on putting them through their paces.

In a number of his plays, but nowhere more obviously than in *Enemy*, Miller seems to be following a crude primer for would-be writers which requires that a character on his first appearance imprint himself indelibly on the mind of the audience, and that this be brought about through contrast and peculiarities of personality. Kiil's brief part in the first scene is a striking example. He is made colorful to the point of burlesque by his petty pilfering and his eccentricities of eating and speech. Confronted with the stuffed-shirt Mayor, the ill-mannered Kiil expresses his contempt for this official by demonstratively biting into his apple and making a rude exit.

In several instances Miller succeeds in strengthening the roles of the secondary characters. He lets some of them participate more fully in the action and brings about a fiercer interaction between them and Dr. Stockmann. Captain Horster's role, which is shadowy in the original, is rounded out to make him a man of disinterested conviction in the adaptation. He is the one person who has the courage to vote against the resolution declaring the Doctor an enemy of the people. Mrs. Stockmann, who is mostly passive and fearful about the welfare of her family in the original, is more willing to speak her own mind in the adaptation and attempts to support her husband with her own conviction.

On the other hand, in a number of instances Miller has condensed the original at the expense of the play's complexity and those passages which were too unconventional for him to handle. Petra, the Stockmann's daughter, is stripped of all her genuinely controversial ideas. In Ibsen's act I, Billing playfully encourages the two Stockmann boys to be atheists, whereupon Mrs. Stockmann, who is uneasy about the subject, sends the boys to bed. Miller lets the matter rest there by bringing Dr. Stockmann back on the stage and having the conversation turn to something else. In Ibsen's play, however, Petra has something further to say: "All this hypocrisy! At home we're taught to hold our tongues; and at school we have to teach the children lies!"[7] Petra insists on putting into words what Mrs. Stockmann is trying to evade. In Ibsen's act III, Petra appears in the newspaper office to inform Hovstad that she will not translate the religious novel for publication in the newspaper, as he and Billing had hoped, and then proceeds to voice her critical views on religion. Miller found it impossible to eliminate Petra's appearance, but this episode does lose most of its original import.

In the town meeting of Ibsen's fourth act this theme occurs again. Dr. Stockmann taunts Hovstad about his claims to being a freethinker. When the latter, because of the presence of the local citizenry, indignantly disavows any such thing, the Doctor states that he himself is the only freethinker in the community. Miller, of course, has retained none of this in his adaptation.

III

In like manner, contrary to the original, Miller has made his hero shallow and uncomplicated. A comparison of the two Dr. Stockmanns will demonstrate how Ibsen and Miller, for all the idealism they supposedly have in common, diverge categorically in their concept of the hero.

Miller's idea of a hero is indirectly revealed in an account of how he happened on the bit of information that led him to write *All My Sons:*

> It came out of an idle conversation with one of Miller's in-laws, who told of a woman in her neighborhood who turned in her own father for having shipped faulty materials to the government during the war. "The action astounded me," Miller said. "An absolute response to a moral command."[8]

Both in life and in a dramatic work "an absolute response to a moral command" is an inadequate justification for intolerance of letting people be what they are. Ibsen, the author of *Brand*, whose title character asserts the claim of "all or nothing," understood that no human being could sustain the life of the ideal without being oppressively forbidding or unbearably priggish. Brand is a monumental champion of the ideal who excites the imagination, yet is in the end condemned by God. He is an eminently dramatic figure because he lives in conflict with himself and produces tension in those about him. Evidently Miller has a low tolerance for internal contradiction, complex behavior and genuine social non-conformity. Ibsen, by contrast, consistently portrays heroes in whom the good is only partial, and admixed with less desirable traits. Miller's descriptions of two of his characters in *The Crucible*, for instance, represent his conception of the rough-hewn, ruggedly individualistic man who thinks his own thoughts and goes his own way. Of John Proctor he writes:

> He was the kind of man—powerful of body, even-tempered, and not easily led—who cannot refuse support to partisans without drawing their deepest resentment. In Proctor's presence a fool felt his foolishness instantly—and a Proctor is always marked for calumny therefore. (*Collected Plays*, p. 239)

And of Giles Corey the author observes: "He was a crank and a nuisance, but withal a deeply innocent and brave man" (*Collected Plays*, p. 254). It was no doubt in the light of such characters that Eric Bentley was moved to make some significant distinctions:

> *Othello* is not a melodrama, because, though its villain is wholly evil, its hero is not wholly virtuous. *The Crucible* is a melodrama because though the hero has weaknesses, he has no faults. His innocence is unreal because it is total. . . . Innocence is, for a mere human being, and especially for an artist, insufficient baggage.[9]

Ibsen, who conceived of Gregor Werle's quest for absolute truth and virtue in *The Wild Duck* as pathological, presents us in *Enemy* with a hero who is driven by dubious motivation and injudicious measures to achieve a good. Miller gives us a Dr. Stockmann whose principles are pure and whose motivations are not open to question—who can deliver himself of a simple-minded battle cry to stand up for what one holds to be right. Miller proves himself less of the artist in having to simplify Stockmann in order to make his play prove its thesis. That Miller, by his character abridgement, has made his task considerably easier goes without saying. James Joyce recognized the nature of Ibsen's achievement in *Enemy* years before Miller was born, when he remarked,

> How easy it would have been to have written *An Enemy of the People* on a spec-
> iously loftier level—to have replaced the *bourgeois* by the legitimate hero! Critics
> might then have extolled as grand what they have so often condemned as banal.[10]

Ibsen was less interested in proving the moral innocence of Dr. Stockmann than in pointing up the self-seeking nature of his opponents and the deviousness of their tactics in getting their way. It was all right for Dr. Stockmann to be on the "right" side for some wrong reasons; the author could let his hero be wrongheaded and misguided. The Doctor's heroism still has aspects of nobility, but is not to be subscribed to without reservation. Ibsen is skillful enough to make the audience incensed at the injustice done Dr. Stockmann without re-quiring that it side with him completely. Like a bourgeois version of Brand, the Doctor is admirable and reprehensible at the same time.

Miller gives his hero minor failings, which do not stand in the way of his actions being endorsed in entirety. He is more nearly the ideal figure, with the right edges rounded off. The views of Miller's Dr. Stockmann coincide with those of the author. Ibsen, on the other hand, does not identify himself in all respects with his hero. Ibsen clarified this matter in a letter to his publisher:

> Dr. Stockmann and I . . . agree on so many subjects. But the Doctor is a more muddle-
> headed person than I am, and he has, moreover, several other characteristics for the
> sake of which people will stand hearing a good many things from him which they
> might perhaps not have taken in such very good part had they been said by me.[11]

And years later Ibsen remarked to a friend, "Stockmann is in part an oddball and a hothead."[12]

Ibsen has chosen as his Dr. Stockmann a man who has ulterior motives for championing the truth. The Doctor's first announcement of the chemical analy-sis demonstrating the pollution of the springs is given in the form of a personal vindication. In a speech to his wife he observes of his father-in-law: "That'll give the old man something to gape at! He thinks I'm cracked in the head—and a lot of other people think so too, I've noticed. But I'll show them! Yes—this time I'll show them" (Ibsen, p. 172)! Although the health and wellbeing of a good many people are at stake, the Doctor's unreflecting elation would be more appropriate for a reporter savoring the credit and praise which will be his for a scoop he has made: "I'll let them have it now! I've prepared a report for the Board of Directors; it's been ready for a week—I was only waiting for this" (Ibsen, p. 173).

Miller's Doctor, who is mostly a sensible and self-controlled man, with none of the abandonment and self-indulgence of Ibsen's character, merely voices righteous indignation that his professional opinion had not been heeded earlier, so that the public welfare could be served. In contrast to this prim selflessness, Ibsen's Doctor hungers for recognition and appreciation, which leads him to expressions of false modesty that give his true feelings away: "if the Board of Directors should think of offering me a raise in salary—I shall refuse it. I simply won't accept" (Ibsen, p. 174)! Miller, for his part, lets Billing make this suggestion, which the Doctor then rejects out of hand. Subsequently, Ibsen's

Doctor, once again protesting too much, insists that he will have no part of any celebrations in his honor. This bit of unveiled braggadocio is muted in the adaptation by an allusion of Miller's Dr. Stockmann to the common people, whose supposed innocence might carry them away in their desire to honor him.

The egotist in Ibsen's Stockmann permits himself a naive expression of his conceit. When Hovstad, in answering the question as to what he thinks about the Doctor's article, replies, "I think it's an absolute masterpiece—," Stockmann responds, "Yes, isn't it" (Ibsen, p. 197)? Miller's Doctor is of course too strait-laced to talk like that, and the adaptation omits the line.

This egotism of Ibsen's Doctor, which manifests itself again in an excessive concern about the printing of the report, is transformed in the same breath into a suspiciousness bordering on paranoia at not having been granted the acclaim which his vanity was counting on:

> You've no idea what I've been through today. I've been exposed to every kind of pressure; my rights as an individual have been threatened—. . . .
> Yes! I was expected to crawl and humble myself. My deepest—my most sacred convictions are to be sacrificed for purely personal ends—. (Ibsen, p. 198)

In Miller's version the impulsive hyperbole is dispensed with and the suggestion of generalized persecution is altered by the clear identification of the source of imposition:

> DR. STOCKMANN. The Mayor has declared war, so war is what it's going to be! . . .
> And this is only the beginning! You know what he tried to do? . . . He actually tried to blackmail me! He's got the nerve to tell me that I'm not allowed to speak my mind without his permission! Imagine the shameless effrontery! (Miller, p. 140)

Along with a sincere desire to spell out the truth, Ibsen's Stockmann has anti-social and even anarchic elements in his make-up, so that unlike his counterpart in the adaptation, the sum total of his thoughts and actions amounts to less than the cogent unity of a lawyer's brief. Ibsen's Doctor quickly grows infatuated with his mission as a reformer, and says as much when he tells his wife to go home and look after the house and leave him to look after the community. In his concern for his reputation he is shown not to be unlike his brother, the Mayor, who stands on the other side of the political fence. The Mayor maintains, "If I am concerned with protecting my reputation, it is only for the good of the town" (Ibsen, p. 188). Ibsen established that the two brothers are cut of the same cloth. Each in his own way rationalizes his concern for reputation by identifying himself with the welfare of the community. The Doctor is of course more nearly in the right, but the motivations behind the actions of the two mark their similarity of character and blur the borderlines of their commitments.

Ibsen, then, was not merely interested, as Miller was, in a mouthpiece for his own points of view, but in the infinitely more challenging presentation of a power play between egos and vested interests. In Ibsen's play the life-lie is to be found on both sides, and yet in this welter of half-right and half-wrong and the seemingly universal venality of self-interest, the drama does not succumb to relativism and the Doctor's moral stand is sustained despite all its surrounding vagaries.

In his preface Miller observes,

> it has become the fashion for plays to reduce the "thickness" of life to a fragile facsimile, to avoid portraying the complexities of life, the contradictions of character, the fascinating interplay of cause and effect. . . .

Here, too, Miller is unconsciously passing judgment on himself and his own failings—what one critic has termed "Mr. Miller's steadfast . . . refusal of complexity, the assured simplicity of his view of human behavior. . . ."[13]

Nowhere is Miller's recoil from complexity more in evidence than in the scene in which Dr. Stockmann is confronted by his father-in-law with the information that his failure to compromise can cost the Stockmann family its inheritance. Miller's Doctor weathers the confrontation as a man of unyielding principle, his eyes fixed unerringly on the shining light of his inviolable ideal. "I am ready to hang for my convictions" (Miller, p. 180), he broadcasts loftily. But for Ibsen's Doctor, Kiil proves to be a genuine tempter who shakes his integrity for several bad moments. Stockmann's troubled wish becomes father to a thought that occurs to him for the first time: "Damn it! Surely there must be some scientific way of purifying the water—some sort of disinfectant—" (Ibsen, p. 247). He reminds himself of the injustice done him, that he has been called an enemy of the people, and affirms that he has a duty to his family. "And since everyone says it's merely an illusion on my part—why not let it be an illusion then! Let them have their way" (Ibsen, p. 247)! However, what looks like it could become a sell-out is reversed by an access of anger on the Doctor's part over the imputation of Hovstad and Aslaksen that he is engaged in a conspiracy with his father-in-law for the sake of personal profit.

By reducing the Doctor to a package of virtue, Miller not only flattens the character, he also deprives the play of the subtle irony of the original. The bumptiousness of Stockmann's idealism in the first half of the play is lost, as is the satire on his swelled head in those scenes in which he rejects public honors and banquets on his behalf. In the hat scene some of the more memorable stage action of the play is toned down to the point of eliminating all the underlying mockery. In the original the Doctor puts on the Mayor's hat and seizes his cane to taunt his brother and act out his threat of "taking over." He reverses the tables and the equations of power by this symbolic gesture. For good measure, he adds, "You may be chief of police, but I'm the Mayor—I'm king of the whole town" (Ibsen, p. 213)! In Miller's version the ironic implications of the episode are lost and nothing new is revealed about the Doctor's character. Here the Doctor dons the hat almost as an afterthought and only when the supercilious Mayor demands that it be turned over to him. Ibsen's Doctor, defiant to the end, lays the hat and cane on the table. Miller's Stockmann, being more docile, hands both of them over to the Mayor.

For a variety of reasons, Ibsen's fourth act, with its big assembly scene, poses special problems for a stage performance, and here Miller's adaptation represents a real improvement in several places. At the same time it introduces weaknesses of its own. Miller abridged this act more than any of the others, reducings its last 14 pages to 6, while allowing himself the greatest liberties in making his changes. Ibsen's fourth act is the high point of the play, but because of its length and rambling quality it has limited dramatic staying power. In his frustration over being denied the right to read his report Dr. Stockmann says more than he has reflected upon, and his arguments become a blunderbuss intended to provoke and give hurt; in sheer *non sequitur* he digs up the story of the pirate ancestry in the Stockmann family to embarrass his brother the Mayor. The Doctor's sudden discoveries are harebrained and his thoughts are a discursive crazy quilt. While much of this partakes of the grotesque, its aimlessness inevitably tries the patience of a modern audience.

We can understand that Ibsen was counting on the sympathy of the audience for the persecuted Doctor, at the same time that he was revealing his own ambivalence towards the man who is a rebel at all costs. But by presuming so much, the act oversteps the bounds within which the audience is willing to do what Ibsen's letter says, namely to accept from Dr. Stockmann what they would not accept from the author. The Doctor's self-righteousness and ill-advised preachments simply come off too badly here. Miller economizes greatly at the expense of the overly controversial and irrelevant material, letting his Doctor become excited, but not inarticulate or merely rash. To compensate for the loss of richness of the verbal free-for-all in the original, the adaptation more strongly emphasizes the possibility of physical violence: the Stockmann family, on leaving the meeting, has to pass through a hostile gantlet.

Ibsen's Doctor discovers his contempt for the solid majority relatively late in life and only after the solid majority that he was so delighted to have behind him turns against him. His radicalism, inspired by the frustration and antagonism of the moment, repeatedly overshoots the mark: "In our Society, the worst enemy to truth and freedom is the majority. . . . It's the minority that's always right" (Ibsen, pp. 225–26)! In his ardor the Doctor raises the issue of the springs to national significance and ends by damning the entire country:

> This poison will spread throughout the country, and eventually the whole country
> will deserve to be destroyed; and, should it ever come to that, I'd say from the bottom
> of my heart: let it be destroyed, and let all its people perish! (Ibsen, p. 232)

Miller, on the other hand, does not really challenge the primacy of democracy, nor does he let his hero claim that the majority is always wrong. Instead, he sets forth a few well-tempered arguments showing that the majority can err, and concludes: "The majority is never right until it does right" (Miller, pp. 164–65). It is only natural that Miller should delete the references by Ibsen's Stockmann to animal eugenics, innate racial superiority and extermination of human beings like so much vermin, all of which is too painful a reminder of Nazi ideology. That Ibsen's Doctor, given the chance to calm down, does not really set great store by such racism is evidenced by the fact that in the last act, when he is making plans for a new school, he remarks, "I'm going to experiment with a few mongrels for a change; there's plenty of good raw material there" (Ibsen, p. 254)

IV

One of Miller's more sympathetic critics, Robert Hogan, has pointed out that in the eyes of this playwright "the most valid and fertile subject for the drama is the attempt to show man struggling to be at one with society."[14] Hogan goes on to establish that in most of his mature plays Miller postulates man's need for the respect of his neighbors. These perceptive comments serve to account for the difficulties that Miller clearly had with this play. By using the super-structure of Ibsen's drama, Miller has been obliged not merely to adapt the original, but also to do violence to it, because there is no common ground in their conflicting theses. Miller's preface demonstrates to what extent he miscon-ceives the significance of Ibsen's play:

> I believe this play could be alive for us because its central theme is, in my opinion, the central theme of our social life today. Simply, it is the question of whether the democratic guarantees protecting political minorities ought to be set aside in time of crisis.

This is what Miller's play is about, not Ibsen's.

Miller does not challenge the principles and workings of democracy, but only its abuses. Ibsen, on the other hand, is bluntly calling into question the democratic ideal of majority rule. Miller is interested in protecting political minorities while Ibsen is speaking out on behalf of a leadership of the elite. In an address he delivered to a group of working men in the Norwegian capital in 1885, Ibsen formulated his view on the subject:

> Democracy alone cannot solve the social question. An element of aristocracy needs to be infused into our life. Of course, I do not mean the aristocracy of birth, or the purse, or even the aristocracy of intellect. I mean the aristocracy of character, of will, of mind. That only can free us.[15]

Three years earlier he had explained in a letter to the Danish critic Georg Brandes what he meant by his contention, "It's the minority that's always right!":

> I am of course not thinking of the minority of reactionaries who have been left astern by the big central party which we call liberal; I mean the minority which forges ahead in territory which the majority has not yet reached. (Meyer, p. 201)

The elite, as Ibsen conceived it, is forced to compromise itself if it affiliates with parties and collectives. "An intellectual pioneer," according to Ibsen, "can never gather a majority about him" (Meyer, p. 210). The distance that separates Miller's thinking from the concept of an aristocratic elite is evidenced by his essay "Tragedy and the Common Man," which consigns tragedy to the "heart and spirit of the average man."[16]

Both Ibsen's play and Miller's adaptation raise the question, how much can a man give in and still remain true to himself? Each author provides his own answer to this question by means of the aphorism he devises to conclude the play. Ibsen's reads, "the strongest man in the world is the man who stands alone" (Ibsen, p. 225). Ibsen gave expression to this thought as a *Weltanschauung* ten years before he wrote *Enemy*. Its first and apparently tentative formulation appears in a letter to a friend, which defines the statement that the minority is always right as "my fundamental principle in every field and domain."[17] In another letter directed two weeks later to Georg Brandes, the thought has become more clearly crystallized and is virtually identical with that spoken by Dr. Stockmann: "To me it appears that the man who stands alone is the strongest."[18] This is a position close to Kierkegaard's philosophy and a variation of that enunciated in Schiller's *Wilhelm Tell*, "Der Starke ist am mächtigsten allein." For Ibsen as for Kierkegaard and Schiller, this statement is an affirmation of the self and starts not with a concern for social action, which is the case for Miller, but with an insistence on one's own freedom to act.

Miller's Doctor is stating something quite different when he says of those who fight for truth, "We're the strongest people in the world [. . .] and the strong must learn to be lonely" (Miller, p. 188)! This remark takes its departure not from the individual, but from the plural pronoun "we," and is part of the thinking pattern of the author of *The Crucible*, which depicts the individual as largely helpless until he begins to influence the mass. Miller is, in democratic fashion, setting forth a campaign platform to win over others, a process which requires a union of interests with society.

Ibsen's standpoint is essentially different. He is maintaining that he, like Camus's Sisyphus, finds greater strength and finds it possible to take a firmer stand with regard to his beliefs precisely because of the resistance he encounters. Ibsen implicitly criticizes the view espoused by Miller with the hypocritical words of the provost in *Brand:* "Every man must curb his individuality, / . . . The man who fights alone / Will never achieve anything of lasting value."[19] In *Enemy* Ibsen has the Mayor, whom he identifies with the spirit of democracy,[20] say, "The individual must subordinate himself to Society as a whole . . ." (Ibsen, p. 164). Miller's version makes the Mayor garble these lines because they represent a dictum he is not willing to oppose (Miller, p. 111). And it omits altogether a later speech by the Doctor—"I don't care if the whole world crumbles, I refuse to be a slave to any man" (Ibsen, p. 195)! Here again the two playwrights part company. A letter by Ibsen testifies to this fact:

> I have never really had a strong feeling for solidarity with society and have gone along with it only as a traditional principle; if one had the courage to dismiss it entirely, perhaps one would get rid of the ballast which weighs down most heavily on the personality. There are times when the whole history of the world seems to me like one big shipwreck, in which it is up to everybody to save himself.[21]

Such an attitude partakes, of course, of anarchy, and to an extent translates the motto, "the strongest man in the world is the man who stands alone," into a philosophy of "every man for himself." It makes society the great antagonist against which the individual must rebel. While Miller's heroes doom themselves to frustration by isolating themselves, Ibsen's mostly require separation from the mass if they are to realize themselves. It follows that Miller's primary impetus is his social consciousness. Ibsen, as well as a number of his heroes, on the other hand, develop social consciousness when they discover that they cannot attain self-realization in a corrupt or repressive society.

It is significant that when Ibsen was reproached by the King of Norway for writing *Ghosts*, he did not defend himself by alleging the hopes for social melioration which had impelled him to write the play. Instead, he replied, "But, Your Majesty, I *had* to write *Ghosts*."[22] Here too, self-expression and self-realization are made paramount. Ibsen was affirming that his duty to himself, not the social conscience, came first. *Enemy* implies all this, and something more. Indirectly, it is also saying that true self-realization is to be found in struggle. It makes clear that despite the corruption of society and the fact that the establishment wins its victories by lies and illusions, the individual must answer to his own conscience and speak out against what he thinks is wrong. He must make his stand against all odds and not necessarily with a hope of victory, but for the sheer privilege and necessity of being true to one's self. In a like manner Lessing once stated that if God offered him liberty in His right hand, and the struggle for liberty in His left, he would seize God's left hand in gratitude.[23]

Ibsen demonstrates that it is only when the individual has painfully struggled for self-realization that he is able to make the Doctor's discovery that one is strongest when one stands alone. When Stockmann has pushed himself to the limit, when he has unmasked society, he also ends by removing his own masks and various deceits. Because he has found what he really stands for, he can part with the egocentricity and desire for approbation that had earlier motivated him.

V

It should be clear from a literary point of view that Ibsen's perspective makes for the richer drama. Miller's over-insistence on a moral stance allowed his Dr. Stockmann too little individuality and made him mostly a stock character. Such straitened confines would leave too little latitude for Ibsen's considerably more interesting and complex figure and deny in psychological terms this author's statement that "For me liberty is the first condition of life, and the highest" (Meyer, p. 202).

Unlike Ibsen, who has succeeded in making his case clear against a background of ambivalence and psychological relativism, Miller, to make his point, has in the past needed a clear-cut delineation of good and evil. Quentin, in *After the Fall*, standing outside the concentration camp, observes, "and I, without belief, stand here disarmed."[24] Miller has to have his belief written large and his morality explicit, even if the content of that morality is subject to change. Thus it is also Quentin who enumerates his varying hopes for salvation: "Socialism once, then love . . ." (*Fall*, p. 16).

Ibsen in *Enemy* shows that everyone supports his own truth and that "truth" itself is not always easily identifiable or readily isolated. Miller, by contrast, protects himself and his audience from the uneasiness that must stem from such insights. The problems Miller investigates are comfortably compartmentalized, moral disorder is prophylactically excluded, so that no self-doubt need enter the minds of the playwright and his audience. Truth-seeking in Miller's dramas takes on some of the characteristics of martyrdom: a man of essential purity, by the gesture of his commitment, is putting himself on the stake, secure in the knowledge that his cause is righteous and a great reward— the preservation of the rectitude of his conscience—is assured him. Miller's central character is not really subject to human temptation, because of the desideratum that Miller has described as "the fanatic insistence on his self-conceived role . . ." (*Collected Plays*, p. 33).

There are signs in *After the Fall* that Miller has discovered a greater complexity of vision, in which good and evil are more closely interwoven and the hero is called upon to challenge his own innocence. In an article on this play Miller states, "Man needs to recognize and be aware of the destructive elements in himself."[25] There are lines in this play which read like a retraction of everything Miller had written previously. In that uneven mixture of smugness, flatness and lyricism which frequently in the past has characterized his essayistic writings, Miller once held forth on his own drama production:

> Time, characterizations, and other elements are treated differently from play to play, but all to the end that that moment of commitment be brought forth, that moment when, in my eyes, a man differentiates himself from every other man, that moment when out of a sky full of stars he fixes on one star. (*Collected Plays*, p. 7)

Quentin is of a very different mind in his painful announcement,

> I keep looking back to when there seemed to be some duty in the sky. I had a dinner table and a wife— . . . a child and the world so wonderfully threatened by injustices I was born to correct! It seems so fine! Remember—when there were good people and bad people? And how easy it was to tell! The worst son of a bitch, if he loved Jews and hated Hitler, he was a buddy. Like some kind of paradise compared to this. (*Fall*, p. 22)

In his process of self-discovery Quentin finds that he had been acting out of deeper motivations than those for which he had been congratulating himself; he had prided himself on his desire to help until he discovered it was a desire for power. In a flash of insight that is akin to that afforded by *The Wild Duck* Quentin comes to understand:

> So the truth, after all, may merely be murderous? The truth killed Lou, destroyed Mickey. Then how do you live? A workable lie? But that comes from a clear conscience! Or a dead one. Not to see one's own evil—there's power! And rightness too!—so kill conscience. Kill it. (*Fall*, p. 61)

This play makes it clear that "humanity" also means culpability. Holga avows, "no one they didn't kill can be innocent again" (*Fall*, p. 21), and the play symbolically incorporates a reminder of universal guilt by means of the stone tower of the German concentration camp.

It is impossible for Miller to hold such views as these without questioning his own affirmation of high principle and without being suspicious of the self-assuring sentiment that goes with being a reformer. Apparently, however, Miller has found it difficult to live with his own insight that the lack of innocence is an integral part of man. In *Incident at Vichy* he refutes Quentin's withering line, inspired by the vision of the stone tower, "no man lives who would not rather be the sole survivor of this place than all its finest victims" (*Fall*, p. 113)! *Incident at Vichy* represents an attempt, within the configuration of an existential situation, to reinstate the possibility of innocence. Von Berg, an inarticulate and unpolemical, but high-minded person who remains a confirmation of purity in a corrupt world, chooses to be a victim in the name of innocence and gives up his life so that Leduc, the Jewish psychiatrist, can go free.

Leduc, who gives the play its dialectic of good and evil, has learned about man that "he is full of murder, . . . his ideals are only the little tax he pays for the right to kill with a clear conscience."[26] He also poses the injunction, "know theyself": "Part of knowing who we are is knowing we are not someone else. . . . And that is why there is nothing and will be nothing—until you face your own complicity with this [. . .] your own humanity."[27] This play retains the insight of *After the Fall* about the dubious quality of man's ideals, at the same time that it returns to the earlier transcendence of the ideal. It takes the way out of giving awareness of evil to one character and sheer innocence to another.

Miller's most recent play, *The Price*, couples the problem of attaining success with that of being true to oneself, themes which are central to all his major works. Walter, the successful surgeon, whose primary loyalty has been to himself and who abandoned his father and brother when they needed his help, reveals the price he paid to gain wealth and power when he says, "there's simply no time for people."[28] Walter's brother Victor, on the other hand, has sacrificed his chance for a professional career out of a sense of duty to the father he felt he had to support. On the surface the situation seems to be a recapitulation of familiar instances in which Miller has pitted rectitude against egoism. In reality, however, both brothers, in looking for justification of their past, have been deceiving themselves about their underlying motivations. It is significant that in the dramatically effective second act the audience is led to change its mind several times as to which of the brothers has been in the right.

Each brother is battling conflicting forces in himself which remain partially incomprehensible. The parallel to *Fall* is obvious. Victor, no less than Walter, is forced to challenge his own innocence and discovers that he has acted out of considerations he has been unwilling to recognize. What seemed to be rational decisions have in reality masked life-lies which are part of the self-image of both brothers. The echoes of Ibsen and more especially of the original version of *Enemy* become evident when Walter tells his brother, "we're like two halves of the same guy" (Price, p. 110). Miller's relinquishing of the absolute is borne out by the "Author's Production Note": "A fine balance of sympathy should be maintained in the playing of the roles of Victor and Walter. . . . As the world now operates, the qualities of both brothers are necessary to it . . . (*Price*, p. 117).

Solomon, the old Jewish second-hand dealer, is playing raisonneur when he tells Victor, "Let me give you a piece of advice—it's not that you can't believe nothing, that's not so hard—it's that you still got to believe. . . . That's hard. And if you can't do that, my friend—you're a dead man" (*Price*, p. 37)! All of which is to say that man errs, but he must go on living and believing in himself. This eighty-nine year old Jew, who ends the play with explosive laughter, symbolizes the vitality that affirms life despite the suffering and disappointments brought about by existence and one's own misguided acts.

The Price is not a great play, but it is an absorbing one which does not pretend to deliver final answers to life's problems. It remains to be seen what Miller will do in future plays with his newly-won perception.

In any case, after his own fall from innocence, it is not likely that he will retreat to that period of his production, amply illustrated by his prosy adaptation of *Enemy*. Here he measured out mutually exclusive portions of good and evil and dispensed with the substance of life, the individuality and extravagance, the irony and grotesqueness of Ibsen's Stockmann, so that, devoid of all distractions, he could say, like his model, "Now listen here!"

Notes

1. William Archer, in John Northam, *Ibsen's Dramatic Method: A Study of the Prose Dramas* (London, 1953), p. 77; Robert Brustein, *The Theatre of Revolt* (Boston, 1964), p. 72; and Eric Bentley, "Henrik Ibsen: A Personal Statement," *Ibsen: A Collection of Critical Essays*, ed. Rolf Fjelde (Englewood Cliffs, N.J., 1965), p. 16.

2. Brustein, p. 71.

3. *Ghosts and Three Other Plays*, trans. by Michael Meyer (Garden City, N.Y. 1966), p. 203. All other references to this work will be identified in the text as "Meyer."

4. *A Grammar of Motives* (New York, 1955), pp. 3f.

5. *An Enemy of the People*, adapted by Arthur Miller, in *Seeds of Modern Drama*, III (New York, 1963), 108. All further references to this work will be cited in the text as "Miller."

6. *Arthur Miller's Collected plays* (New York, 1957), p. 22. All other references to this work will be identified in the text as "*Collected Plays*."

7. *Six Plays by Henrik Ibsen*, trans. by Eva Le Gallienne (New York, 1957), p. 169. All other references to Ibsen's *Enemy* will be quoted from this work and identified in the text as "Ibsen."

8. Allan Seager, "The Creative Agony of Arthur Miller," *Esquire*, LII (October, 1959), 123.

[9. Eric Bentley, "The Innocence of Arthur Miller," *The Dramatic Event* (New York, 1954), pp. 90, 94.—Ed. Note]

10 "When We Dead Awaken," ed. James Walter McFarlane, *Discussions of Henrik Ibsen* (Boston, 1962), p. 62.

11. Hermann Weigand, *The Modern Ibsen* (New York, 1960), pp. 120–21.

12. Halvdan Koht, *The Life of Ibsen*, II (New York, 1931), 184. The text of the original, which

I have translated, reads: " 'Stockmann,' he said many years later to a German friend, . . . 'ist zum Teil ein grotesker Bursche und ein Strudelkopf'."

13. Robert Warshow, "The Liberal Conscience in 'The Crucible.' Arthur Miller and His Audience," *Commentary*, XV (March, 1953), 267.

14. Robert Hogan, *Arthur Miller* (Minneapolis, 1964), p. 8.

15. Montrose J. Moses, *Henrik Ibsen: The Man and His Plays* (Boston, 1908), p. 383.

16. In Robert W. Corrigan, ed., *Tragedy: Vision and Form* (San Francisco, 1965), p. 151.

17. Hermann Weigand, p. 121.

18. Ibid.

19. Ibid., p. 136.

20. Dr. Stockmann, after having provoked his brother's ire by donning his insignia of office, says mockingly, "Listen to him! We've roused the spirit of democracy— . . ." (Ibsen, p. 213).

21. In Johannes Mayrhofer, *Henrik Ibsen: Ein literarisches Charakterbild* (Berlin, 1911), p. 111. The translation is mine; the letter, which bears the date September 24, 1871, is directed to Georg Brandes.

22. F. L. Lucas, *The Drama of Ibsen and Strindberg* (London, 1962), p. 169.

23. Gotthold Ephraim Lessing, "Eine Duplik," *Gesammelte Werke*, VII (Berlin, 1956), 27.

24. (New York, 1964), p. 15. All other references to this work will be identified in the text as "*Fall.*"

25. In Sheila Huftel, *Arthur Miller: The Burning Glass* (New York, 1965), p. 192. The article originally appeared in *The Stage* (February 13, 1965).

26. *Incident at Vichy* (New York, 1965), p. 65.

27. Ibid., p. 66.

28. *The Price* (New York, 1968), p. 74. All other references to this work will be cited in the text as "*Price.*"

The Crucible

Mr. Miller Looks at
Witch-Hunting

Richard Watts, Jr.°

Arthur Miller's "The Crucible," which opened at the Martin Beck last night, is a drama of emotional power and impact. In it, the author of "Death of a Salesman" is contemplating the rise of mass hysteria and intolerance as represented by the horrible Salem witch trials of 1692, and, although he clearly would not be averse to having his spectator's notice certain disquieting resemblances to present-day conditions, he doesn't press the parallels too closely. The result is a hardhitting and effective play that demands and deserves audience attention, even though it lacks some of the compelling excellence I had expected of it.

This is certainly not to say that "The Crucible" is without the spirit and eloquence that we have come to expect of Mr. Miller. Almost throughout, the play's emotional forthrightness grips the attention and holds it amid a succession of scenes of unrelenting excitement. It is written with feeling and indignation, and the importance of what it is saying by implication gives it dignity, largeness and inescapable distinction. In scene after scene, it has the sort of ringing intensity that is fairly irresistable.

Emotionally, I think it is vastly successful. Where I found it a little disappointing in its final effectiveness is in Mr. Miller's inability to combine with it the kind of intellectual insight that was so notable in "Death of a Salesman" and made it one of the most distinguished dramas of the American theater. To a certain extent, the author does delve into the causes and motives that created the background of the terrors which marked one of the darkest spots in our history. But he is chiefly concerned with what happened, rather than why, and this neglect sometimes gives his work a hint of superficiality.

It is no doubt highly unfair to compare Miller's treatment of intolerance with Bernard Shaw's magnificent use of the theme in "Saint Joan," but I hope I can show what I mean by contrasting the Inquisitor in the latter drama with Deputy-Governor Danforth in "The Crucible." Shaw made his Inquisitor a man of great intellectual gifts and moral stature, and was all the more impressive by showing that intolerance could force even such a person into the terrible act of burning Joan at the stake. Miller's Deputy-Governor is also a well-meaning man doing frightful things, but, despite Walter Hampden's excellent playing, he emerges as pretty much a cardboard villain.

While there is, to my mind, an unfortunate superficiality in "The Crucible," the playwright deserves considerable credit for using implication, rather than too heavy an underlining to make his valuable points for today. There are, indeed, only a few moments when he doesn't let his sinister story speak for itself, and they are chiefly in the last act. But his characters tend to be dramatized points of view, or points of emotional hysteria, rather than the human beings that would have made them more striking in the theater. Nevertheless, despite such weaknesses, there is much emotional fire and indignation which can approach the overwhelming.

It seems a little fantastic to say that the veteran Mr. Hampden, at his age, is improving as an actor, but I don't think I have seen him finer than he is in "The Crucible." Arthur Kennedy proves once more his right to be considered one of the ablest of our younger actors by the moving honesty with which he plays an outraged and unheroic man trying to fight hysteria, and there are excellent portrayals by Beatrice Straight, E. G. Marshall, Fred Stewart, Madeleine Sherwood, Joseph Sweeney, Raymond Bramley, Jenny Egan and Jean Adair. Jed Harris has directed vigorously. Despite its frailties, "The Crucible" is not easily to be forgotten.

The Long Shadow of the Law:
The Crucible

Thomas E. Porter[*]

Among popular forms perennially in favor on Broadway and in the television ratings, the courtroom drama ranks with the leaders. Numerous television series have used the format, from simple whodunits like *Perry Mason*, in which the trial is a device for discovering the criminal, to *The Defenders*, which used the courtroom drama to present controversial issues in legal principle and in practice. Recent Broadway seasons have featured a wide spectrum: *Billy Budd*, *The Caine Mutiny Court Martial*, *Witness for the Prosecution*, *The Andersonville Trial*, *Twelve Angry Men*. This format has inherent qualities that attract the playwright of any age: a clear division between protagonist and antagonist, gradual revelation of the facts, application of facts to principles, suspense leading to the climax of verdict. Though the formula has never been neglected (*Oresteia*, *Measure for Measure*, *Volpone*, *St. Joan*), it is most favored in democracies, where the Law is venerated and the Court the principle instrument of justice. Beneath the trial formula and the trappings of the Law, there is a complex of attitudes that includes veneration for these institutions. The courtroom has become the sanctuary of modern secularized society and the trial the only true ritual it has left.

The development of these attitudes toward the Law and its ritual began early in American history. Our society from its beginnings had a respect for, and confidence in, the Law. Tom Paine, in *Common Sense*, voiced an ideal which, though it has been variously interpreted, has retained its fascination for the American mind:

> But where say some is the King of America? I'll tell you Friend he reigns above; and doth not make havoc of mankind like the Royal Brute of Great Britain. Yet that we may not appear to be defective even in earthly honors, let a day be solemnly set apart for the proclaiming of the Charter; let it be brought forth placed on the Devine Law, the Word of God; let a crown be placed thereon, by which the World may know, that so far as we approve of monarchy, that in America THE LAW IS KING.

For the contemporary bureaucrat as for the revolutionary patriot, "government

[*]Reprinted from Thomas E. Porter, *Myth and Modern American Drama* (Detroit: Wayne State Univ. Press, 1969), pp. 177-99, by permission of Wayne State University Press and the author. Copyright © 1969 by Wayne State University Press.

under the Law" expresses the democratic ideal: equal rights for all, protection both for the individual in his legitimate endeavors and for society from the depredations of unprincipled individuals, justice meted out with an impersonal, unprejudiced hand according to ordinance. In the Law, so the democrat holds, all opposites are reconciled; the individual and the community, freedom and regimentation, the rule of principle and the rule of men. As the King is the principle of order in a monarchy, so the Law is considered the source of order in a democracy.

In America more obviously than elsewhere, there has been a tendency to regard the Law as the embodiement of "moral law" and "natural law," as well as a *corpus juris* inherited from legal tradition. The nineteenth-century concept of "fundamental law" was made up of these two and was looked on as absolute and immutable.[1] This attitude, foreshadowed in Paine's juxtaposition of Bible and Charter, received concrete expression in the dominance of church and courthouse in the nineteenth-century village and town. When the influence of the church declined, the Law necessarily exerted a greater influence than ever. The corpus of the common law and the system by which it is administered has acquired an aura of permanence and infallibility. On these elements, according to the American creed, rests the security of the citizen and the stability of his way of life.

Belief in this idea has engendered a veneration also for the courts and the lawyers who practice in them. Every culture has some sort of spiritual government that is entrusted with the ideals of that culture. In America the Courts are at once the receptacle and the guardian of those ideals. "Our spiritual government today centers in the judicial system. Here is the bulwark of all the older symbols and theories both legal and economic. Here is the stage on which the ideals of society are given concrete reality."[2] This attitude is most manifest when the courts come under attack.

> Americans alone of Western people made constitutionalism a religion and the judiciary a religious order and surrounded both with an aura of piety. They made the Constitution supreme law, and placed responsibility for the functioning of the federal system on the courts. The Supreme Court, in time, became the most nearly sacrosanct of American institutions.[3]

The dignity and inviolability accorded the Supreme Court is shared by the whole judicial system. The judge, *ex officio*, holds a position of influence and respect, and in his own courtroom, he is absolute master. The legal profession, while not so exalted, shares some of this distinction with the judiciary. Reverence for the Court and respect for the lawyer is a reflection of an abiding belief in justice and equality administered under the Law.

One of the most persistent attitudes embodied in the myth of the Law is the notion of a "fair trial." "The notion that every man however lowly is entitled to a fair trial and an impartial hearing is regarded as the cornerstone of civilized government."[4] The Law is seen as watching over legal procedures and

guaranteeing impartiality by "due process." The general outlines of the procedure are: a preliminary hearing; an indictment which discloses to the accused
the nature of the offense; a trial in which evidence is presented fully and an
opportunity given to the accused to introduce and respond to all relevant issues;
an appellate review of both the law and the evidence; a permanent written
record of the entire proceedings.[5] The "fair trial" aspect of our view of the Law
provides for the protection of the individual from "mob rule" and tyranny.

Another attitude, generally and vaguely opposed to the ideal of fair trial, is
the sacredness of law enforcement. As the Law protects the individual from
injustice, it also secures the rights of society against the criminal. This aspect of
the myth emphasizes the absolute nature of the principles involved and demands that principles be applied to the facts impersonally, beyond purely
personal discretion. If laws are not enforced, and disrespect for the law allowed
to flourish, then chaos results.

If we look at the two attitudes expressed by the myth, in theory they seem
to involve a number of contradictions: the individual in the democracy must be
free, yet the rules laid down by society constrain him; a permanent unyielding
code must be enforced without respect to persons, yet justice can never ignore
persons; the majority must rule, yet minorities are entitled to their rights. When
these theories are applied to criminal law, the same type of contradiction
appears:

> An attorney should not take cases the winning of which imperils the forces of law and
> order; every criminal, however, is entitled to a defense; criminal lawyers, however,
> should not resort to mere technicalities; nevertheless, they should do everything
> legally possible for their clients.[6]

These contradictions, if spelled out and adverted to, would paralyze the legal
system; they can subsist together only because they are resolved in practice. In
the American system, the trial reconciles these attitudes in a ritual action. It is a
genuine ritual—a communal, sacrosanct ceremony that expresses the beliefs of
the community and, within the limits of the myth, provides for the purgation of
the individual and order in the society.

The trial ritual—the structure of the action and the actors involved—
dramatizes both the fair-trial and the law-enforcement aspects of the myth. It is
an investigation of innocence and guilt in terms of an application of facts and
motives to principles. There is a clear declaration of the issues, a marshalling of
forces into opposing camps, a verdict in which justice is done. The opposing
camps—prosecution and defense—represent, broadly speaking, the two extremes; the prosecution maintaining the rights of society and the defense the
rights of the individual. The judge represents the absolute nature of the law and
arbitrates the application of facts to principles. In its verdict, the jury resolves
the opposition between these two forces under the direction of the judge. As
peers who can evaluate the motives and actions of the accused and as citizens
who respect the law, the members of this body represent both the individual

and society. Thus they can weigh the case and make an objective judgment. Ideally, the verdict has the status of absolute truth that encompasses all the attitudes of society. Dramatically, it is the epiphany that resolves the agon.

The ceremonial nature of this action is underscored by the circumstances that surround it and by the formalized treatment it is given. Even the criminal taken red-handed is not considered guilty until the jury is in and the verdict rendered. The protocol of the courtroom—the baliff's cry, the judge's robes, the formal language—are all part of the ritual atmosphere. The set procedure, with its rubrical consistency, also emphasizes the ceremonial structure. These details declare that the trial is a ritual in which (ideally) justice is done and in which the contradictions in the democratic system are reconciled.

One of the most instructive attempts by a contemporary playwright to make use of the trial ritual and the attitudes that surround it is Arthur Miller's *The Crucible*. Plays like *The Caine Mutiny Court Martial* use the formula in a straight-forward way to vindicate the hero's actions or, at least, his motives; in such plays the trial is a convenient dramatic device for presenting the action. The probity of the court is taken for granted; due process is the means by which the defense can insure justice for the individual. Miller's play not only uses the formula as a dramatic framing device, but also raises the question about the value of the trial itself as an instrument of justice. At the heart of *The Crucible* is the relation of the individual to the Law, and the author's probing into this area makes the play a significant work. Miller has described the playwright's art in terms of the Law: "In one sense a play is a species of jurisprudence, and some part of it must take the advocate's role, something else must act in defense, and the entirety must engage the Law."[7] Whether or not this analogy holds true for his other efforts is a moot point; in *The Crucible* he consciously uses history and the trial formula to investigate the American attitude toward the Law.

Miller's play is based on actual records of a seventeenth-century incident in colonial Salem, but it has clear parallels with contemporary events. Attempts to write historical drama for the modern theatre have not been notably success-ful; perhaps they have never been except when the past is dealt with in terms of the present. Maxwell Anderson failed in spite of his Shakespearean style, and his *Elizabeth the Queen* and *Mary of Scotland*, while they tap a remote sense of Anglo-Saxon pride, today seem almost as dated as Boker's *Francesca da Rimini*. Conversely, currently popular history plays—*Man for All Seasons*, *Luther*, *Becket*—make the story a vehicle for modern themes: the folly of depending on the common man or the purity of the law, religion as a psychophysical phe-nomenon, the inevitability of a cultural clash even when individuals are person-ally engaged. For the dramatist, history serves as a glass in which the audience sees its own image.

The Crucible opened on Broadway January 22, 1953, at the height of the furor stirred up by the accusations of Senator Joe McCarthy. In February of 1950 McCarthy had addressed the Ohio County Women's Republican Club in Wheeling, West Virginia. In his speech, as the Wheeling *Intelligencer* reported it, he claimed to have "in his hand" a list of two-hundred-and-five known

Communists in the State Department. With this broadside the panic was on. The "threat of Communism from within" became a serious consideration in national politics and in the attitudes of Americans; McCarthy became a rallying point for conservatives the country over. By 1953 investigations of this charge (and the variants which McCarthy later added) were being undertaken on a nation-wide scale. The Senator used his Congressional privilege to investigate people in public life, and everyone who had had any connection with the Party felt the pressure of public opinion and a sense of insecurity about their position and their public image. Miller's own record in this regard was not unblemished and the matter became a personal threat.

> It was the fact that a political, objective, knowledgeable campaign from the far Right was capable of creating not only a terror but a new subjective reality, a veritable mystique which was gradually assuming even a holy resonance. The wonder of it all struck me that so practical and picayune a cause, carried forward by such manifestly ridiculous men, should be capable of paralyzing thought itself, and worse, causing to billow up such persuasive clouds of "mysterious" feelings within people.[8]

He was deeply disturbed as he watched men who had known him well for years pass him by "without a word" because of this terror "knowingly planned and consciously engineered." McCarthyism was in the air and it had all the qualities—for those personally affected—of the witch-hunt. Miller consciously draws the parallel; his plays are efforts to deal with what was "in the air." "They are one man's way of saying to his fellow men, 'This is what you see every day, or think or feel; now I will show you what you really know but have not had the time or the disinterestedness, or the insight, or the information to understand consciously.'"[9] Once the Communist issue settled into the background, the playwright could protest that the real inner meaning of the play is not simply an attack on McCarthyism, but a treatment of the perennial conflict between individual conscience and civil society—"the handing over of conscience to another and the realization that with conscience goes the person, the soul immortal, and the 'Name.'"[10] In any event, there is a parallel between what happened in Salem under the Puritan theocracy and what happened in Washington under the aegis of anti-Communism, and this parallel has its impact on Miller's treatment of the historical record. In a broader perspective, the myth of the Law and the ritual of the trial shape the structure of the play and help determine its ultimate dramatic meaning.

If the reign of Law is central to the American democratic ideal and if the "fair trial" is the ritual which insures its inviolability, the worst of all perversions in this area is a "bad" law enforced by a "corrupt" court. It is quite clear that, in the real order of things, any particular law is judged not by an absolute standard, but by one relative to a public consensus, and that this consensus can change. Thus, for instance, the trial of Joan of Arc seems a blatant miscarriage of justice, not because the judges failed to adhere to due process or to apply the letter of the law, but because a heresy law itself no longer compels any agreement from society at large. Prosecutions for heresy no longer fit into popular notions about the area of legal inquiry. Therefore, Joan's trial, by standards of due process "so eminently fair," has long appeared to be a travesty of justice.[11] Because the last appeal in a democratic system is to the courts and because the Law is the bulwark of social order, any vision of corruption in the judiciary, any use of the law against the tenor of the popular mind, becomes the occasion for a general outcry. So, after the fact, the Sacco-Vanzetti case and the McCarthy investigations can be dubbed witch-hunts, whether due process was observed or not. This corruption is always laid at the door of particular individuals or a particular community because it cannot be attributed to the idea of the Law itself. Miller, in *The Crucible*, deals with the perversion of the Law in the township of Salem and, by extension, with a persistent threat to any democratic system.

In the light of this belief—that corruption is of the individual—it is worth noting that Miller found inspiration for the play in a bit of personal information embedded in the trial records:

> I had known of the Salem witch-hunt for many years before "McCarthyism" had arrived. . . . I doubt I should even have tempted agony by actually writing a play upon the subject had I not come upon a single fact. It was that Abigail Williams, the prime mover of the Salem hysteria, so far as the hysterical children were concerned, had a short time earlier been the house servant of the Proctors, and now was crying out Elizabeth Proctor as a witch, but more—it was clear from the record that with entirely uncharacteristic fastidiousness she was refusing to include John Proctor, Elizabeth's husband, in her accusations, despite the urging of the prosecutors.[12]

Though the major issue in the play deals with the individual and society and with judicial corruption, Miller found his dramatic motivation in a domestic triangle. There is no question of the law as such being at fault; it is the motivations of individuals that are to provide an understanding of the hysteria that created and prolonged the witch-hunt. Within the structure of the trial formula Miller investigates these motivations and the actions which flow from them in relation to the guilt or innocence of individuals and of the community.

The trial formula, when it is not simply a framing device for a detective-story plot, is an investigation of innocence and guilt in terms of an application of facts and motives to principles. In order that guilt or innocence be proven, the individual declared responsible for evil or exonerated of it, the ritual provides for a clear definition of the issues, and a marshalling of forces into opposing camps. The resulting agon is presided over by judge and/or jury representing the impartiality of the principles (which are not always included in any particular law or set of laws) from which justice emanates.

The dramatic uses of this formula can be various. In the melodramatic treatment, the hero is falsely accused and vindicated by the verdict with the onus falling on a clearly defined group of villians or on a single vicious individual. More complex versions of the pattern depend on a less definite division of responsibility. For instance, the hero can be declared legally guilty according to a "bad" law or by a corrupt court, thus throwing the real guilt on the community that supports the law or fails to impeach the court. The implied result is the purgation of society for whose renewed sense of justice the hero is responsible. A third version declares the hero really guilty under a good law, thus revealing a hitherto unacknowledged guilt to him (and to the audience). When the protagonist as individual or type stands convicted in the light of genuine principles, the trial is essentially a purification ritual, its dramatic effect varies according to the distribution of guilt and innocence. *The Crucible*, even though it does indict the community, includes a complicating variant because the protagonist, besides answering a formal charge, must satisfy his own conscience about his innocence.

The structure of events, then, involves two investigations, two indictments, and two verdicts. Proctor is arraigned by the court for witchcraft; Proctor weighs the guilt of his infidelity to his wife. These two issues are carefully interwoven by the playwright, for Proctor's guilty relationship with Abigail Williams provides him with the evidence to prove the official testimony of Abby and the girls fraudulent. Thus the investigation of the witchcraft charge involves his confessing to adultery. These two issues, both of which involve Proctor's guilt, interrelate to determine the meaning of the play. What is ultimately at stake is the relation of the individual to a society governed by men under the Law. Whatever Miller intended to do in his play, *The Crucible* makes a statement about this relationship.

In one of his headnotes Miller makes a claim for his historical accuracy in depicting the events of the witch trials. The play is situated in the appropriate historical context of time and place. Salem of 1692 is depicted as an isolated community, self-contained by the surrounding forest; its spiritual government and the secular arm are in the hands of Puritan divines and the law is the law of the covenanter; the dialogue has a suitable seventeenth-century flavor. The action runs chronologically within the setting so that the realistic progression fits with the logic of the trial formula and the historical event. But the playwright adds to this perspective another dimension—a consciousness of the significance of these events to a present-day democracy. The "good people" in the cast of characters have attitudes which reflect contemporary ideals rather than the historical Puritan outlook. Thus the playwright does not mechanically reproduce the 1692 situation and exploit it for its inherent dramatic values; rather through the attitudes of the protagonist, his allies among the villagers and one of the inquisitors, he includes a perspective relevant to the audience. Miller himself was aware of this broader dimension. He explains that his realism does not imply an attempt at slice-of-life drama; he felt that the expressionism of *Death of a Salesman* would be unnecessary:

> I had found a kind of self-awareness in the bloody book of Salem and had thought that since the natural realistic surface of that society was one already immersed in the questions of meaning and the relations of men to God, to write a realistic play of that world was already to write in a style beyond contemporary realism.[13]

Perhaps this self-awareness is better attributed to the playwright than to the trial records; in any event, there is a dimension in the play which anticipates the modern attitude toward the Salem incident, whether history includes it or not.[14]

As a defendant in the courtroom and protagonist in the drama John Proctor is very recognizable. He is a farmer, a man of substance in the community without being a land-grabber like the malicious Thomas Putnam. Though he lives outside the ambit of the village, he acts as a respected member of the community. In his dealings with others, neighbors and servants, he is straightforward, honest and somewhat unpolished. When he comes looking for his delinquent servant girl, there will be no nonsense: "I'll show you a great doin' on your arse one of these days. Now get you home; my wife is waitin' with your work!"[15] This rugged individualism also informs his attitude toward religion—positive, undogmatic with more than a touch of scepticism on the witchcraft issue.

> *Putnam.* I do not think I saw you at Sabbath meeting since the snow flew.
> *Proctor.* I have trouble enough without I come five miles to hear him preach only hellfire and bloody damnation. Take it to heart, Mr. Parris. There are many others who stay away from church these days because you hardly ever mention God any more. (CRUCIBLE, p. 245.)

He cannot brook the idea of the minister who should be a servant to the parish making himself the authority: "I do not like the smell of this 'authority.'" Neither is he a sombre or a solemn man; he has that quality which distinguishes a line of American heroes, a love of nature and the outdoors. His first scene with Elizabeth dwells on fertility and the beauties of nature.

> *Proctor.* This farm's a continent when you go foot by foot droppin' seeds in it.
> *Elizabeth.* (coming with the cider) It must be.
> *Proctor.* (drinks a long draught; then, putting the glass down) You ought to bring some flowers in the house.
> *Elizabeth.* Oh, I forgot! I will tomorrow.
> *Proctor.* It's winter in here yet. On Sunday let you come with me, and we'll walk the farm together; I never see such a load of flowers on the earth. . . . Lilacs has a purple smell. Lilac is a smell of nightfall, I think. Massachusetts is a beauty in the spring. (CRUCIBLE, p. 262.)

This quality—the touch of the poet, the appreciation of nature—relates to Proctor's predicament with Abby. The girl has gauged his temper, he is no "cold man." She tempted him and, being a man of strong passions, he fell. By the time the play opens, the nagging of conscience has produced a resolve not to touch her again. The affair, as far as Proctor is concerned, is over and done with; he has confessed to his wife and honestly is trying to make it up to her. In short, Miller's protagonist is no Puritan, no hypocrite; he has the democratic virtues (and vices) that render him recognizable to the audience.

With Proctor are associated the "good people" of the village. Giles Corey, the homespun old curmudgeon who battles for his rights in court, Rebecca Nurse, the sainted lady of the village with a wide reputation for charity, are also caught in the web of the law, the one because he injudiciously wanted to know what his wife was reading in her books, the other because she could not save

Goody Putnam's children. Corey manifests the same kind of individualism as Proctor; he will not accept the tyranny of his neighbors or the injustice of the court. Rebecca Nurse also shows a blessed scepticism by suggesting perhaps the malice of the villagers, rather than the practice of witchcraft, is responsible for the evil that is abroad. During the course of the action one of the prosecutors, Mr. Hale, is converted in a dramatic acknowledgement of Proctor's position. These personae reflect the protagonist's qualities and so are related to him in the course of the action.

The opposition is concentrated in Abigail Williams who bridges the official investigation and Proctor's personal struggle. The "evil" in the play focuses on Abigail as fountainhead, even though she is not its most chilling expression. It is not her actions that condemn her: dancing in the woods by modern standards is no crime, her desire for John Proctor is rendered quite understandable, her uncle's superciliousness is riding for a fall. Rather, it is the means she uses to pursue her ends. She is willing to sacrifice the community and everyone in it, to subvert the function of the Law, in order to gain her objectives. Her wickedness, then, amounts to a shrewd use of the hypocrisy, greed and spite that thrive in her neighbors under the pretext of seeing justice done. Her power arises from her ability to convert her psychic energies and the willful pursuit of her own objectives into a genuine visionary hysteria. At bottom Abby knows that her prophetic fit is self-induced, that the witchcraft she denounces is non-existent; but once the fit is on her, she can produce a convincing performance and induce the same kind of hysteria in the children. Her real diabolism is her misuse of the sacrosanct office of witness to gain her own ends.

With her are associated the "bad people" of Salem, those who are shown to be greedy and spiteful like the Putnams, those who are envious of power and status like Parris and Cheever. When witchcraft is murmured in the streets, the concealed feelings and grudges come to the surface. Thus the sterile Putnams cry out on Giles Corey for his land and Rebecca Nurse for her good name and her large brood. Parris sees an opportunity to put down the rebellious "faction" (Proctor and Corey) in the parish which refuses him ownership of his house and golden candlesticks for his altar. They can invoke the letter of the law, the witchcraft ordinance, for their own purposes. Conventional belief supports the mischief they do in the name of tradition. Their evil, like Abigail's, is a misuse of law and the court, institutions which everyone must respect as the source of order in the community. This evil, if execrable, is intelligible, for it looks to personal gain and satisfaction of the ego.

Between the Proctor faction and the bad people is the official judiciary, the judges and members of the court. The court represents the force of the Law, impersonal and impartial, which reconciles letter and spirit, law enforcement and individual rights. An attitude of reverence for the Law permeates the play. Mr. Hale comes armed with its authority, "allied to the best minds of Europe— kings, philosophers, scientists, and ecclesiasts of all churches." His armful of tomes, he pompously declares, are weighted with authority. Here are principles with the certainty of law to test by:

> *Hale.* Now let me instruct you. We cannot look to superstition in this. The Devil
> is precise; the marks of his presence are definite as stone, and I must tell you all that I
> shall not proceed unless you are prepared to believe me if I should find no bruise of
> hell upon her. (CRUCIBLE, p. 252.)

Hale proceeds with his investigation calmly, impersonally, sounding his warning about going beyond the facts, and relying on his authoritative books. When
the official inquiry opens, the court possesses the same sense of solemnity and
definitiveness. Elizabeth calls it "a proper court, four judges sent out of Boston,
weighty magistrates of the General Court." When Proctor threatens to rip the
Governor's warrant, Cheever, the clerk of the court, warns him not to touch it.
Constable Herrick's nine men must arrest Elizabeth—it is so ordered by the
court. (CRUCIBLE, p. 281.) When, in the third act, Judge Danforth is introduced, he is wrapped in the dignity of his office and knowledge of the law. After
a disturbance in the courtroom and an outcry by Giles Corey, he interrogates
the old man:

> *Danforth.* Who is this man? . . .
> *Giles.* My name is Corey, sir, Giles Corey. I have six hundred acres, and timber
> in addition. It is my wife you be condemning now.
> *Danforth.* And how do you imagine to help her cause with such contemptuous
> riot? Now be gone. Your old age alone keeps you out of jail for this.
> *Giles.* They be tellin' lies about my wife, sir, I—
> *Danforth.* Do you take it upon yourself to determine what this court shall
> believe and what it shall set aside?
> *Giles.* Your Excellency, we mean no disrespect for—
> *Danforth.* Disrespect, indeed! This is disruption, Mister. This is the highest court
> of the supreme government of this division. (CRUCIBLE, p. 287.)

Even the rough old yeoman is impressed with Danforth and has no doubts
about his being a good judge. On this point the record shows, and Miller
acknowledges, that due process is Danforth's middle name. Even in the face of
Proctor who ripped his warrant and damned the court, the judge is prepared to
"hear the evidence." Whatever motives they might have, the men-at-law conduct their cases with a fine show of impartiality. In the end Danforth and Hale
are shown to have been on different sides of the fence; Danforth is joined to
Abigail and the forces of evil and Hale becomes an advocate of the individual
with Proctor. But this fourth-act epiphany derives its full significance only in
contrast to the image of dignity and impartiality that the judges and the lawyers
demonstrate in the first three acts.

Though she is one of the accused and John Proctor's wife, Elizabeth, in the
early scenes, shares this dramatic function of the judiciary because she rules on
Proctor's personal guilt with regard to his infidelity. Proctor makes this function
clear:

> *Proctor.* I cannot speak but I am doubted, every moment judged for lies, as
> though I come into a court when I come into this house!
> *Elizabeth.* John, you are not open with me. You saw her in a crowd, you said.
> Now you—

Proctor. No more! I should have roared you down when first you told me your suspicion. But I wilted, and, like a Christian, I confessed. Confessed! Some dream I had must have mistaken you for God that day. But you're not, you're not, and let you remember it! Let you look sometimes for the goodness in me, and judge me not.

Elizabeth. I do not judge you. The magistrate sits in your heart that judges you. I never thought you but a good man, John—(with a smile)—only somewhat bewildered.

Proctor. (laughing bitterly) Oh, Elizabeth, your justice would freeze beer! (CRUCIBLE, p. 265.)

The wife is a mirror of the magistrate; she is unemotional, impersonal about the relationship. She stands in much the same position with regard to John and Abigail as Danforth does to the witches and the community. This is another link between the two plot-lines. The "cold wife" cannot arrive at a fair decision about her husband because she relies on the "evidence" and the letter of the law.

The opposing camps are finally drawn up according to their attitude toward the Law. The protagonist and his allies, whether or not they believe in the existence of witchcraft, do not believe in the rigid enforcement of this law in Salem. They see that, literally, the letter killeth. The antagonists, whether believers or not, stand by the rigid enforcement of the letter for their own purposes. The judiciary, bound by the Law to do justice, is charged with deciding between these two camps.

By choosing the witchcraft law and by giving his protagonist modern attitudes, Miller puts audience judgment and sympathy beyond all doubt. Today's audience cannot take the possibility of witchcraft seriously; the implication for us is that no enlightened citizen of any age would be able to take it seriously. When some of the citizens of a community see a law as outmoded, that is, when a significant minority take a contrary stance, any rigid enforcement of such a law must be considered unjust and undemocratic. (Consider the civil rights issues of the recent past.) The audience can reasonably anticipate that the trial, as a ritual that reconciles differences and vindicates the right, will justify the position of Proctor and his allies.

The events that precede the trial dramatize at once a fear that reason may not prevail and a confidence that the Court will acknowledge the right. In spite of the hysteria of the children, the malevolence of townsfolk like the Putnams and the self-interest of Pastor Parris, Hale is convinced that the innocent have nothing to fear. The orderly course of official inquiry by an impartial investigator should guarantee the outcome, but it is clear that Hale cannot control the forces at work. Though we want to share his confidence in the legal process, the indictments, based on Abby's evidence, raise serious doubts about the outcome of the trial.

In the trial itself Miller carefully compounds faith in the ritual as the instrument of justice with the fear that it cannot cope with the irrational forces at work in Salem. The solemnity of the Court and Danforth's attention to due process accords with the sense of confidence in the ritual. The Judge follows its prescriptions faithfully, he works calmly and impersonally with the govern-ment at his side. "This is the highest court of the supreme government of this province," he thunders at Giles Corey, "do you know it?" (CRUCIBLE, p. 287.) When Giles wishes to present evidence in his wife's defense, Danforth insists on form: "Let him submit his evidence in proper affidavit. You certainly are aware of our procedure here, Mr. Hale." (CRUCIBLE, p. 287). When John Proctor protests that the children have been lying and that the Putnams are guilty of collusion, Danforth replies that he has found their evidence convincing:

> You know, Mr. Proctor, that the entire contention of the state in these trials is that the voice of Heaven is speaking through the children? . . . I tell you straight, Mister, I have seen marvels in this court. I have seen people choked before my eyes by spirits; I have seen them stuck with pins and slashed by daggers. I have until this moment not the slightest reason to suspect that the children may be deceiving me. (CRUCIBLE, pp. 289, 291.)

With this warning Danforth hears Proctor's evidence. He is too good a lawyer to act arbitrarily. When Cheever cries out that Proctor plows on Sunday and Hale breaks in to protest that a man cannot be judged on such evidence, Danforth replies: "I judge nothing." Hale then pleads for a lawyer to plead Proctor's case, and Danforth replies, logically enough, that since witchcraft is an invisible crime, only the witch and the victim know the facts and that there is nothing left for a lawyer to bring out. Proctor's case is built on Mary Warren's confes-sion, and Danforth properly charges the children to consider the seriousness of their position:

> Now, children, this is a court of law. The law, based upon the Bible, writ by Almighty God, forbid the practice of witchcraft, and describe death as the penalty thereof. But likewise, children, the law and the Bible damn all bearers of false witness. (Slight pause.) Now then. It does not escape me that this deposition may well be devised to blind us; it may well be that Mary Warren has been conquered by Satan, who send her here to distract our sacred purpose. If so, her neck will break for it. But if she speak true, I bid you now drop your guile and confess your pretense, for a quick confession will go easier with you. (CRUCIBLE, p. 299.)

The rhetoric of this charge to the witnesses may lean toward raising doubts about the advisability of retraction, but its burden is fair enough. Danforth applies the rules of procedure scrupulously, yet the tide is running against Proctor and the good people. The ritual is seen to be no guarantee that justice will be done as it becomes painfully clear that the Court, with the blessing of the Law, is going—as Giles Corey cried out earlier—*to hang all these people.*

There is a factor missing from Danforth's administration of the law; Miller dramatizes one aspect of this missing ingredient in the actions and attitudes of Mr. Hale. When he first appears on the scene to conduct his inquiry, Hale uses the conventional tests that he finds in his books. John Proctor is suspect when he is able to recite only nine of the Commandments; his wife has to prompt the tenth: "Adultery, John." From his experience in Salem the minister learns to see beyond logic and authority and assess the human motives necessary to balance the scales of justice. In the courtroom John Proctor finally has to play his trump card and accuse Abby of lechery; his wife Elizabeth alone can support his allegation. Though Proctor testifies that he has never known his wife to lie, rather than expose her husband to infamy she speaks "nothing of lechery." (CRUCIBLE, p. 307.) Danforth has his answer; Proctor has perjured himself. But Hale speaks out for intuition against the legal process:

> *Hale.* Excellency, it is a natural lie to tell; I beg you, stop now before another is condemned! I may shut my conscience no more—private vengeance is working through this testimony! From the beginning this man Proctor has struck me as true. . . . (Pointing at Abigail) This girl has always struck me false. (CRUCIBLE, p. 307.)

Though the minister has no law to back up his intuition, he is willing to make it a conscience matter. As Proctor has used "common sense" to object to the witchcraft investigation, Hale invokes his feelings to support Proctor's accusations against Abigail. But the Law as due process has no room for intuition. Danforth refuses to add this in; Hale's intuition and Proctor's common sense are not evidence. Because the Judge refuses to admit this human factor, the good people have no recourse.

The other aspect of the human factor for which the Law makes no provision is emotion. Due process provides no tool for coping with the kind of hysteria that the children's shrieking generates. Emotional reactions have a real impact on the Court (and the audience), yet this impact cannot be included in the record. "The witness cried out" or "(confusion in the courtroom)" is no substitute for the atmosphere of mystery and/or conviction that results from the emotional outburst. From the beginning of the investigations Abigail has been able to turn this weapon against logic and common sense. Whenever her probity is called into question, she transmutes the dry, question-and-answer proceedings into enthusiastic pulsings. In his preliminary investigation, Hale is searching for the truth about the dancing in the forest and begins to close in:

> *Abigail.* I want to open myself! (They turn to her, startled. She is enraptured, as though in a pearly light.) I want the light of God, I want the sweet love of Jesus! I danced for the Devil; I saw him; I wrote in his book; I want to go back to Jesus; I kiss his hand. I saw Sarah Good with the Devil! I saw Goody Osburn with the Devil! I saw Bridget Bishop with the Devil! (CRUCIBLE, p. 259.)

Neither Hale's authoritative books nor his fledgling intuition are proof against this kind of outburst. Here Abby discovers a power that can be summoned up at will against her enemies.

The source of this emotional power, as is evident from the imagery, lies in Abby's sexual experience. Her outbursts are orgiastic, full of latent sexuality. It is this energy that cannot be weighed in the balance, that initially paralyzes Hale and terrifies the onlookers. Abby's experience with Proctor, hidden from the town, is channeled into her vision, producing a real hysteria in herself and the rest of the children. She introduced them to this mystery in the forest—the naked dancing—and so established a covenant of secret guilt and desire that supports their conspiracy in court. At this point John Proctor's "private sin" has implications for the community.

This emotional outburst has as much to do with Proctor's downfall as Elizabeth's lie. At the crisis of the trial, when Mary Warren's testimony threatens her, Abby calls up this hysteria. Danforth has turned his questioning on her: "Is it possible, child, that the spirits you have seen are illusion only, some deception that may cross your mind when—" (CRUCIBLE, p. 303.) Abby calls up a "cold wind" and all the girls shiver. She sees a yellow bird on the rafters—Mary Warren's spirit tempted from her by John Proctor's diabolism. Threatened by the same fate she has helped thrust on others, Mary Warren breaks and cries out against Proctor. Again this hysteria has a complement of sexual overtones. The yellow bird with claws and spreading wings recalls Tituba's flying to Barbados and the sexual freedom of the forest; the serving girl responds by describing Proctor's tempting in sexual images: "He wake me every night, his eyes were like coals, and his fingers claw my neck, and I sign, I sign . . . " (CRUCIBLE, p. 310.) Though Abby is shamming and the children recognize it, the emotions that fly about the courtroom are very real, the more so because they tap that forbidden well-spring, sexuality, which the Puritan community cannot (or will not) recognize for what it is.

This emotional factor in the case is not accounted for by the rules. It is irrational, a-logical, but very real. Once the witchcraft scare has spread through town, it becomes the channel by which fear, greed, sexual repressions, irresponsibility can be sublimated into "evidence." The Law can help create a scapegoat on which the secret sins of the community can be visited. Judge and jury must ferret out the secret source of such emotion and expose it to view. This is asking a great deal of the judiciary; yet if the trial is to work at all, it works because judge and jury manage to have proper intuitons about human values in a case. So the conditions by which the Law is an effective tool of justice include an ability to perceive, through a maze of technicalties, the whole issue and to deal with it in a humane fashion. The "evil" in Danforth and in Abigail is their lack of this humanity.

Because the Law cannot cope with emotion and its irrational springs and because the ritual cannot substitute for a lack of intuition (wilful or not), the verdict goes against John Proctor and his allies, the order of things is reversed, justice is not done and the Law itself becomes the instrument of perversion.

In the trial, Miller has dramatized the deficiencies of the Law in the hands of an evil court interpreting a bad law. In the fourth act he attempts to frame a solution to this problem. He reintroduces Danforth and Hale, representatives, respectively, of the letter and of the humane view of the Law. Danforth visits the jail to find Parris overwrought because of Abby's treachery and Hale defiantly working to persuade the prisoners to confess. It becomes perfectly clear to the Judge that the girls' testimony was fradulent, if he had not known this all along. But the hanging verdicts are now on record; twelve have been hanged for the crime of witchcraft, and pardon for the rest would necessarily be a confession of error on the part of the court. Rebellion is stirring in a neighboring town and chaos threatens the theocracy that Danforth represents. So the decision must be upheld and the law enforced.

> *Danforth*. Now hear me, and beguile yourselves no more. I will not receive a single plea for pardon or postponement. Them that will not confess will hang. . . . Postponement now speaks a floundering on my part; reprieve or pardon must cast doubt upon the guilt of them that died till now. While I speak God's law, I will not crack its voice with whimpering. If retaliation is your fear, know this—I should hang ten thousand that dared to rise against the law. (CRUCIBLE, p. 318.)

Danforth makes explicit here an attitude which underlies his role during the trial sequence. Though misapplied, the principle of law enforcement is recognized as valid by the audience.

As we have seen above, law enforcement is part of the American attitude toward the Law; it must be upheld or anarchy follows. It is just as important to the American ideal as the fair trial. When the individual takes upon himself the prerogative of deciding which law may be obeyed and which disregarded, the community feels that the bulwark of order has been breached. Thus the icy wind that blows when Danforth speaks is not the chill of his malevolence and inhumanity only, as some critics claim and as Miller himself seems to think.[16] Danforth appeals to a principle that the audience recognizes as plausible. Otherwise, he would pose no real threat. In spite of the fact that his own personal motives include the preservation of his own position in power, and thus are evil, he is defending an attitude that Americans recognize as necessary. Thus the tension in the position between respect for the Law as such—even a bad law— and a respect for the right of the individual to dissent.

Miller finally tries to reconcile these polarities by turning attention to John Proctor. Proctor is no Puritan and no hypocrite; he has, as pointed out above, all those qualities that make a man acceptable to modern society, including a sense of isolation in his guilt. His private sin which, through Abby, contributed to the conviction of the innocent remains unabsolved. His wife, in their final confrontation before the execution, confesses that his guilt is also hers: "It needs a cold wife to prompt lechery." (CRUCIBLE, p. 323.) But Proctor, who has set himself outside the law, cannot accept martyrdom; he is not fit to die with Rebecca Nurse in the odor of sanctity. There is no final assurance that he is worthy, either in his sacrificial defense of the innocent before the court or in Elizabeth's assumption of responsibility for his sin.

> *Elizabeth*. You take my sins upon you, John—
> *Proctor*. (in agony) No, I take my own, my own! . . .
>
> *Elizabeth*. Do what you will. But let none be your judge.
> There be no higher judge under Heaven than Proctor is! (CRUCIBLE, p. 323.)

The ultimate verdict of the play, then, is to be Proctor's decision about his own state of soul.

To clarify this situation dramatically, Miller has his hero hesitate before the prospect of dying for his beliefs. Mr. Hale, who has failed to move Danforth from his purpose, has been urging the condemned to confess because "Life is God's most precious gift; no principle, however glorious, may justify the taking of it." (CRUCIBLE, p. 320.) Though Proctor confesses in Hale's terms: "I want to live," a natural fear of death is not his only motive, it is rather a continuing sense of guilt and unworthiness. Elizabeth has to remind him that he is his own judge now; he cannot find justification or condemnation except in his own conscience.

John Proctor does find justification within; his "motive" lies in the discovery that Danforth intends to publish his confession. He will neither implicate others in his "crime" of witchcraft, nor allow Danforth to use his name to justify their deaths. When he discovers that he cannot concur in their legal lie, he is able to absolve himself and so die for his convictions:

> *Hale*. Man, you will hang. You cannot!
> *Proctor*. I can. Now there's your first marvel, that I can. You have your magic now, for now I think I see some shred of goodness in John Proctor. Not enough to weave a banner with, but white enough to keep it from the dogs. (CRUCIBLE, p. 328.)

When Proctor goes to execution, personal honor triumphs over the deficiencies of the Law and the conspiracy of malicious clique and corrupt court.

This epiphany satisfies the exigencies of the structure; Proctor goes to his death purged of guilt and seeing meaning in his sacrifice. But his triumph is an individual victory only; it does not touch the radical oppositions dramatized in the play. In fact, it only adds another dimension to them. The legal system in America, because it is the font of order and justice, has acquired a sacral aura. Progressively it has been dealing, not only with crime, but also with moral guilt. Because, in the popular mind, the verdict of the court is also a moral judgment, we tend to operate on the assumption that the Law, institution and ritual, can one day become a *perfect* instrument of justice, that is, it can become an instrument of absolution as well as acquittal.[17] So in contemporary criminal law, the issue is not confined to the fact of commission, but is equally engaged with the motive. Psychiatric observation is increasingly admissible as evidence. Thus the law reaches out toward those hitherto private areas, dealt with in the past by pastor or priest, to create a strategy that will deal with the communitarian forgiveness of guilt. (Whether or not we can ever hope to achieve this objective is not at issue here.) Miller, in *The Crucible*, dramatizes the tensions that make the trial a questionable instrument of justice and the contradiction that lurks at the center of our myth of the Law. He tries to resolve these polarities by insisting that only the individual can be an adequate judge of his own private actions. The hero, all his sins upon him, must cope with the spectre of guilt alone. The audience is left with the suspicion that self-absolution begs the question; the old adage applies: no man is a good judge in his own case.

In stereotype, dramatic use of the trial pattern depends on the public's faith that this ritual infallibly reconciles contraries, *solvuntur ambulando*. When it is used as a framework in conventional drama, for instance, the verdict of the court resolves all differences between individual and society and makes evident the innocence or guilt of the individual and his society. The logical progression of the ritual gives the verdict the appearance of absolute truth (or as close an approximation as man can reasonably expect). In plays like *The Caine Mutiny Court Martial* or *Saint Joan*, the trial reveals the truth even when the verdict is one-sided. The audience, whose posture is that of the jury, can detect prejudice in the judge, or a vicious prosecutor, or an inept defense counsel. The dramatist can see to it that they do. So this ritual, at least on the stage, ordinarily does what a ritual should do, that is, guarantee the desired result.

The Crucible, however, uses the trial pattern, not as a framework, but to explore the attitudes that underlie the ritual itself. The formal symmetry of orderly investigation, indictment, presentation of evidence and verdict is broken by hysterical outbursts; the support that due process, in the hands of an humane and unbiased judiciary, provides the truth is undermined by the inhumanity of Danforth. The man who is caught between the grinding stones of a corrupt court and an evil law may save himself in the end by becoming his own judge and jury, but the dramatic fact in *The Crucible* is the grinding. The ritual fails, and the hero is isolated with his guilt.

In his epilogue, Miller tries to insist that sacrifices like Proctor's eventually do have a relationship to the whole community.

> In solemn meeting, the congregation rescinded the excommunications—this in March 1712. But they did so upon orders of the government. The jury, however, wrote a statement praying forgiveness for all who had suffered. . . . To all intents and purposes, the power of the theocracy in Massachusetts was broken. (CRUCIBLE, p. 330.)

This comment may allay the playwright's scruples, but it is not part of the dramatic experience. The play makes its own statement by conveying, with a sense of urgency, the opposition between two American ideals: the need for Law and law enforcement and the right of the minority to dissent. In dramatizing this tension, it also calls attention to the need for a ritual that can deal with communal and individual guilt. In the absence of such a ritual John Proctor's triumph is finally a mystery, unaccommodated man holding, for personal reasons, to a personal vision. The black-gowned shadow of Danforth is not blotted out by the rising sun and Proctor's sacrifice.

Notes

1. Ralph Henry Gabriel, *The Course of American Democratic Thought* (New York, 1940), p. 16.

2. Thurman W. Arnold, *The Symbols of Government* (New Haven, 1935), p. 127.

3. Henry Steele Commager, *The American Mind* (New Haven, 1950), p. 363.

4. Arnold, *Symbols of Government*, p. 134.

5. Ibid., pp. 136-37.

6. Ibid., pp. 143-44.

7. Arthur Miller, *Collected Plays* (New York, 1957), pp. 24-25 (Introduction). In view of this remark, Miller's choice of lawyer as hero in his autobiographical play *After the Fall* is not surprising.

8. Ibid., p. 39.

9. Ibid., p. 11.

10. Ibid., p. 47.

11. Arnold, *Symbols of Government*, p. 141.

12. *Collected Plays*, p. 41. It speaks well of the judges of the Salem trials that Miller was able to draw on official records in constructing his play. The preservation of these documents indicates that the judges felt fully justified in their course of action. For them, the letter of the law was clear and they applied it with what they considered a rigorous fairness. Had the witches been stabbed in the dark and the record either not taken or destroyed, no redress would have been possible. The material is so complete that Miller could not only reconstruct the event and include accurate historical detail, but he was also able to supply credible motivations from hints in the testimony.

13. Ibid., p. 47.

14. The modified realism of the setting used in the 1953 production—rough wooden beams and period set-pieces—was changed to black draperies in the more successful 1958 revival. This change underscored the modern dimension by giving the *mise en scene* more universality.

15. *The Crucible* in *Collected Plays*, p. 239. Quotations from the play are from this version, hereafter referred to as CRUCIBLE.

16. "So critics have taken exception, for instance, to the unrelieved badness of the prosecution in my play. I understand how this is possible and I plead no mitigation, but I was up against historical facts which were immutable. I do not think that either the record itself or the numerous commentaries upon it reveal any mitigation of the unrelieved, straightforward, and absolute dedication to evil displayed by the judges of these trials and the prosecutors." (Miller, *Collected Plays*, p. 43.)

17. The "secularization" of American society is a point at issue here. For Justice Holmes, a leading American jurist, the American system of morality is "a body of imperfect social generalizations expressed in terms of emotion." The Law can dispense with emotion and evolve toward a better understanding of the deepest instincts of man. Through this understanding men can connect the Law with "the universe and catch an echo of the infinite, a glimpse of its unfathomable process, a hint of the universal law." Practically, then, without prejudice to a higher order, the Law can become an ever more effective instrument for justice here and now. (Oliver Wendell Holmes, *Collected Legal Papers* [New York, 1952], pp. 306, 202.)

Arthur Miller's *The Crucible:*
Background and Sources

Robert A. Martin[*]

When *The Crucible* opened on January 22, 1953,[1] the term "witchhunt" was nearly synonymous in the public mind with the Congressional investigations then being conducted into allegedly subversive activities. Arthur Miller's plays have always been closely identified with contemporary issues, and to many observers the parallel between the witchcraft trials at Salem, Massachusetts in 1692 and the current Congressional hearings was the central issue of the play.

Miller has said that he could not have written *The Crucible* at any other time,[2] a statement which reflects both his reaction to the McCarthy era and the creative process by which he finds his way to the thematic center of a play. If it is true, however, that a play cannot be successful in its own time unless it speaks to its own time, it is also true that a play cannot endure unless it speaks to new audiences in new times. The latter truism may apply particularly to *The Crucible*, which is presently being approached more and more frequently as a cultural and historical study rather than as a political allegory.

Although *The Crucible* was written in response to its own time, popular interest in the Salem witchcraft trials had actually begun to surface long before the emergence of McCarthyism. There were at least two other plays based on the witchcraft trials that were produced shortly before *The Crucible* opened: *Child's Play* by Florence Stevenson was produced in November, 1952 at the Oklahoma Civic Playhouse; and *The Witchfinders* by Louis O. Coxe appeared at about the same time in a studio production at the University of Minnesota.[3] Among numerous other works dealing with Salem witchcraft, a novel, *Peace, My Daughter* by Shirley Barker, had appeared as recently as 1949, and in the same year Marion L. Starkey had combined an interest in history and psychology to produce *The Devil in Massachusetts*, which was based on her extensive research of the original documents and records. Starkey's announced purpose was "to review the records in the light of the findings of modern psychology," and to supplement the work of earlier investigators by calling attention to "a number of vital primary sources of which they seem to have been ignorant."[4]

The events that eventually found their way into *The Crucible* are largely

[*]Reprinted from *Modern Drama*, 20 (1977), 279–92, by permission of the journal.

contained in the massive two volume record of the trials located in the Essex County Archives at Salem, Massachusetts, where Miller went to do his research. Although he has been careful to point out in a prefatory note that *The Crucible* is not history in the academic sense, a study of the play and its sources indicates that Miller did his research carefully and well. He found in the records of the trials at Salem that between June 10 and September 22, 1692, nineteen men and women and two dogs were hanged for witchcraft, and one man was pressed to death for standing mute.[5] Before the affair ended, fifty-five people had confessed to being witches, and another hundred and fifty were in jail awaiting trial.

Focusing primarily upon the story of John Proctor, one of the nineteen who were hanged, Miller almost literally retells the story of a panic-stricken society that held a doctrinal belief in the existence of the Devil and the reality of witchcraft. The people of Salem did not, of course, invent a belief in witchcraft; they were, however, the inheritors of a witchcraft tradition that had a long and bloody history in their native England and throughout most of Europe. To the Puritans of Massachusetts, witchcraft was as real a manifestation of the Devil's efforts to overthrow "God's kingdom" as the periodic raids of his Indian disciples against the frontier settlements.

There were, surprisingly, few executions for witchcraft in Massachusetts before 1692. According to George Lyman Kittredge in his *Witchcraft in Old and New England,* "not more than half-a-dozen executions can be shown to have occurred."[6] But the people of Salem village in 1692 had recent and—to them—reliable evidence that the Devil was at work in the Massachusetts Bay Colony. In 1688 in Boston, four children of John Goodwin had been seriously afflicted by a "witch" named Glover, who was also an Irish washwoman. In spite of her hasty execution and the prayers of four of the most devout Boston ministers, the Goodwin children were possessed by spirits of the "invisible world" for some months afterward. One of the leading Puritan ministers of the time was Cotton Mather, who in 1689 published his observations on the incident in "Memorable Providences, Relating to Witchcrafts and Possession."[7] Although the work was intended to warn against witchcraft, Mather's account can also be read as a handbook of instructions for feigning possession by demonic spirits. Among numerous other manifestations and torments, Mather reported that the Goodwin children were most often afflicted by "fits":

> Sometimes they would be Deaf, sometimes Dumb, and sometimes Blind, and often, all this at once. One while their Tongues would be drawn down their Throats; another-while they would be pull'd out upon their Chins, to a prodigious length. They would have their Mouths opened unto such a Wideness, that their Jaws went out of joint; and anon they would clap together again with a Force like that of a strong Spring Lock.[8]

Four years later, in February, 1692, the daughter and niece of the Reverend Samuel Parris of Salem village began to have "fits" very similar to those experienced by the Goodwin children as reported and described by Mather. According to Marion Starkey, Parris had a copy of Mather's book, and, in addition, "the Parrises had probably had first-hand experience of the case, since they appear to have been living in Boston at the time. The little girls might even have been taken to see the hanging."[9]

In spite of an apparent abundance of historical material, the play did not become dramatically conceivable for Miller until he came upon "a single fact" concerning Abigail Williams, the niece of Reverend Parris:

> It was that Abigail Williams, the prime mover of the Salem hysteria, so far as the hysterical children were concerned, had a short time earlier been the house servant of the Proctors and now was crying out Elizabeth Proctor as a witch; but more—it was clear from the record that with entirely uncharacteristic fastidiousness she was refusing to include John Proctor, Elizabeth's husband, in her accusations despite the urgings of the prosecutors. Why? I searched the records of the trials in the courthouse at Salem but in no other instance could I find such a careful avoidance of the implicating stutter, the murderous, ambivalent answer to the sharp questions of the prosecutors. Only here, in Proctor's case, was there so clear an attempt to differentiate between a wife's culpability and a husband's.[10]

As in history, the play begins when the Reverend Samuel Parris begins to suspect that his daughter Betty has become ill because she and his niece Abigail Williams have "trafficked with spirits in the forest." The real danger Parris fears, however, is less from diabolical spirits than from the ruin that may fall upon him when his enemies learn that his daughter is suffering from the effects of witchcraft:

> *Parris.* There is a faction that is sworn to drive me from my pulpit. Do you understand that?
> *Abigail.* I think so, sir.
> *Parris.* Now then, in the midst of such disruption, my own household is discovered to be the very center of some obscene practice. Abominations are done in the forest—
> *Abigail.* It were sport, uncle![11]

As Miller relates at a later point in the play, Parris was a petty man who was historically in a state of continual bickering with his congregation over such matters as his salary, housing, and firewood. The irony of the above conversation in the play, however, is that while Parris is attempting to discover the "truth" to prevent it from damaging his already precarious reputation as Salem's minister, Abigail actually is telling him the historical truth when she says "it were sport." Whatever perverse motives may have subsequently prompted the adult citizens of Salem to cry "witch" upon their neighbors, the initiators of the Salem misfortune were young girls like Abigail Williams who began playing with spirits simply for the "sport" of it, as a release from an emotionally oppressive society. A portion of the actual trial testimony given in favor of Elizabeth Proctor (John Proctor's wife) by one Daniel Elliott suggests that initially, at least, not everyone accepted the girls' spectral visions without question:

> The testimony of Daniel Elliott, aged 27 years or thereabouts, who testifieth and saith that I being at the house of lieutenant Ingersoll on the 28 of March, in the year 1692,

there being present one of the afflicted persons which cried out and said, there's Goody Proctor. William Raiment being there present, told the girl he believed she lied, for he saw nothing: then Goody Ingersoll told the girl she told a lie, for there was nothing; then the girl said that she did it for sport, they must have some sport .[12] [punctuation added]

Miller's addition in *The Crucible* of an adulterous relationship between Abigail Williams and Proctor serves primarily as a dramatically imperative motive for Abigail's later charges of witchcraft against Elizabeth Proctor. Although it might appear that Miller is rewriting history for his own dramatic purposes by introducing a sexual relationship between Abigail and Proctor, his invention of the affair is psychologically and historically appropriate. As he makes clear in the prefatory note preceding the play, "dramatic purposes have sometimes required many characters to be fused into one; the number of girls . . . has been reduced; Abigail's age has been raised; . . ." Although Miller found that Abigail's refusal to testify against Proctor was the single historical dramatic "fact" he was looking for, there are two additional considerations that make adultery and Abigail's altered age plausible within the historical context of the events.

The first is that Mary Warren, in the play and in history, was simultaneously an accuser in court and a servant in Proctor's household. If an adulterous affair was probable, it would more likely have occurred between Mary Warren and Proctor than between Abigail Williams and Proctor; but it could easily have occurred. At the time, Mary Warren was a fairly mature young woman who would have had the features Miller has represented in Abigail: every emotional and sexual impulse, as well as the opportunity to be involved with Proctor. Historically, it was Mary Warren who attempted to stop the proceedings as early as April 19 by stating during her examination in court that the afflected girls "did but dissemble": "Afterwards she started up, and said I will speak and cried out, Oh! I am sorry for it, I am sorry for it, and wringed her hands, and fell a little while into a fit again and then came to speak, but immediately her teeth were set, and then she fell into a violent fit and cried out, oh Lord help me! Oh Good Lord save me!"[13] As in the play, the rest of the girls prevailed by immediately falling into fits and spontaneously accusing her of witchcraft. As her testimony of April 21 and later indicates, however, she soon returned to the side of her fellow accusers. On June 30, she testified:

The deposition of Mary Warren aged 20 years here testifieth. I have seen the apparition of John Proctor senior among the witches and he hath often tortured me by pinching me and biting me and choking me, and pressing me on my Stomach till the blood came out of my mouth and also I saw him torture Mis Pope and Mercy Lewis and John Indian upon the day of his examination and he hath also tempted me to write in his book, and to eat bread which he brought to me, which I refusing to do, Jno Proctor did most grievously torture me with a variety of tortures, almost Ready to kill me .[14]

Miller has reduced Mary Warren's lengthy and ambiguous trial testimony to four pages in the play by focusing on her difficulty in attempting to tell the truth after the proceedings were under way. The truth that Mary has to tell—

"It were only sport in the beginning, sir"—is the same that Abigail tried to tell Parris earlier; but the telling has become compounded by the courtroom presence of Proctor, Parris, Hathorne and Danforth (two of the judges), the rest of the afflected girls, and the spectators. In a scene taken directly from the trial records, Mary confesses that she and the other girls have been only pretending and that they have deceived the court. She has never seen the spirits or apparitions of the witches:

> *Hathorne.* How could you think you saw them unless you saw them?
> *Mary Warren.* I—I cannot tell how, but I did. I—I heard the other girls screaming, and you, Your Honor, you seemed to believe them, and I—It were only sport in the beginning, sir, but then the whole world cried spirits, and I—I promise you, Mr. Danforth, I only thought I saw them but I did not.[15]

The second, additional consideration is that although Miller has raised Abigail's age from her actual eleven to seventeen, and has reduced the number of girls in the play to five only, such alterations for purposes of dramatic motivation and compression do not significantly affect the psychological or historical validity of the play. As the trial records clearly establish, individual and family hostilities played a large role in much of the damaging testimony given against those accused of witchcraft. Of the ten girls who were most directly involved in crying out against the witches, only three—Betty Parris (nine years old), Abigail Williams (eleven years), and Ann Putnam (twelve years)—were below the age of sexual maturity. The rest were considerably older: Mary Walcott and Elizabeth Booth were both sixteen; Elizabeth Hubbard was seventeen; Susanna Sheldon was eighteen; Mercy Lewis was nineteen; Sara Churchill and Mary Warren (Proctor's servant) were twenty. In a time when marriage and motherhood were not uncommon at the age of fourteen, the hypothesis of repressed sexuality emerging disguised into the emotionally charged atmosphere of witchcraft and Calvinism does not seem unlikely; it seems, on the contrary, an inevitable supposition. And it may be worth pointing out in this context that Abigail Williams was not the only one of the girls who refused to include John Proctor in her accusations against his wife, Elizabeth. In her examination of April 21, Mary Warren testified that her mistress was a witch and that "her master had told her that he had been about sometimes to make away with himself because of his wife's quarreling with him. . . ." A few lines later the entry reads: "but she would not own that she knew her master to be a witch or wizzard."[16]

With the exception of Abigail and Proctor's adultery, the events and characters of *The Crucible* are not so much "invented" data in a fictional sense as highly compressed representations of the underlying forces of hatred, hysteria, and fear that paralyzed Salem during the spring and summer of 1692. And even in this context Abigail Williams's characterization in the play may be more restrained in the light of the records than Miller's dramatization suggests. For example, one of the major witnesses against John Proctor was twelve year old Ann Putnam, who testified on June 30 that "on the day of his examination I saw the apparition of Jno: Proctor senior go and afflict and most grievously torture the bodies of Mistress Pope, Mary Walcott, Mercy Lewis, Abigail Williams. . . ."[17] In projecting several of the girls into Abigail, Miller has used the surface of the trial records to suggest that her hatred for Proctor's wife is a dramatic equivalent for the much wider spread hatred and tension that existed within the Salem community. Abigail, although morally corrupt, ironically insists upon her "good" name, and reveals at an early point in the play that she hates Elizabeth Proctor for ruining her reputation:

> Parris. [to the point] Abigail, is there any other cause than you have told me, for your being discharged from Goody Proctor's service? I have heard it said, and I tell you as I heard it, that she comes so rarely to the church this year for she will not sit so close to something soiled. What signified that remark?
> Abigail. She hates me uncle, she must, for I would not be her slave. It's a bitter woman, a lying, cold, sniveling woman, and I will not work for such a woman![18]

On a larger scale, Miller brings together the forces of personal and social malfunction through the arrival of the Reverend John Hale, who appears, appropriately, in the midst of a bitter quarrel among Proctor, Parris, and Thomas Putnam over deeds and land boundaries. Hale, in life as in the play, had encountered witchcraft previously and was called to Salem to determine if the Devil was in fact responsible for the illness of the afflicted children. In the play, he conceives of himself, Miller says, "much as a young doctor on his first call":

> [He appears loaded down with half a dozen heavy books.]
> Hale. Pray you, someone take these!
> Parris. [delighted] Mr. Hale! Oh! it's good to see you again! [Taking some books] My, they're heavy!
> Hale. [setting down his books] They must be; they are weighted with authority.[19]

Hale's entrance at this particular point in the play is significant in that he interrupts an argument based on private and secular interests to bring "authority" to the question of witchcraft. His confidence in himself and his subsequent examination of the girls and Tituba (Parris's slave who inadvertently started the entire affair) represent and foreshadow the arrival of outside religious authority in the community. As an outsider who has come to weigh the evidence, Hale also helps to elevate the issue from a local to a regional level, and from an unofficial to an official theological inquiry. His heavy books of authority also symbolically anticipate the heavy authority of the judges who, as he will realize too late, are as susceptible to misinterpreting testimony based on spectral evidence as he is:

> Hale. [with a tasty love of intellectual pursuit] Here is all the invisible world, caught, defined, and calculated. In these books the Devil stands stripped of all his brute disguises. Here are all your familiar spirits—your incubi and succubi; your witches that go by land, by air, and by sea; your wizards of the night and of the day. Have no fear now—we shall find him out if he has come among us, and I mean to crush him utterly if he has shown his face![20]

The Reverend Hale is an extremely interesting figure historically, and following the trials he set down an account of his repentance entitled "A Modest Inquiry into the Nature of Witchcraft" (Boston, 1702). Although he was at first as overly zealous in his pursuit of witches as everyone else, very much as Miller has portrayed him in *The Crucible*, Hale began to be tormented by doubts early in the proceedings. His uncertainty concerning the reliability of the witnesses and their testimony was considerably heightened when his own wife was also accused of being a witch. Hale appears to have been as tortured spiritually and as dedicated to the "middle way" in his later life as Miller has portrayed him in *The Crucible*. Five years after Salem, he wrote in his "Inquiry":

> The middle way is commonly the way of truth. And if any can show me a better middle way than I have here laid down, I shall be ready to embrace it: But the conviction must not be by vinegar or drollery, but by strength of argument. . . . I have had a deep sence of the sad consequence of mistakes in matters Capital; and their impossibility of recovering when compleated. And what grief of heart it brings to a tender conscience, to have been unwittingly encouraging of the Sufferings of the innocent.[21]

Hale further commented that although he presently believed the executions to be the unfortunate result of human error, the integrity of the court officials was unquestionable: "I observed in the prosecution of these affairs, that there was in the Justices, Judges and others concerned, a conscientious endeavour to do the thing that was right. And to that end they consulted the Presidents [Precedents] of former times and precepts laid down by Learned Writers about Witchcraft."[22]

In *The Crucible*, Hale's examination of Tituba is very nearly an edited transcription of her testimony at the trial of Sarah Good, who is the first person Abigail accuses of consorting with the Devil. At the time of the trials, Sarah Good had long been an outcast member of the Salem community, "unpopular because of her slothfulness, her sullen temper, and her poverty; she had recently taken to begging, an occupation the Puritans detested."[23] When she was about to be hanged, her minister, the Reverend Nicholas Noyes, made a last appeal to her for a confession and said he knew she was a witch. Her prophetic reply was probably seen later as proof of her guilt when she said to Noyes: "you are a lyer; I am no more a Witch than you are a Wizard, and if you take away my Life, God will give you Blood to drink."[24] A few years after she was hanged, Reverend Noyes died as a result of a sudden and severe hemorrhage.

Largely through the Reverend Hale, Miller reflects the change that took place in Salem from an initial belief in the justice of the court to a suspicion that testimony based on spectral evidence was insufficient for execution. This transformation begins to reveal itself in Act Two, as Hale tells Francis Nurse that the court will clear his wife of the charges against her: "Believe me, Mr. Nurse, if Rebecca Nurse be tainted, then nothing's left to stop the whole green world from burning. Let you rest upon the justice of the court; the court will send her home, I know it."[25] By Act Three, however, Hale's confidence in the justice of the court has been badly shaken by the arrest and conviction of people like

Rebecca Nurse who were highly respected members of the church and community. Hale, like his historical model, has discovered that "the whole green world" is burning indeed, and fears that he has helped to set the fire.

Partially as a result of Hale's preliminary investigation into the reality of Salem witchcraft, the Court of Oyer and Terminer was appointed to hear testimony and conduct the examinations. The members of the court immediately encountered a serious obstacle: namely, that although the Bible does not define witchcraft, it states unequivocally that "Thou shalt not suffer a witch to live" (Exodus 22:18). As Proctor attempts to save his wife from hanging, Hale attempts to save his conscience by demanding visible proof of the guilt of those who have been convicted on the basis of spectral testimony:

> Hale. Excellency, I have signed seventy-two death warrants; I am a minister of the Lord, and I dare not take a life without there be a proof so immaculate no slightest qualm of conscience may doubt it.
> Danforth. Mr. Hale, you surely do not doubt my justice.
> Hale. I have this morning signed away the soul of Rebecca Nurse, Your Honor. I'll not conceal it, my hand shakes yet as with a wound![26]

At first, the witches who were brought to trial and convicted were generally old and eccentric women like Sarah Good who were of questionable character long before the trials began. But people like Rebecca Nurse and John Proctor were not. As Miller has Parris say to Judge Hathorne in Act Four: "it were another sort that hanged till now. Rebecca Nurse is no Bridget that lived three year with Bishop before she married him. John Proctor is not Isaac Ward that drank his family to ruin."[27] In late June, Rebecca Nurse was found guilty and sentenced to hang after an earlier verdict of "not guilty" was curiously reversed. Her minister, the Reverend Nicholas Noyes again, decided along with his congregation that she should be excommunicated for the good of the church. Miller seems to have been especially moved by her character and her almost unbelievable trial and conviction, as he indicates by his comments in the "Introduction" and his interpolated remarks in Act One. On Tuesday, July 19, 1692, she was hanged on Gallows Hill along with four others, all women. She was seventy-one years old. After the hanging, according to Starkey:

> The bodies of the witches were thrust into a shallow grave in a crevice of Gallows Hill's outcropping of felsite. But the body of Rebecca did not remain there. Her children bided their time . . . and at night when the crowds and the executioners had gone home again, they gathered up the body of their mother and took it home. Just where they laid it none can know, for this was a secret thing and not even Parris, whose parsonage was not a quarter of a mile up the road past the grove where the Nurses buried their dead, must see that a new grave had been opened and prayers said. This was the hour and the power of darkness when a son could not say where he had buried his mother.[28]

Historically, Proctor was even more of a victim of the laws of his time than Miller details in *The Crucible*. Although the real John Proctor fought against his arrest and conviction as fervently as anyone could under the circumstances, he, like Miller's Proctor, was adamant in his refusal to confess to witchcraft because he did not believe it existed. And although fifty-two of his friends and neighbors risked their own safety to sign a petition in his behalf, nothing was done to re-examine the evidence against him. Ironically, Proctor's wife—in whose interest he had originally become involved in the affair—had become pregnant and, although sentenced, would never hang. She was eventually released after en-during her husband's public execution, the birth of her child in prison, and the seizure and loss of all her possessions.

Under the law, the goods and property of witches could be confiscated after their trial and conviction. In Proctor's case, however, the sheriff did not wait for the trial or the conviction. A contemporary account of the seizure indicates that neither Proctor nor his wife were ever expected to return from prison:

> John Proctor and his Wife being in Prison, the Sheriff came to his House and seized all the Goods, Provisions, and Cattle that he could come at, and sold some of the Cattle at half-price, and killed others, and put them up for the West-Indies; threw out the Beer out of a Barrel, and carried away the Barrel; emptied a Pot of Broath, and took away the Pot, and left nothing in the House for the support of the Children: No part of the said Goods are known to be returned.[29]

(The Proctors had five children, the youngest of whom were three and seven.) Along with three other men and one woman, John Proctor was hanged on August 19. On September 22, seven more witches and one wizard were hanged, and then the executions suddenly ended.

Miller has symbolized all the judges of the witchcraft trials in the figures of Danforth and Hathorne (Nathaniel Hawthorne's ancestor), and presented them as being more "official" in a legal sense than their historical models actually were. None of the judges in the trials had any legal training, and, apparently, neither had anyone else who was administering the law in the Massachusetts Bay Colony. According to Starkey, the curious nature of the trials was in part due to the Puritans' limited understanding of the law, their contempt for law-yers, and their nearly total reliance on the Bible as a guide for all matters of legal and moral authority:

> The Puritans had a low opinion of lawyers and did not permit the professional practice of law in the colony. In effect the administration of the law was in the hands of laymen, most of them second-generation colonists who had an incomplete grasp of current principles of English jurisdiction. For that matter, this chosen people, this community which submitted itself to the direct rule of God, looked less to England for its precepts than to God's ancient and holy word. So far as was practicable the Puritans were living by a legal system that antedated the Magna Carta by at least two millennia, the Decalogue and the tribal laws codified in the Pentateuch.[30]

As historians occasionally have pointed out, the executions did not stop because the people in Massachusetts suddenly ceased to believe in either the Devil or witchcraft; they stopped, simply and ironically, because of a legal question. There never was any doubt for most people living in New England in 1692 whether or not witchcraft was real or whether witches should be executed; the question centered around the reliability of spectral evidence coming from the testimony of the afflicted. It was largely through the determinations of Increase Mather and fourteen other Boston ministers that such testimony was declared to be insufficient for conviction and therefore became inadmissable as evidence. It was better, they concluded, to allow ten witches to escape than to hang one innocent person. In late October, Governor Phips officially dismissed the Court of Oyer and Terminer, and—although the trials continued through the following April—in May, 1693 he issued a proclamation discharging all the remaining "witches" and pardoning those who had fled the colony rather than face arrest, trial, and certain conviction.

Miller has said that if he were to rewrite *The Crucible*, he would make an open thematic issue of the evil he now believes to be represented by the Salem judges. His altered viewpoint toward the play may be accounted for partially as a reconsideration of his intensive examination of the trial records which, he has said, do not "reveal any mitigation of the unrelieved, straightforward, and absolute dedication to evil displayed by the judges of these trials and the prosecutors. After days of study it became quite incredible how perfect they were in this respect."[31]

Miller's subsequent view of evil, however, did not come entirely from his study of the trial records. Between writing *The Crucible* in 1952 and producing the "Introduction" to the *Collected Plays* in 1957, he underwent a personal crucible when he appeared before the House Un-American Activities Committee in 1956. Although the experience was understandably not without its effect on his later attitude toward Congressional "witchhunters," it should, nevertheless, be considered in relation to his comments on the judges and evil quoted above. A more accurate reflection of Miller's attitude while writing *The Crucible* appears perhaps most clearly in the account published in February, 1953 of his thoughts while standing on the rock at Gallows Hill:

> Here hung Rebecca, John Proctor, George Jacobs—people more real to me than the living can ever be. The sense of a terrible marvel again; that people could have such a belief in themselves and in the rightness of their consciences as to give their lives rather than say what they thought was false. Or, perhaps, they only feared Hell so much? Yet, Rebecca said, and it is written in the record, "I cannot belie myself." And she knew it would kill her. . . . The rock stands forever in Salem. They knew who they were. Nineteen.[32]

Like the rock at Salem, *The Crucible* has endured beyond the immediate events of its own time. If it was originally seen as a political allegory, it is presently seen by contemporary audiences almost entirely as a distinguished American play by an equally distinguished American playwright. As one of the most frequently produced plays in the American theater, *The Crucible* has attained a life of its own; one that both interprets and defines the cultural and historical background of American society. Given the general lack of plays in the American theater that have seriously undertaken to explore the meaning and significance of the American past in relation to the present, *The Crucible* stands virtually alone as a dramatically coherent rendition of one of the most terrifying chapters in American history.

Notes

1. *The Crucible* opened at the Martin Beck Theater in New York City. Directed by Jed Harris, the cast included Arthur Kennedy as John Proctor, E. G. Marshall as the Reverend John Hale, and Beatrice Straight as Elizabeth Proctor. After 197 performances, the play closed on July 11, 1953.

2. John and Alice Griffin, "Arthur Miller Discusses *The Crucible*," *Theatre Arts* 37 (October, 1953), 33.

3. Dennis Welland, *Arthur Miller* (New York, 1961), p. 74.

4. Marion L. Starkey, *The Devil in Massachusetts* (New York, 1949), p. 12; hereafter cited as *The Devil*.

5. For this and other information of an historical and factual nature, I am indebted to *What Happened in Salem?*, ed. David Levin (New York, 1960), hereafter cited as *Salem; Narratives of the Witchcraft Cases, 1648–1706*, ed. George Lincoln Burr (New York, 1914), hereinafter cited as *Narratives;* and *Salem Witchcraft* by Charles W. Upham (Boston, 1867). I have also drawn upon material located in the Essex County Archives, particularly the Works Progress Administration transcript of *Salem Witchcraft, 1692* on file in the Essex County Court House at Salem. For a perspective of the events as social history, see Paul Boyer and Stephen Nissenbaum, *Salem Possessed: The Social Origins of Witchcraft* (Cambridge, Massachusetts, 1974).

6. George Lyman Kittredge, *Witchcraft in Old and New England* (Cambridge, Massachusetts, 1929), p. 367. Frederick C. Drake, however, in "Witchcraft in the American Colonies, 1647–62," documents by names, dates, and places twenty executions for witchcraft between 1647–62, the majority of which took place in Massachusetts and Connecticut. Only two executions, Drake says, took place in the colonies between 1662 and 1691, one of which was the result of the Goodwin case in Boston in 1688 (*American Quarterly* 20 [1968], 694–725).

7. Cotton Mather, "Memorable Providences . . .," (Boston, 1689); rpt. in Burr, *Narratives*, pp. 93–143.

8. Burr, *Narratives*, p. 101.

9. Starkey, *The Devil*, p. 24.

10. Arthur Miller, *Arthur Miller's Collected Plays* (New York, 1957), p. 41; hereinafter cited as *C. P.* Present-day Salem is not where the witchcraft began in 1692. The town of Danvers, originally called "Salem Village," is the location of Miller's play and the historical site in Essex County where the tragedy began. Danvers, or Salem Village, is a few miles northwest of present-day Salem, which was then called "Salem Town."

11. *C. P.*, p. 231.

12. Levin, *Salem*, p. 64.

13. Ibid., pp. 52–53.

14. Ibid., p. 61.

15. *C. P.*, pp. 302–303.

16. Levin, *Salem*, p. 56.

17. Ibid., pp. 60–61.

18. *C. P.*, p. 232.

19. Ibid., p. 251.

20. Ibid., p. 253. *Incubi, succubi:* in the mythology of witchcraft, incubi are evil spirits capable of assuming the human male form to have sexual intercourse with women at night, while succubi assume the female form to have sexual intercourse with men in their sleep.

21. Burr, *Narratives*, pp. 404–405. Hale's account was written in 1697; published in 1702 after his death.

22. Burr, *Narratives*, p. 415.

23. Levin, *Salem*, p. xviii.

24. Burr, *Narratives*, p. 358.

25. *C. P.*, p. 277.

26. Ibid., p. 297.

27. Ibid., p. 316.

28. Starkey, *The Devil*, p. 177.

29. Burr, *Narratives*, p. 361.

30. Starkey, *The Devil*, p. 36. In addition to Starkey's conclusion, George Lincoln Burr has noted that "in these trials of 1692 the jurors were chosen from among church-members only, not, as later, from all who had the property to make them voters under the new charter." *Narratives*, p. 362, n. 2.

31. *C. P.*, pp. 42–43.

32. Arthur Miller, "Journey to 'The Crucible,'" *New York Times*, February 8, 1953, Sec. 2, p. 3. Miller's admiration for the "Salem Nineteen" is presumably also extended to the twentieth person who died there—the eighty year old Giles Corey, who was pressed to death on September 19 for standing mute before the judges and the court. "Pressing" involved placing rocks on the accused's chest until he died or consented to enter a plea and stand trial. Tradition has it that Corey's last words were "more weight," just before he died, but a less heroic end was recorded by a contemporary who probably witnessed the gruesome procedure: "In pressing [,] his Tongue being prest out of his Mouth, the Sheriff with his Cane forced it in again, when he was dying. He was the first in New-England, that was ever prest to Death." Burr, *Narratives*, p. 367.

A View From The Bridge

Miller's *View from the Bridge* Is Splendid, Stunning Theatre

Under the general title of "A View from the Bridge," Arthur Miller has written two superlatively fine plays, and they were given a superlatively fine production at the Coronet Theatre last evening. They are the American theatre in its most vigorous aspect, and with them Miller whose work has already commanded great respect, shows further development in his human insight, his theatrical skill and his quality as a poet. These plays are in the vernacular of the lowly—of the inarticulate, even—yet they emerge as works of beauty. And a most exciting company under the direction of Martin Ritt brings them to throbbing life.

The first of them might be called a mood-setter, rather than a curtain-raiser. Called "A Memory of Two Mondays," it is a one-act fragment about people who work in an automobile parts warehouse in the early Roosevelt days. Properly speaking, it has no plot—yet something does happen to almost everybody. A youth gets a chance to go to college. A drunk reforms. Another drunk rebels. A young man with a song in his soul finds himself forgetting the song as poverty and a lack of opportunity grind him down.

The principal performance in the opener is given by J. Carrol Naish in the role of a hard-drinking, short-tempered, ceaselessly profane old German, a warehouse shipping boss who has slaved there for 22 years. It is a slashing and wonderfully pictorial characterization.

Indeed, all the roles are character parts and they are excellently done. The players include Leo Penn, Russell Collins, Van Heflin, Curt Conway and Tom Pedi. The warehouse setting by Boris Aronson is a masterpiece of dusty gloom.

The second play, "A View from the Bridge," concerns present-day life in a colony of Italian-American longshoremen on the Brooklyn waterfront. Although it is vibrant with characters, this is no slice-of-life essay; it is a tragedy in the classic form, and I think it is a modern classic. What happens in it simply has to happen, and this is the inevitability of true tragedy. In it, Van Heflin gives a magnificent performance as a longshoreman who, though his mind is limited and he cannot find words for his thoughts, is an admirable man. He is popular, kind, loyal, loving and generous.

[*]Reprinted from *New York Daily News*, September 30, 1955. Copyright 1955 by the New York News, Inc. Reprinted by permission.

When two of his wife's Italian cousins—submarines they are, in waterfront argot—are smuggled into this country, he makes room for them in his home. Gratefully they move in among his wife, his children and the teen-age niece whom he has brought up and whom he has come to love, he thinks, as a daughter.

And now the stage is set for tragedy. One of the illegal immigrants has a family in Italy for whom he is working; the other, young, extraordinarily handsome and exceedingly blond, is single. He wants to become an American, and he falls in love with his benefactor's niece. If he marries the girl he will no longer have to hide from immigration officials.

A monstrous change creeps upon the kind and loving uncle. He is violently opposed to this romance and is not intelligent enough to realize that this opposition is not motivated as he thinks, by a dislike of the boy and a suspicion that he is too pretty to be a man, but by his own too-intense love for his niece. Not even the wise and kindly neighborhood lawyer can persuade him to let the girl go.

The play is told as the lawyer's recollection of what happened—of the events that ultimately spell death for a man who would have scoffed at death only a brief time ago. The lawyer, played with quiet persuasiveness by Naish, sits at the side of the stage apron and now and again tells the audience of the things that came about.

This is an intensely absorbing drama, sure of itself every step of the way. It makes no false moves, wastes no time and has the beauty that comes from directness and simplicity. Some of the language in both the Miller works is rough or bawdy, but it is true and it belongs and is not there for shoddy sensationalism.

There are several other fine performances in the second play, particularly those of Gloria Marlowe as the girl, Eileen Heckart as Heflin's wife, Richard Davalos as the boy and Jack Warden as the boy's brother. And for the tragedy Aronson has designed a miraculously fluid and poetically imaginative section of the Red Hook waterfront.

Arthur Miller has come a long way in our theatre, and he will go much farther, for his mind is a mind that won't stay still.

A Look at
A View From The Bridge

Arthur D. Epstein *

Arthur Miller's original version of *A View from the Bridge*, a one-act play, had its New York premiere on September 29, 1955. Broadway audiences have never seen Miller's two-act version, which was produced both in London and Paris. Because the script that is now usually published in the revision, and since this revision was the one selected for publication in the standard edition of Miller's plays,[1] my criticism will generally center upon this version as a working text.

Available criticism of the play is not extensive. What commentary we do have exists in the nature of reviews. Scholarly critiques are scant; most Miller critics, unfortunately, are still preoccupying themselves with Willy Loman. Eddie Carbone merits, I think, a somewhat kinder critical fate than his actual destiny in *A View from the Bridge*.

The setting of *A View from the Bridge* is the Red Hook section of Brooklyn, facing seaward from the Brooklyn Bridge, a section which Miller intimately knows. The central character, Eddie Carbone, is a Brooklyn longshoreman who lives with his wife, Beatrice, and his seventeen-year-old niece, Catherine (his ward), in a tenement building in Red Hook. The other two major characters are Marco and Rodolpho, Beatrice's Italian cousins, who come illegally to the United States and move in to live in Eddie's apartment. The introduction of the two "submarines" into the small world of Eddie Carbone sets the action of the play in motion.

A frame device is used in *A View from the Bridge* in the form of a modified Greek chorus. Miller creates Alfieri, a wise neighborhood lawyer of Italian ancestry, as the "engaged narrator"[2] of the story. In addition to his choric role, Alfieri functions as Eddie's confidant, further evidence of Miller's reliance upon Greek convention. In Alfieri's initial address to the audience, it is made perfectly clear that one of the themes of the play is to be man's relation to secular law:

> In this neighborhood to meet a lawyer or a priest in the street is unlucky. We're only thought of in connection with disasters, and they'd rather not get too close. I often

* Reprinted from *Texas Studies In Literature and Language*, 7, No. 1 (1965), 109–22. Copyright © 1965 by the University of Texas Press. Reprinted by permission of University of Texas Press and the author.

> think that behind that suspicious little nod of theirs lie three thousand years of
> distrust. A lawyer means the law, and in Sicily, from where their fathers came, the
> law has not been a friendly idea since the Greeks were beaten.[3]

Alfieri goes on to explain that the people of Red Hook not only distrust the law, but that essentially their heritage is one of primitive justice. Alfieri's references to Al Capone and Frankie Yale stress the violent forms of the "justice" that once prevailed during the first waves of Italian immigration.

Much of the physical danger of Red Hook has diminished, and Alfieri tells the audience: "I no longer keep a pistol in my filing cabinet."[4] Today these Italian immigrants who people Red Hook are "quite civilized, quite American. Now we settle for half."[5] What we have in *A View from the Bridge*, ironically, is an action which involves a man, Eddie Carbone, who will not settle for half. His primitive passions, more reminiscent of the ancient ancestors to whom Alfieri alludes in his choric moments, admit no compromise and throw him into violent conflict with his milieu.

Alfieri is a romantic; his references to Sicily, the dreariness of his years of unromantic legal practice, his frequent allusions to antiquity and to his heritage, all suggest that Miller wished to frame his action through the persona of Alfieri. It is worth noting that only Alfieri sees anything of larger significance in Eddie's tragedy than the self-interested views of the familial participants in it. To this extent I think Dennis Welland is correct in suggesting that "This play is 'a view from the bridge' not only because its setting is Brooklyn, but more importantly because it tries to show all sides of the situation from the detached eminence of the external observer. Alfieri is essential to the play because he is the bridge from which it is seen."[6] As far as Welland goes he is perceptive; yet he fails to note that Alfieri's view, although detached, is essentially romantic. I should also like to suggest that it is helpful to think of the word "Bridge" as the bridge linking modern Brooklyn with ancient Sicily, and furthermore, in the abstract, the bridge of Time.

Interestingly enough, this bridge between past and present was portrayed vividly by the original New York set, which stressed the Greek influence upon the play. Two massive columns were used to frame (paralleling the choric frame) the Brooklyn house in which Eddie lives. Skeletal in form, shorn of any intrusive adornment, this set avoided realistic detail. It was unfortunately changed in the two-act London and Paris versions. If, as the play seems to suggest, Miller was interested in the timelessness of Eddie's tragic deed, then a set emphasizing that timelessness would indeed be appropriate. I did not see the British version, but it is interesting to note that Margaret Webster, who did, has commented:

> Gone is the sense—so impressive to me in New York—of a people of ancient lineage
> reborn on the Brooklyn waterfront, yet still the prey of those smoldering buried
> passions which wrought the Classic tragedies. The dynamite is not less, but the scale is
> smaller.[7]

Although Miller defends his change to a more realistic set on the basis of making

Eddie's social context clearer,[8] no further clarity actually emerges. In essence, Miller, in his attempt to portray more vividly a realistic milieu, diminished the universality of his theme and the myth-like atmosphere of his piece.

Most obvious of all the changes, of course, is the division into two acts.[9] This hurts the play; the propelling force of Eddie's obsessive movement toward self-destruction is interrupted and lessens the power and spiraling intensity of the work.

In addition to the change in set and the division into two acts, Miller has made another change that by and large weakens his original version. One of the strengths of the one-act version was the more effective use of the narrator. "Good evening. Welcome to the theater," Alfieri greeted his audience. "This is the end of the story. Good night," were his final words. This representational device, which deliberately framed the play *as a play,* is absent in the revised version. Such a difference in representation may seem minor at first glance; but consider that Alfieri narrates and participates in a tale whose power is positively stunning; to snap the thread of audience involvement, as was the case in the original version, with a casual "Good night," is a theatrical tour de force. Psychologically, Miller's alteration was unsound.[10]

In his revised Prologue to the tragedy, Alfieri romanticizes and waxes nostalgic:

> . . . in Calabria perhaps or one the cliff at Syracuse, another lawyer quite differently dressed, heard the same complaint and sat there as powerless as I, and watched it run its bloody course.[11]

Two points should be made here. This passage stresses, first, the timelessness of Eddie's tragedy and the human condition, and second, the inevitability of the happenings the audience is about to see presented on the stage. In the Prologue the audience is prepared for violence. Repeatedly throughout the play Alfieri stresses his powerlessness to halt the movements of Eddie's path toward disaster. And of course the irony involved is that we too, the audience, shall sit as dumbfounded and powerless to stop Eddie Carbone from self-destruction as Alfieri. Miller comments upon this emotional reaction of the audience:

> I wanted the audience to feel toward it [the story] as I had on hearing it for the first time—not so much with heart-wringing sympathy as with wonder. For when it was told to me I knew its ending a few minutes after the teller had begun to speak. I wanted to create suspense but not by withholding information. It must be suspenseful because one knew too well how it would come out, so that the basic feeling would be the desire to stop this man and tell him what he was really doing to his life.[12]

Eddie's subliminal incestuous love for Catherine exists prior to Rodolpho's appearance. Catherine is cautioned about her "walkin' wavy," and the looks the local candy-story cowboys give her. Until Rodolpho the threat of sexual rivals is remote—the rivalry does not intrude into Eddie's household. Until the arrival of the blond submarine, male dominance in his own house is un-challenged. Underlying Eddie's fear of sexual rivals is suspicion; he is basically distrustful of other people, and this is one of the major differences between him and Catherine and Beatrice. This central motif of suspicion is illuminated in a conversation that focuses upon Catherine's receiving Eddie's reluctant permission to work as a stenographer in a plumbing factory. Compare the polar viewpoints expressed in the advice given to Catherine by Eddie and Beatrice:

> *Eddie:* I only ask you one thing—don't trust nobody. You got a good aunt but she's got too big a heart, you learned bad from her. Believe me.
> *Beatrice:* Be the way you are, Katie, don't listen to him.[13]

This suspicion and caution help to explain Eddie's attitude toward hiding the two submarines. Eddie demands of Catherine and Beatrice complete silence. In recounting the story of Vinny Bolzano, a boy who informed on his submarine uncle, Miller establishes the tribal attitude of the Italian immigrants who people Red Hook toward an informer. The boy was set upon by his own family, was dragged by his feet with his head banging against the stairs, into the streets, and was never heard from again. Informing, the unforgivable sin of betrayal, is punishable by ostracism, expulsion from the tribe. Eddie's narration of the circumstances of Vinny Bolzano's story dramatically foreshadows his own fate after he is similarly guilty of betrayal. It is ironic that the Bolzano story is first mentioned by Eddie; Miller thus underscores from the beginning Eddie's keen awareness of the code of justice in the polis of which he is a part. *Despite* this unwritten neighborhood law, he eventually turns informer. His betrayal is evidence of the intensity of his passion for Catherine and the unswerving direction of his obsessive love for her.

II

Critics have completely overlooked, evidently viewing it as purely representational, Rodolpho's singing of "Paper Doll," except to indicate that Martin Ritt, the stage director of the New York production, caught the satire of Italian singers who consciously imitate the singing style of American crooners.[14] However, what is much more crucial is that, like many of the songs in Shakespeare's plays, the lyrics of "Paper Doll" in *A View from the Bridge* illuminate the dilemma of the tragic hero. Quite clearly, Arthur Miller, who could have selected any of a plethora of Tin Pan Alley favorites, chose "Paper Doll" for definite reasons. The lyrics explain his choice:

> "I'll tell you boys it's tough to be alone,
> And it's tough to love a doll that's not your own.
> I'm through with all of them,
> I'll never fall again,
> Hey, boy, what you gonna do?
> *I'm gonna buy a paper doll that I can call my own, A doll*
> *that other fellows cannot steal (Eddie rises and moves upstage.)*
> And then those flirty, flirty guys
> With their flirty, flirty eyes
> Will have to flirt with dollies that are real—[15]

The dominant theme of the lyric is that the singer is going to buy a paper doll that other fellows cannot steal; in other words, an object of love which will obviate the possibility of rivalry and theft. The relevance to Eddie Carbone is striking. Throughout the play (which incidentally is interwoven with imagery of thievery) Eddie repeatedly accuses Rodolpho of having stolen Catherine from him or alludes to it. Catherine is Eddie's paper doll. Rodolpho is the flirty, flirty guy, and the interesting fact that the singer intends to "buy" a paper doll parallels exactly Eddie's attitude that he has a basic right to control Catherine's actions because of the enormous personal sacrifices he has made in order to raise her:

> I worked like a dog twenty years so a punk could have her, so that's what I done. I mean, in the worst times, in the worst, when there wasn't a ship comin' in the harbor, I didn't stand around lookin' for relief—I hustled. When there was empty piers in Brooklyn I went to Hoboken, Staten Island, the West Side, Jersey, all over—because I made a promise. I took out of my own mouth to give to her. I took out of my wife's mouth. I walked hungry plenty days in this city![16]

Eddie's hostility toward Rodolpho is revealed in his thinly veiled suggestion of his suspicion of Rodolpho's homosexuality, first mentioned to Beatrice. Never concrete in his accusation, the closest Eddie comes to specific identification is to label Rodolpho a "weird."[17] "Queer," the more common pejorative for a homosexual, could easily have been used by Miller,[18] but the selection of the word "weird" subtilizes Eddie's suggestion and is more appropriate to the texture of shadowy innuendo in which he is working. Rodolpho, we and Beatrice are informed, is now known by Eddie's longshoreman pals as "Paper Doll . . . Canary."[19] He does "a regular free show"; and it is unnecessary, I think, to belabor the sexual overtones of this phrase. His hair is "wacky . . . he's like a chorus girl or sump'm,"[20] Eddie tells us. In this dialogue Eddie is the accuser, making sly, damaging suggestions, while Beatrice attempts to defend Rodolpho against such innuendoes and to dismiss their relevance. Set in striking juxtaposition to this scene is the following with Eddie and his friends, Louis and Mike. A surface glance reveals its comic relief. But there is something more. Actually what Miller has done (again reminiscent of Shakespeare's use of comic scenes) is to illuminate the earlier scene by reversing Eddie's role. In his meeting with Louis and Mike, it is Eddie who is placed in the uncomfortable position of defending Rodolpho against the same innuendoes now being leveled at him by Mike and Louis. This has gone completely unnoted by critics. Notice the striking similarity between Beatrice's and Eddie's language in trying to explain Rodolpho's odd behavior on the waterfront piers:

> *Beatrice* [to Eddie]: Well, he's a kid; he don't know how to behave himself yet.[21]
> *Eddie* [to Louis and Mike]: Yeah, I know. But he's a kid yet, y'know? He—he's just a kid, that's all.[22]

An echo of Beatrice's words. An ironic reversal of roles. Furthermore it is Mike, in the comic scene, who assumes Eddie's role of the insinuator in the previous scene. Not only does this scene help to illuminate through comedy and juxtaposition the earlier scene and help to establish the discomfort of Eddie's dilemma, but it lends credence to Eddie's suspicion that Rodolpho is a homosexual by buttressing through representation the reactions of Eddie's pals to Rodolpho, reactions which Eddie had just described to Beatrice in the previous scene. It seems to me to be one of the major deficiencies of the criticism of *A View from the Bridge* that no recognition has been made of Miller's abundantly clear attempt to make *some* case for Eddie's behavior. Eddie's reaction to Rodolpho is not as isolated, as bizarre and monstrous, as the critics suggest.[23] On the contrary, we have seen (and I shall later point out additional textual evidence) that other characters in the play, namely, Eddie's longshoreman pals—whose background is similar to Eddie's and whose views are not distorted by incestuous desire for Catherine—also read Rodolpho as a "weird." Eddie Carbone, as Arthur Miller has carefully created him, is not isolated in his reactions to Rodolpho.

Eddie's meetings with his confidant, Alfieri, provides a closer look into Eddie's private world. The suggestion that Rodolpho is a homosexual, which he never makes concretely to Beatrice, is more directly stated to Alfieri (although the word "homosexual" is never used). The jibs of Eddie's peers are revealed as he attempts to construct a case against Rodolpho to convince Alfieri that the young submarine is a homosexual. What emerges as a central issue in this scene is that under the written law Eddie Carbone has no recourse *even* if his accusation is true.

Eddie's accusation reveals a mind tortured by the fear that he is about to lose Catherine, and his distress is compounded by his suspicion that Rodolpho is a homosexual. Yet this suspicion, ironically, provides Eddie with a seemingly innocent motive for opposing the marriage of Catherine and Rodolpho. Eddie's accusation of inversion is the foundation upon which he attempts to structure a case against Rodolpho. His efforts to enlist the assistance of Alfieri on his behalf are based upon convincing Alfieri of Rodolpho's homosexuality—of convincing Alfieri that Rodolpho "ain't right." The zeal with which he takes up his hostility to Rodolpho externalizes the intensity of his own passion for Catherine, and obviates any necessity for self-examination which might expose this underlying passion—an exposure Eddie is unable to face. Witness, for example, Eddie's horror when Beatrice confronts him at the end of the play with an open declaration of his subconscious feelings for his niece:

> *Eddie, crying out in agony:* That's what you think of me—that I would have such a thought? *His fists clench his head as though it will burst.*[24]

And, similarly, during his first interview with Alfieri, Eddie reacts furiously to Alfieri's suggestion that he may want Catherine for himself: "What're you talkin' about, marry me! I don't know what the hell you're talkin' about!"[25]

Alfieri, with sagacity and insight, realizes that the real problem involved is Eddie's excessive love for Catherine:

You know, sometimes God mixes up the people. We all love somebody, the wife, the kids—every man's got somebody that he loves, heh? But sometimes . . . there's too much, and it goes where it mustn't.[26]

Alfieri suggests that this excess of love (and Alfieri never challenges Eddie's genuine protective love for Catherine) may begin to overflow in unnatural directions. Law, Alfieri explains to Eddie, is merely a codification of what is natural and has a right to happen. Eddie's frustration in learning that the law is uninterested in his case against Rodolpho breaks through in an impassioned speech which echoes the theme of "Paper Doll":

And now I gotta sit in my own house and look at a son-of-a-bitch punk like that— which he came out of nowhere! I give him my house to sleep! I take the blankets off my bed for him, and he takes and puts his dirty filthy hands on her *like a goddam thief!*[27]

Let us listen again to those all-important lyrics: "I'm gonna buy a paper doll that I can call my own. / A doll that other fellows cannot steal." And now Eddie crying to Alfieri: "He's stealing from me!"[28] The robbery motif, the imagery of thievery in Eddie's anguished speech and in the lyrics of "Paper Doll" is clearly not accidental.

Symbolically, Alfieri (Reason) is contrasted with Eddie (Passion); Eddie is a man governed by his passions, and in *A View from the Bridge* Miller is showing us the deficiencies of an impulsive man who operates without the moderation imposed by reason. Yet, one of the elemental ironies of the play is that Alfieri, a symbol of rational thought, a man of legal training, ordered procedure, wisdom, and basic native intelligence, is also powerless to stop the onrushing tide and sweep of the horrible events in this play. Alfieri realizes the direction in which Eddie is heading, but is puzzled by his own inability to halt him. His only gesture is to consult, in an admission of personal helplessness, "a certain old lady in the neighborhood, a very wise old woman" (a practice common among many clannish societies), and is told to "Pray for him."[29] The written law, man's own law, is inadequate here, Miller seems to be saying. Eddie Carbone's fate is in the hands of the Gods. How much like Greek tragedy!

Earlier I mentioned that there is additional evidence to support Eddie's view that Rodolpho is a homosexual, evidence which suggests that not only Eddie thinks Rodolpho is a homosexual. Eddie, recall, visits Alfieri after the famous scene in which he seizes Rodolpho and, in front of Catherine, kisses him.[30] Alfieri, who tries to dissuade Eddie from informing and senses that he is now so inclined, shouts to Eddie after an interview: "You won't have a friend in the world, Eddie! Even those who understand will turn against you, *even the ones who feel the same* will despise you!"[31]

Despite the fact that he recognizes the thoughtlessness of Eddie's action, Alfieri is nevertheless unmistakably aware that others, namely Eddie's fellow longshoremen, also suspect that Rodolpho is a homosexual. Moreover, the scene with Eddie and his friends, Louis and Mike, is instructive here in pointing up that others besides Eddie share his suspicions about Rodolpho. The diction and the tenor of the dialogue clearly suggest that the longshoremen, of whom Louis and Mike are representative, respond to Rodolpho as does Eddie. In the conversation outside Eddie's house, for instance, Louis and Mike, after expressing amazement at Marco's masculine strength, confirm Eddie in his suspicions. Immediately following their words about Marco, we have this glaring contrast:

> *Mike, grinning:* That blond one, though—*Eddie looks at him.* He's got a sense of humor. *Louis snickers.*[32]

Miller is careful to note that Mike's words about the "blond one" are framed with a grin, and that Louis then snickers, a direction that significantly reveals that something is being withheld in this conversation. The character of what Mike has to say to Eddie reinforced by Louis' response, does not indicate an appreciation of Rodolpho's humor *per se*; on the contrary, Mike's words refer to the young submarine's odd behavior on the waterfront. Continuing, Mike relates to Eddie in a fit of hysterical laughter: "You take one look at him—everybody's happy."[33] One day while working with Rodolpho at the Moore MacCormack Line, the other longshoremen "was all hysterical."[34] Miller's stage directions following these words should not be neglected: "*Louis and he* [Mike] *explode in laughter.*"[35] Furthermore, it is worth noting that Eddie, Miller tells us, is "*Troubled*" by this conversation. In essence, the significance of this scene is to solidify Eddie's private suspicions of Rodolpho's weird behavior by displaying a public representation and confirmation of these suspicions through the personae of Louis and Mike.

The working environment of which Eddie is a part, specifically, longshoremen, consists of a group of men who depend for their livelihood upon their physical power. Loading and unloading cargo is grueling, physical, masculine labor. I emphasize what is obvious because I wish to make strikingly clear that longshoremen would quite naturally associate physical labor with masculinity. Rodolpho, on the other hand, can sew, sing (in a very high voice, perhaps somewhat effeminate?) and cook—all aptitudes which in the minds of longshoremen, or for that matter any working group which relies upon sheer masculine physical power, are associated with feminity. Plainly Rodolpho is not a homosexual because he sings in a high voice and can cook and sew. But because of their background and work it is understandable that Eddie and his peers regard Rodolpho as they do. And this is why Alfieri, who appreciates the psychology of his Red Hook clients, can say "*even the ones who feel the same will despise you.*" It is fallacious to suggest that Eddie Carbone is isolated in his response to Rodolpho. What does finally isolate Eddie from his community is not his innuendoes or even his attempt to degrade Rodolpho in front of Catherine. Rather, it is his overt act of betrayal, of informing the immigration authorities that Rodolpho and Marco are submarines. By this one decisive act, Eddie commits the unforgivable sin of informing, with the inevitable consequence of isolation from his social context.

For betrayal, Marco's spitting in Eddie's face is a symbolic murder which foreshadows his act of murder at the conclusion of the play. The spitting, coupled with a public accusation ("That one! He killed my children! That one stole the food from my children"[36]), underscores the imagery of theft. According to Eddie, Rodolpho has stolen Catherine; Marco has stolen Eddie's "good name." Balancing Eddie's victimization, Marco feels that Eddie has stolen a chance for the life of his children. We might also note that although Eddie's betrayal was not designed to net the two submarine nephews of the butcher, Lipari, both the neighborhood and Lipari condemn and punish Eddie just as severely as if Eddie's act had been originally perpetrated against Lipari and his family. In other words, it is inconsequential against *whom* Eddie informs; the act of informing is what is unforgivable and unforgettable in the Red Hook mind.

Marco is a symbol of primitive justice. Like Eddie, he will not settle for half. The symbolic murder of spitting in Eddie's face does not satisfy his appetite for revenge. As he says to a fearful Alfieri: "In my country he would be dead now. He would not live this long."[37] Marco is a product of the Old World. "Not quite civilized, not quite American," he insists upon a primitive form of justice.[38] Ironically, Marco is as dissatisfied with the law as Eddie. Both want from the law what the law has not been designed to provide—indiscriminate punishment; in a word, retributive justice. An interesting parallel is evident: Eddie seeks recourse to the law to prevent Catherine from marrying someone who "ain't right." When recourse to the law fails, he informs. Marco too wants Eddie punished for degrading his brother, robbing his children, mocking his work. Learning there is no law for that, he reneges on his word to Alfieri and ultimately kills Eddie. Marco's code of law is primitive, punitive justice. As he takes Marco's hand (the same hand that held the chair as a threatening weapon) Alfieri counsels him: "This is not God, Marco. You hear? Only God makes justice."[39] Interestingly enough, both Eddie and Marco receive warnings from Alfieri; both men reject his advice.

Alfieri, the romantic, makes the clearest statement of authorial opinion we have in A *View from the Bridge*. He recognizes the waste of Eddie's death and the violation of a code of honor. But Alfieri, in his Epilogue following Eddie's death, assigns a dignity to Eddie's action which would otherwise be ambiguous:

> I confess that something perversely pure calls to me from his memory—not purely good, but himself purely, for he allowed himself to be wholly known and for that I think I will love him more than all my sensible clients.[40]

Eddie Carbone is a tragic figure, Miller clearly feels, because in the intransigence of his actions there is an implicit fidelity to the self, an integrity to one's own beliefs no matter how perverse they may be. However wrong he may have been, and Alfieri is not unmindful of Eddie's tragic deed, Eddie nonetheless pursues what he regards as a proper course of action.[41] Reason was absent in his behavior, but the irony is that Alfieri, a product of the compromising attitude of the Italian-American community of Red Hook ("we settle for half"), still loves a man who did not settle for half. Alfieri, the romantic, admires the purity of

Eddie's emotions, not the rightness or wrongness of them. Of Alfieri's rewritten Epilogue in the revised version of *A View from the Bridge* Miller has this to say, which I think suggests how desperately he wanted to make clear that Eddie is a tragic figure:

> In revising the play it became possible to accept for myself the implication I had sought to make clear in the original version, which was that however one might dislike this man, who does all sorts of frightful things, he possesses or exemplifies the wondrous and humane fact that he too can be driven to what in the last analysis is a sacrifice of himself for his conception, however misguided, of right, dignity, and justice.[42]

Although Miller considers Eddie a tragic figure, he nonetheless apparently has never had any clearly defined outline of the emotions toward Eddie which he wanted to elicit from his audience. A comparison of his own statements reveals this uncertainty. In the introduction of his *Collected Plays*, Miller suggests that the changes he made in revising the original version had this result: "It was finally possible to mourn this man."[43] On the other hand, three years later, in a new introduction to the paperback reprint of the play, Miller had this to say: "Eddie is still not a man to weep over."[44] Miller's confusion, I think, is the result of his preoccupation with the moral element in *A View from the Bridge* rather than eliciting specific emotions. The dilemma of a man—Eddie—betraying the code of his social milieu is of paramount consequence to Miller, and is what engages his creative energy. His failure to clarify what emotions the audience will feel reveals itself even in the statement about Eddie that he makes Alfieri deliver in the Epilogue to the play. Alfieri, like Miller, has ambivalent feelings toward Eddie: "And yet, it is better to settle for half, it must be! And so I mourn him—I admit it—with a certain . . . alarm."[45]

Despite Miller's recognition of Eddie's moral flaw, he (and I think this is typical of Miller's vision of life) cannot ignore the essential humanity of his characters. His faith in the dignity of man is what leaves him unable to dismiss completely the humanly fallible Eddie Carbone from the race of humanity. Perhaps Linda's words in *Death of a Salesman* can illuminate for us what Miller really thinks of Eddie Carbone:

> I don't say he's a great man. Willy Loman [Eddie Carbone?] never made a lot of money. His name was never in the paper. He's not the finest character that ever lived. But he's a human being, and a terrible thing is happening to him. So attention must be paid. He's not to be allowed to fall into his grave like an old dog. Attention, attention must be finally paid to such a person.

Notes

1. *Arthur Miller's Collected Plays* (New York, 1957).

2. *Collected Plays*, p. 47.

3. Ibid., p. 379.

4. Ibid.

5. Ibid.

6. Dennis Welland, *Arthur Miller* (New York, 1961), p. 105.

7. Margaret Webster, "A Look at the London Season," *Theatre Arts*, XLI (May, 1957), 29.

8. *Collected Plays*, pp. 50–51.

9. This became necessary, Miller explains in the paperback edition of the play, because of the expansion of Beatrice's role. This accounts for almost all of the additional dialogue, of which Margared Webster observed after covering the play's London premiere: "This [*A View from the Bridge*] has been expanded by about twenty minutes of new dialogue, most of which seemed to me to be dotting i's and crossing t's, and is split in half by a long interval, much to its detriment." See Webster, "A Look at the London Season," *Theatre Arts*, XLI (May, 1957), 28–29.

10. One change from the original is advantageous. Eddie no longer is the parent of two children. Childlessness intensifies his passion for Catherine; she is in fact his only baby, and this change makes his dilemma more pitiable. Without Catherine he would be left truly childless and lonely, and his anguish is thereby magnified.

11. *Collected Plays*, p. 379.

12. From Arthur Miller's introduction to the paperback edition of *A View from the Bridge* (New York, 1960), p. vii.

13. *Collected Plays*, pp. 386–387.

14. Henry Hewes, "Broadway Postscript: Death of a Longshoreman," *Saturday Review*, XXXVIII (October 15, 1955), 26.

15. *Collected Plays*, p. 396. With the exception of Miller's italicized stage directions, the italics are mine.

16. Ibid., p. 404–410.

17. Ibid., p. 398.

18. Gerald Weales in a different context has briefly noted Eddie's avoidance of the word "queer." See his "Arthur Miller: Man and His Image," *Tulane Drama Review*, VII (Fall, 1962), 175.

19. *Collected Plays*, p. 398.

20. Ibid.

21. Ibid.

22. Ibid., p. 400.

23. Of all the play's reviewers, only Eric Bentley has recognized Miller's ambiguity concerning the fact that Rodolpho may be a homosexual: ". . . we don't feel sure the accusation is false." See "Theatre," *New Republic*, CXXXIII (December 19, 1955), 22.

24. *Collected Plays*, p. 438.

25. Ibid., p. 410.

26. Ibid., p. 409.

27. Ibid., p. 410. Italics mine.

28. Ibid.

29. Ibid.

30. It is notable that Miller relies upon translatable physical action—not dialogue—to represent Eddie's contempt for Rodolpho. An earlier instance of action to represent passion occurs in the scene in which Eddie proposes to teach Rodolpho how to box. This fight scene also establishes the play's vendetta motif. After Eddie staggers Rodolpho, Marco, generally reticent, arises and challenges Eddie to lift a chair by one of its front legs, a feat which Eddie cannot accomplish. In a terrifying display of strength and determination, Marco raises the chair in a symbolic gesture of triumph, and holds it as a weapon over Eddie's head. Stunning in its power, this scene directly parallels the final scene: both acts conclude with Eddie on his knees before Marco.

31. *Collected Plays*, p. 424. Italics mine.

32. Ibid., p. 400.

33. Ibid.

34. Ibid.

35. Ibid. During Eddie's first interview with Alfieri, we have a telling passage in which the character of Louis and Mike's convulsive laughter, which punctuates the conversation about Rodolpho, and its effect upon Eddie's mind are movingly illuminated for us: *EDDIE*: "Mr. Alfieri, they're laughin' at him on the piers. I'm ashamed. Paper Doll they call him. Blondie now. His brother thinks it's because he's got a sense of humor, see—which he's got—but that ain't what they're laughin'. Which they're not goin' to come out with it because they know he's my relative, which they have to see me if they make a crack, y'know? But I know what they're laughin' at, and when I think of that guy layin' his hands on her I could—I mean it's eatin' me out, Mr. Alfieri, because I struggled for that girl." See *Collected Plays*, p. 408.

36. *Collected Plays*, p. 433.

37. Ibid.

38. It is worth noting how carefully Miller has drawn a contrast between Marco and Rodolpho. Clearly distinguishable are Marco's primitive intransigence (his refusal to forgive Eddie and his desire for revenge); his loyalty to the Old World (he does not wish to become an American citizen); and his physical characteristics (dark). In contrast we have Rodolpho's civilized conciliation to Eddie (he apologizes for causing all the trouble); his renunciation of Italy (he wishes to become an American citizen); and his physical characteristics (light).

39. *Collected Plays*, p. 435.

40. Ibid., p. 439.

41. Dennis Welland notes Eddie's "moral intransigence," and makes the shrewd observation that Alfieri's rewritten curtain speech "prevents our seeing Eddie as the animal—which is what Marco has just called him." See *Arthur Miller*, p. 104.

42. *Collected Plays*, p. 51.

43. Ibid., p. 52.

44. *A View from the Bridge*, p. x.

45. *Collected Plays*, p. 439.

After The Fall

Review of *After The Fall*

John Simon*

A far more imposing dramatic gossip column, and a considerably more massive example of how to *épater les bourgeois*, is Arthur Miller's *After the Fall*. Miller's mind has always loomed bulky on the stage—not like a genuine largeness, but like the elephantiasis of a flea. Imagine, to be precise, an enormous photographic enlargement of a microbe: instead of being majestic, it is merely distorted, grotesque, and blurred in its detail. This is emblematically manifest in the very opening stage direction of *After the Fall*: "The action takes place in the mind, thought, and memory of Quentin." Though *mind* would seem to cover the whole thing very nicely, one might, pedantically, wish to throw in *memory*. But what on earth is that pleonastic *thought* for? To satisfy Miller's need for magnifying grandiloquence: Damn the tautologies, full speed to the stars!

The most painful flaw of *After the Fall* is its megalomania combind with hypocrisy. A forthright, smiling self-love can be harmless and even likable. But here we have Miller telling us that he is relentlessly baring his, or his blantantly autobiographical hero's, chest—only to emerge as someone whose faults are as nothing compared to those of almost everybody else. True, Quentin is a bit cold to his women; true, when, as a lawyer, he undertakes to defend a man forsaken by all his other friends as he comes up for Congressional investigation, Quentin is scared about his own future and momentarily relieved when the man commits suicide. But at least Quentin reasons patiently with these women and freely admits his small failings; whereas they, unself-critical, hurl castrating abuse or violently absurd demands at him—in fact, we see four wives in the play calling their husbands "moron" or "idiot" and, at crucial points, maltreating them accordingly. And at least Quentin does stand up for the victim of McCarthyism when no one else will. In short, a classic case of what Wilde called washing one's clean linen in public.

And the megalomania! What are we to make of a play whose chief purpose, or, at any rate, only lively element, is the laying of Marilyn Monroe's ghost, but which cannot do this without dragging in everything from McCarthy to Auschwitz, from the Communism of the Thirties to the Garden of Eden and a symbolic self-crucifixion? Quentin-Miller's humdrum peccadilloes are played

*From *Hudson Review*, 17 (1964), 234–36. Copyright © 1964 by John Simon. Reprinted by permission of Random House, Inc. and John Simon.

out under the gaze of a Nazi death camp; a characteristic stage image shows us Quentin towering over three prostrate, spurned or adoring, women; and, in a particularly gross scene, "Maggie" Monroe's naked mating-dance is superimposed on a Congressional hearing. Similarly, in statements about his play, Miller is regularly invoking Goethe, Tolstoy, the Book of Genesis, or the attacks on Hannah Arendt's *Eichmann in Jerusalem* (which he equates with unfavorable notices of his play), or informing us that it reveals "a hidden process which underlies the destructiveness hanging over this age," as though *After the Fall* had made some giant psychic discovery that hitherto eluded all analysis. Actually, the play's only discovery is a new form of contrition called *tua culpa*.

Perhaps the most preposterous statement of Miller's is this: "*After the Fall* is experimental in any terms. It involves what is not a new theatrical style so much as a new style of thinking about the world, the unification, the synthesis of individual psychology and social and moral considerations to make a moral biology on the stage. Instead of having a work concentrate on one element of man, I have tried to put him on in totality." This about a play which has for its sum total of newness a narrator who comments on or steps into remembered events—muddying their sequence and creating formlessness—and which has for its only solution to all the injustice, lovelessness, cruelty, loneliness, disaffection in this world an utterance made by the character representing Miller's new wife, to the effect that "one must finally take one's life in one's arms" and "kiss it" even though it has the "dreadful face" of an idiot child. *O altitudo!* The playwright is requested kindly to refrain from making a moral biology on the stage—or on the rug, either.

What Miller woefully lacks here is the imagination to digest, transpose, transubstantiate the givens of his life, never mind about kissing it. It is this incapacity for any translation beyond the changing of a few names and professions—including the awkward one of turning the theatre and writing of plays into the law and writing of briefs—that forces an audience to see the play, as it were, through a keyhole; that makes the viewer a voyeur, and the critical cogitator a gossip-monger in spite of himself. There would be nothing shocking about a sentence like "But how can you speak of love, she had been chewed and spat out by a long line of grinning men!" (except, perhaps, the triteness of the writing) if one's nose weren't being rubbed in the fact that this is Arthur Miller talking about Marilyn Monroe, his ex-wife. And so it goes, from intimate premarital disclosure to garish marital fracas and all the way to suicide, and we are every man his own Dorothy Kilgallen.

Space allows me only to itemize some of the other lapses. There is the inconsistency in character when Maggie hurtles from a paragon of healthy sexuality to a pathetic, abject, neurotic bitch. There is the incredibly poor taste of showing one's two previous wives as failures, while one's new one (with whom one hasn't had time to fall out as yet) is presented as a wartime heroine and peacetime angel of goodness, wisdom, and, above all, self-abnegation—the key to a woman's success with Mr. Miller. There are ghastly flights of pseudo-prose poetry (as in "How few the days are that hold the mind together like a tapestry hung on four or five hooks"); there is the autobiographical hero's grammar, so bad that it verges on illiteracy. There is the humorlessness, both in the few, feeble attempts at wit and in the ability to write, in complete serious-ness, a line like, "And in the morning, a dagger in that dear little daughter's heart!" Add to this Elia Kazan's uninventive, musical comedy-style direction on a grandiose open stage on which you would expect to see, at the very least, *Prometheus Bound,* and performances which, with the exception of Barbara Loden's penetrant Maggie, are undistinguished, and you have a picture of what the mountain of Lincoln Center Repertory Theatre has labored to give birth to. Instead of toiling away at this overlong brief, Miller should have quietly settled out of court.

The View From The Mirror

Walter Kerr°

After the Fall resembled a confessional which Arthur Miller entered as a penitent and from which he emerged as the priest. It was a tricky quick change, sometimes an almost imperceptible one; but it constituted a neither especially attractive nor especially persuasive performance.

I speak of Arthur Miller directly because the play seemed, quite simply and virtually all of the time, to be about its playwright, not at all about the shadowy alter ego he called Quentin. It seemed to be about Mr. Miller for two reasons, one of them less important than the other.

The less important reason was its patent use of the author's relationship with the late Marilyn Monroe. We were given no cause for doubt here, not in calling her Maggie or in describing her as a cabaret singer. In production, after one brief and appealing scene on a park bench, actress Barbara Loden swiftly acquired a feathery blond wig, a pair of pajama tops, and a moistness of eye and lip that led us without hesitation to the bridal gown, the broken contracts, and the suicidal dedication to sleeping pills by which we still chart in our nightmares one of the legendary careers of our times. About half of the three-hour evening was consumed with the hero's earnest, desperate, harsh and grating efforts to love this girl, to manage her, to chasten her, to save her. We did not attend to the scenes as though we were following characters in a play. We attended to them as though we had geen given Mr. Miller's former address, and asked in.

The use of the materials, however personal, however intimate, need not have been fatal. Mr. Miller is a theatrical craftsman who has earned our respect. A craftsman can always be granted the freedom, indeed the right, to draw upon any sources meaningful to him. We shall not think him insensitive so long as he puts to this clay an imaginative hand, making something new, independent, complete and self-assertive of it.

It was here that the play failed most seriously, for there was no Quentin, no other man, no other life than Mr. Miller's. The nominal Quentin began by speaking to us as though we were on the other end of a telephone. He was exposing his mind to us in tiny bits and pieces, circuitously, sweepingly, handling the past like so many loose kites bobbing helplessly in midair. His father

°From Walter Kerr, *Thirty Plays Hath November* (New York: Simon and Schuster, 1969), pp. 214–17. Copyright © 1969 by Walter Kerr. Reprinted with permission of Walter Kerr.

hissed disbelief as he was told of his wife's death; his mother pounded at a door with a child's sailboat in her hand, frantically; his first wife turned her back on him, in bed and in the living room, because he was cold and remote.

He struggled for the secret of his remoteness, his failures with at least three women. He seemed to find it in his promise, to all of them, of limitless love. But no man could ever have kept such a promise, he now knew. What lesser promise might he make that would be worthy of a man? He brooded, soliloquized, lectured, shouted, shrugged. In all of his search, however, there was nothing concrete, nothing carved out of bone. The search was verbal, pontifical, rhetorical.

He had no sooner cried out, "We are killing one another with abstraction!" than he went on to say, "This is a city full of people, this is a city full of loves." But "people" and "loves" are themselves abstractions. Vague, general nouns tumbled over one another. We heard about "compromise" and "power" and forever about "truth" ("It is contemptible like all truth, covered like truth with slime!"). We heard, in a first-act sequence reliving the plight of former fellow travelers reduced to telling on one another, that "They took our lust for right and used it for Russian purposes!" Jason Robards, who first played the role, seemed to be whirling a vast lasso of spinning words above his head, aching to rope real emotion and to bring it slapping down. He could not do it.

Because the playwright had not stood off a little distance, just enough distance to imagine one other man, he ended up seeming to discuss himself, to indulge himself, and in some measure, with Jehovah's thunderbolt in his hand, to justify himself. Many of us found this *mea culpa* disingenuous. Why, when the same charge might as easily have been lodged against Eugene O'Neill in the matter of *A Long Day's Journey into Night*?

I don't think the answer has much to do with the fact that O'Neill waited until the members of his family were dead, and indeed left instructions that all of us were to wait for the play until he himself was dead, before displaying the drunkenness, the dope addiction, and the lacerating domestic fury that had been the environment of his youth. Time is not of the essence.

A degree of detachment is. In dealing with such materials, and if such materials are to be truly tamed and shaped, an author's eye must move in two ways. It must first surrender its own claims, its egocentric right to stand at the center of the universe taking the measure of all things and passing judgment upon them. It must slip into a side pocket, into a nearly neutral corner where the light is not so blinding and where it may be able to see clearly, as O'Neill's did. The young O'Neill is the least important, the least assertive, of the four major figures in *A Long Day's Journey into Night*, a pale but observant wraith looking, looking, looking—and trying not to judge.

Mr. Miller, instead, thrusts his hero into the center of things and makes him that center—sole reality, sole arbiter. We are given to understand that the fragments and dispersed action we watch takes place inside the hero's head. To follow this conceit, we must imagine that head expanding until it has encompassed the stage and all the people on it, until it contains the whole visible universe. All that exists is bounded and defined by one man's self-centered reaction to it. The eye is "I," and the "truths" we see are wholly subjective. But we do not trust a wholly subjective truth.

Ideally, as an author's eye moves some distance away from the things it hopes to describe, it also finds itself free to move upward, downward, around, across. It begins to see in dimensions, to note weight and line and color, to build up an image out of sculptural properties—an image that will at last have the independence to live and move on its own. Having detached itself sufficiently to become in effect a third party, the eye is in a position to create.

Here we had only the view from the mirror.

Arthur Miller:
Between Pathos and Tragedy

Clinton W. Trowbridge[*]

No one in the American Theater today speaks as passionately and as ide-alistically about the possibilities of drama as Arthur Miller:

> There lies within the dramatic form the ultimate possibility of raising the truth-consciousness of mankind to a level of such intensity as to transform those who observe it.[1]

wrote Miller in 1956. While he was still an undergraduate at the University of Michigan in the 1930's, he dedicated himself to the task of creating such a drama:

> With the greatest of presumption, (he wrote about his earliest ambitions), I conceived that the great writer was the destroyer of chaos, a man privy to the council of the hidden gods who administer the hidden laws that bind us all and destroy us all if we do not know them.[2]

What might be called Miller's commitment to greatness is important to recognize at the outset because it is this that has made him so harshly critical of the modern theater, has driven him to use his talents only for the production of what he considers the highest in dramatic art, and it is this, finally, that has brought him the extraordinary mixture of critical praise and scorn that he has received.

Miller's primary criticism of the American theater is that it has separated the individual from his society and in doing so has merely dramatized man's alienation from the world in which he lives:

> Since 1920, (he wrote in 1953), American drama has been a steady year by year documentation of the frustration of man. I do not believe in this. . . . That is not our fate.[3]

More recently Miller added:

> The fifties became an era of gauze. Tennessee Williams is responsible for this in the main. One of my own feet stands in this stream. It is a cruel, romantic neuroticism, a translation of current life into the war within the self. All conflict tends to be trans-formed into sexual conflict. . . . It is a theatre with the blues. . . . The drama will have to re-address itself to the world beyond the senses, to fate.[4]

[*]Reprinted from *Modern Drama*, 10 (1967), 221–32, by permission of the journal.

In spite of what he says about his own participation in such a theater, Miller has from the beginning addressed himself to the world beyond the senses. All of his plays depict characters who struggle against fate, though in the earlier plays "fate" means the economic, political, and social forces of their times.

Because of Miller's acknowledgement of Ibsen as his earliest master (he wrote an adaptation of *An Enemy of the People* in 1951), and because his original concern was to depict man in conflict with his society, it is not surprising that he has been most often thought of as a writer of problem plays, a latter day Ibsen, whose messages cease to excite with the passing of the problem with which they deal. But such a judgment is as unfair to Miller as it is to Ibsen; and to Miller, at least, it reflects the anti-intellectual bias of the times. Of this bias Miller has spoken continually and vehemently. Answering a criticism of Peter Ustinov, Miller wrote in 1960:

> I am not calling for more ideology, as Ustinov implies. I am simply asking for a theatre in which an adult who wants to live can find plays that will heighten his awareness of what living in our time involves. I am tired of a theatre of sensation, that's all. I am tired of seeing man as merely a bundle of nerves. That way lies pathology, and we have pretty much arrived.[5]

Having in mind his own attempts in *The Crucible*, Miller wrote of the difficulties involved in depicting the thinking man on the stage:

> In our drama the man with convictions has in the past been a comic figure. I believe he fits in our drama more now, though, and I am trying to find a way, a form, a method of depicting people who do think.[6]

Since that time he has gone further, and in *After the Fall* the entire action of the play takes place "in the mind, thought and memory" of its intellectual protagonist. Judging from the critical reception given that work, it would seem that Miller's hope of thirteen years ago was all too optimistic and that people who do think are simply unfit theatrical subjects. But more of this later. It is time to proceed to the question with which this paper deals: has Miller succeeded in dramatizing "what living in our time involves," and has he done so with such power as "to transform the truth consciousness of mankind"?

This may seem an unfair question to ask of any writer, but Miller himself demands that he be judged in such terms: "I ask of a play," he writes, "first, the dramatic question. . . . Second, the human question—What is its ultimate relevancy to the survival of the race?"[7] For Miller the only drama that can so powerfully engage us as to transform our characters is tragedy. Its arch-enemy is pathos. For this reason it is natural that we should consider Miller's plays in view of these two terms.

Miller first raised the question of the writing of modern tragedy in his preface to *Death of a Salesman* in 1949. Most of us are familiar with his argument for the non-aristocratic tragic hero, the protagonist as common man, raised above his fellows not by rank or position but by the nobility of his spirit. More important for our purposes is his distinction between pathos and tragedy in the same preface.

The possibility of victory must be there in tragedy. Where pathos rules, where pathos is finally derived, a character has fought a battle he could not possibly have won. The pathetic is achieved when the protagonist is, by virtue of his witlessness, his insensitivity, or the very air he gives off, incapable of grappling with a much superior force. Pathos truly is the mode for the pessimist. But tragedy requires a nicer balance between what is possible and what is impossible. And it is curious, although edifying, that the plays we revere, century after century, are the tragedies. In them, and in them alone, lies the belief—optimistic, if you will, in the perfectability of man.[8]

The explanation of this "optimism" lies in Miller's understanding of the so-called tragic flaw. Far from being a fault, it is envisioned as that very strength of will that makes the protagonist refuse "to remain passive in the face of what he conceives to be a challenge to his dignity, his image of his rightful status."[9]

It is not Miller's theory of tragedy that I want to discuss here, however. Rather, I would draw attention to one characteristic of tragedy that for Miller, at least, is essential. It is the idea that tragedy deals ultimately with paradox. On the one hand, it posits the destruction of the hero; its line of action must be, in fact, one in which the sense of doom grows stronger and stronger. On the other hand, we must never for a moment regard the tragic hero's struggle against his fate as absurd, which would be the case if his destruction were completely inevitable. The essential paradox of tragedy, then, lies in the fact that even though the tragic hero is destroyed, his struggle "demonstrates the indestructible will of man to achieve his humanity."[10]

A great drama [Miller writes, almost mystically], is a great jurisprudence. Balance is all. It will evade us until we can once again see man as whole, until sensitivity and power, justice and necessity are utterly face to face; until authority's justifications and rebellion's too are tracked even to those heights where the breath fails, where—because the largest point of view as well as the smaller has spoken—truly the rest is silence.[11]

Pathos is "that counterfeit of meaning"[12] because, in addition to stacking the cards against the protagonist, it does not push the dramatic question far enough; it settles for a vision of mankind that is oversimplified and for that reason can have no real power over us.

Nothing is clearer from a study of Miller's plays than the fact of his growth toward tragedy, as he conceives it, and away from pathos, and one way of seeing this growth is to compare the manner in which Miller has handled the problem of dramatic resolution. In *All My Sons*, the resolution of the basic dramatic conflict is clearly stated in the title. Joe Keller, who has thought that there was nothing bigger than the family, comes to the realization that the pilots who died as the result of the faulty engine heads shipped by his factory were "all my sons." As a direct and immediate result of this knowledge, he commits suicide. *All My Sons* never passes beyond its very considerable pathos to tragedy because, for one thing, it resolves its basic dramatic conflict too simply and in so doing falsifies the paradox that lies unexamined at its heart. How can a person keep his sense of right and wrong while grappling for a living in a business world which recognizes only the principle of the survival of the fittest?

It was this question, basic to, though hardly even considered in, *All My Sons* that Miller made the central one in his next, and most widely acclaimed, play, *Death of a Salesman*.

Whereas in *All My Sons*, father and son stood in ideological opposition to each other and so represented the conflicting values that formed the dramatic question of the play, in *Death of a Salesman* the father and the older son, Biff, though antagonists, are more closely related in their values and there is thus more sense of paradox in the resolution of the basic dramatic conflict. Joe Keller lived by the wrong values, and though the question of what the right values are was only superficially examined, we could at least see that his suicide was a logical result of his self-knowledge. On the other hand, Biff Loman's statement about his father: "He had the wrong dreams. All, all wrong."[13] has to be considered in the light of the neighbor Charlie's answer: "A salesman is got to dream, boy. It comes with the territory."[14] and with the heart-rending urging of Willie's wife: "Attention must be paid. . . . There's more good in him than in many other people."[15] Willie, though he has moments of partial awareness, never does learn that he has lived all, all wrong: and thus the dramatic question of the play remains unresolved. Yet his death is ironic as well as far more full of pathos than Joe's because in depicting it as the result of love as well as imagining it as the final act of a man who literally *is* worth more dead than alive, Miller has remained true to the paradox that lies at the basis of the play.

Powerful as *Death of a Salesman* is, however, Miller himself felt that the play did not succeed in passing beyond pathos into tragedy. A few years after the writing of *Death of a Salesman* he wrote:

> There is great danger in pathos, which can destroy any tragedy if you let it go far enough. My weakness is that I can create pathos at will. It is one of the easiest things to do. I feel that Willie Loman lacks sufficient insight into this situation which would have made him a greater, more significant figure.[16]

We might add that Willie could be taken as almost the model for the protagonist who is "by virtue of his witlessness, his insensitivity, or the very air he gives off, incapable of grappling with a much superior force."

Death of a Salesman is one of the enduring plays of our time, but its strength lies more in its ability to stir our pity than our fear. With his next play Miller found a subject that came nearer his concept of tragedy. *The Crucible*, as Miller tells us,

> developed from a paradox . . . in whose grip we still live, and there is no prospect yet that we will discover its resolution. The witch hunt was a perverse manifestation of the panic which set in among all classes when the balance began to turn toward greater individual freedom. When one rises above the individual villainy displayed, one can only pity them all, just as we shall be pitied someday. It is still impossible for man to organize his social life without repressions, and the balance has yet to be struck between order and freedom.[17]

Written at the time of the McCarthy hearings, *The Crucible* calls up fear as well as pity, however. More aware of what they were doing than were any of Miller's earlier protagonists, the people of Salem are much closer to his concept of the tragic hero. Particularly is this so with John Proctor, the chief protagonist, whose final words are spoken out of the agonizing awareness of corporate guilt. To the court, that has condemned him as well as other innocent people, he cries:

> For them that quail to bring man out of ignorance, as I have quailed and as you quail now when you know in all your black hearts that this be fraud—God damns our kind especially, and we will burn, we will burn together.[18]

In *The Crucible* there is also, for the first time in Miller's work, a genuine sense of exaltation; for in the struggles of John Proctor and the other martyrs to the cause of justice, we recognize our own victory over some of the worst elements of our Puritan past. *The Crucible* has, in fact, virtually all of the characteristics of successful tragedy as Miller conceives them to be. Yet it cannot be said to reach "those heights where the breath fails" because it lacks something far more important to drama: that sense of vividly and fully imagined character that made of Willie Loman a kind of modern Everyman. George Jean Nathan, while overstating the case against Miller, recognized this essential failure in the play when he wrote that the couple who fall victim to the persecution exist mainly as a vehicle for Miller's ideas and that "their tragedy accordingly has the distant air of a dramatic recitation rather than of any personal suffering."[19]

We need not consider Miller's next work, *A Memory of Two Mondays*, a sentimentalized and nostalgic one act play about a young workingman who is saving up his money to go to college. *A View from the Bridge*, however, written at the same time, is of prime importance, for it shows a profound change in Miller's concept of fate.

In the earlier plays fate took the form of the social, economic, or political forces of society. In Eddie Carbone's tragic fall, however, Miller sees for the first time the presence of a quite different force; for Eddie's struggle is not primarily with his society but with himself, with a passion that he can neither understand nor control. Like Phaedra, Eddie is possessed by an unnatural and all devouring love, though unlike Phaedra he is never aware of the true nature of his feelings. In his preface to *A View from the Bridge*, Miller draws attention to the classical outlines of the story:

> When I heard the tale first it seemed to me that it must be some re-enactment of a Greek myth which was ringing a long buried bell in my own subconscious mind. . . . It is not designed primarily to draw tears or laughter from an audience but to strike a particular note of astonishment at the way in which, and the reasons for which, a man will endanger and risk and lose his very life.[20]

Eddie Carbone, unable to give up his niece to one of his wife's illegally entered immigrant cousins whom they are sheltering from the authorities, informs on them and, in so doing, betrays the mores of the society in which he lives. Miller has centered his attention, however, not on Eddie's struggle against society but on his defiance of nature. The lawyer, Alfieri, whose manner of expression as well as admonitory function on the play suggests the *choragus* of Greek tragedy, warns Eddie not to interfere with Catherine and Rudolpho:

> The law is nature.
> The law is only a word for what has a right to happen.
> When the law is wrong it's because it's unnatural.
> But in this case it is natural
> And a river will drown you
> If you buck it now.
> Let her go. And bless her.[21]

Eddie thinks he is only protecting his niece from an unworthy husband, but his classical prototype, the Oedipus whose name his own suggests, looms larger and larger until, at the end of the play, after Eddie has been killed in a knife fight with Rudolpho's brother, the lawyer, Alfieri can draw a parallel between Eddie and the protagonists of Greek tragedy and comment on man's apparently unchangeable primitive nature.

This identifying of fate with the natural law represents an important turning point in Miller's concept of tragedy, but it is not until *After the Fall* that we see him making full use of this concept to create in us the exaltation of high tragedy. *A View from the Bridge*, powerful as it is, simply does not have the dimensions of tragedy. Its protagonist is even more unaware of what is happening to him than was Willie Loman, and therefore the physical violence with which the play ends is more suggestive of the horrors of the vendetta than of anything else. Astonishment is not, after all, the tragic emotion, and although Miller has significantly broadened his concept of fate, and in so doing has paved the way for the enlarged vision of *After the Fall*, *A View from the Bridge* stands as the nearest thing to melodrama he has yet written. The revisions Miller made in the play for its New York run in 1965–1966, while they deepen its thematic content, cannot be said to alter its basic dramatic vision.

We need not pause long over Miller's next work, *The Misfits*, though it is certainly rich in dramatic content (every character is eventually put into dramatic opposition with virtually every other), and though it deals with an extraordinary number of basic questions (What is the nature of innocence? Can it, and if it can, should it be protected? Is communication between man and man, man and society, man and the universe, man and himself either possible or desirable? Is life worth living or not, and before we answer that what do we mean by life and what do we mean by living?) *The Misfits* need not concern us here because of its hopefully-happy ending. Technically speaking, it is neither pathos nor tragedy but comedy, and while Miller's paean to marriage as the solution to all problems can be understood in the light of the sun that was then illuminating his private life, as a dramatic resolution the sentimental ending of *The Misfits* represents the triumph of the soapbox over the stage.

It is all the more to Miller's credit that after mawkishly indulging his romantic nature in *The Misfits*, he should have treated much the same material with the dispassionate honesty that he displays in *After the Fall*. Not that many critics saw it this way. Perhaps no recent play written by a major playwright has received more critical abuse than *After the Fall*. "A three-and-one-half hour breach of taste,"[22] wrote Robert Brustein of *The New Republic*. Deploring its absence of meaning and lack of drama, Richard Gilman of *Commonweal* found in it "only wind, shadows, and purple smoke."[23] The *New Yorker* did not deign to review it at all, but in a column and a half of coldly factual prose attempted, apparently, to kill it by neglect. *Time* magazine took the opposite approach and concluded its equally brief review with these caustic words: "The code of the *Fall* is: when life seems unbearable, find a new woman and start a new life."[24] So hostile were most of the reviews that Miller felt forced to answer his critics, and only ten days after the play's opening published a moving and powerful defense of it in *Life* magazine. In many ways it is fortunate that Miller was driven to such a pass, for he not only showed how completely most of the reviewers had misunderstood his intentions but provided us with an invaluable critical introduction to his work.

One thing Miller made most clear: he is more than ever the moralist. The moralist, moreover, who can afford to speak with the tone of the prophet, being convinced that he has discovered the hidden laws of the universe. "I believe *After the Fall*," he writes, "to be a dramatic statement of a hidden process which underlies the destructiveness hanging over this age."[25]Man's complicity with evil, in himself and in his world, the fact of man's destructive nature and the sense of guilt that must follow that knowledge, this is the thematic content of Miller's play. None of us is innocent; we are all born after the fall. Only after facing the knowledge of our own defeat can we hope to progress; only after admitting our own evil can we work for our own good. It is this paradoxical vision that forms the heart of the play; and it is because Miller has forced this vision on us so relentlessly, with such dramatic intensity, that *After the Fall* can be said to be not only his greatest triumph but one of the few genuinely tragic plays of our time.

All of Miller's plays have been concerned with depicting man's relationship to the world he lives in. All of them have aimed at bringing mankind to a tragic vision of that relationship. Yet powerful as they all are in varying degrees, none of them successfully passed beyond pathos into tragedy. One reason for this is that not until *After the Fall* did Miller find a subject and a theme of genuinely tragic proportions.

Quentin is more than just the most intellectual of Miller's protagonists. He is a portrait of thinking man in our society, his tragic flaw (that which elevates him from his fellows) being his inability to lie to himself. "What's moral?" asks Maggie of him at one point in the play, and he replies: "To tell the truth, even against yourself."[26] The truth that he discovers in himself and in his world is that all men are touched with guilt, that consequently it is impossible to see human life in terms of the war between the Good and the Evil. Even the Nazis, especially, the play seems to say, the Nazis, must be recognized as our brothers;

for we are all capable of their atrocities. If no man can be wholly hated, it is equally true that no man can be wholly loved; and Quentin's desire to dispel the adoration of others is as strong as his search for the nature of his own guilt.

Powerful as the thematic content of the play is, however, what gives *After the Fall* its extraordinary intensity and its real dramatic significance is its form. The entire action of the play, as Miller tells us is in "the mind, thought and memory" of its protagonist, Quentin. Since Quentin is imagined as speaking to a silent figure in the audience whom Miller calls the "Listener," there is a framing action to the play which is, in form, a monologue. Yet we could also call the frame of the play the soliloquy, since, as Miller tells us, "The 'Listener,' who to some will be a psychoanalyst, to others God, is Quentin himself turned at the edge of the abyss to look at his own experience."[27] Since the "Listener" is also, in many ways, identified with the audience, another way of conceiving of the frame is as a long aside. Not only is the very frame of the play a dramatic innovation which stirs our imagination and almost forces our involvement, but it provides what would seem to be the ultimate observation of the classical unities: a person's words, thoughts, and memories over a two-hour period during which he is imagined in conference with a silent figure.

Oppressed by the chaos in himself and in his time, Quentin has come to the "Listener" for advice. Having lived through two marriages and feeling as he does generally disillusioned about life, he is afraid to risk a third marriage. The agony he feels stems from his own sense of complicity with evil and his consequent inability to resolve the question of what his future should be. But his choice is not simply whether to marry or not to marry. Basically it is whether to be or not to be. Only at the end of the play does he make a choice. Another characteristic of the frame, then, is that it deals solely with the dramatic resolution of the play.

The real action of the play, of course, is not this framing action but is composed of the dramatized memories and thoughts that come to Quentin during his consultation with the "Listener." Here Miller seems to have realized the great possibilities of the flash-back technique that he so successfully employed in *Death of a Salesman*. The play takes almost twice as long to perform as his imagined conversation lasts, for as Quentin thinks or remembers, the scene from his past is reenacted on the stage. In fact, the significant moments from Quentin's life are presented before us, not in chronological order but in the more intense psychological order of the association of ideas. He hears his brother's voice promising family support in the midst of a painful scene in which support is being withdrawn from him by someone else. His first wife appears on stage momentarily when his second wife unknowingly repeats her accusation. In some of these scenes from his past Quentin becomes so emotionally involved that we forget for the moment the frame of the play. In others he is the detached observer of a painful scene from his childhood, for instance; and this pulling of Quentin in and out of his own past, as it were, is itself intensely dramatic. Time, space, and action are as freely used in the play itself as they are compressed in the framing action, the very counterpoint between the apparent disorder and complexity of the one and the order and simplicity of the other adding still more to the dramatic intensity of the play. The great dramatic innovation of *After the Fall* consists of Miller's method here of juxtaposing scenes from Quentin's past one on the other so that finally his life has been revealed to us with all the richness that we usually associate with the novel as a form. The modern novelist, Joyce and Proust in particular, as well as creators of the modern film, seem to have given Miller what he has been looking for since 1963: "a form, a method of depicting people who do think."

At the end of the play Quentin knows little more about himself than he did at the beginning. After talking to the "Listener" for two hours, he simply feels less afraid of life and has very hesitantly decided to risk another marriage. Our knowledge of him, however, and of life through him, is so deep as to approach wonder. Identified dramatically as we are in part with the "Listener," we partake of this seeming omniscience. Miller once wrote that the central question asked by all serious drama is "How may a man make of the outside world a home?"[28] Miller treats us and our world with such determined honesty and such intellectual scope that *After the Fall* can be said to give an answer to that question, an answer that Quentin characteristically puts in the form of a series of questions to the "Listener" at the end of the play:

> I swear to you, I could love this world again! . . . Is the knowing all? To know, and even happily, that we meet unblessed; not in some garden of wax fruit and painted trees, that lie of Eden, but after the Fall, after many, many deaths. Is the knowing all? . . . And the wish to kill is never killed, but with some gift of courage one may look into its face when it appears, and with a stroke of love—as to an idiot in the house—forgive it; again and again . . . forever? . . . No, it's not certainty, I don't feel that. But it does seem feasible . . . not to be afraid. Perhaps it's all one has.[29]

Essential as the form of *After the Fall* is to the realization of its power as drama, it would have little effect if Miller had not been able to create convincing characters as well. Perhaps the greatest tribute to Miller's powers of characterization in this play is the very fact that he succeeded in shocking so many in his use of his former wife Marily Monroe as the basis for the character of Maggie. No one is shocked by a weak characterization, no matter how recognizable the original. Were she more aware of what was happening to her, she might have taken on the proportions of a tragic heroine. As it is she stands above Willie Loman even as Miller's most fully realized and completely human figure of pathos.

"A great drama is a great jurisprudence. Balance is all," Miller wrote. In no other play of recent times has such a balance been struck as in *After the Fall*, a balance between the forces of hate and the forces of love, between despair and hope, a balance, finally, between pity and fear, the union of which produces the exaltation of great tragedy, tragedy that has the power to carry us both nearer to and beyond ourselves, tragedy that because it envisions man in ultimate conflict with the demon in himself can hope to rid him of that demon, can hope to raise "the truth-consciousness of mankind to a level of such intensity as to transform those who observe it." Miller himself has called *After the Fall* his "happiest" `work.[30] Elia Kazan saw it as "one of the few truly great plays with which he has come in contact."[31] Howard Taubman of the *New York Times* found the play to be "Miller's maturest."[32]

Coming, as it does, less than a year after *After the Fall*, Miller's most recent play, *Incident at Vichy*,[33] seems particularly disappointing. Generally recognized as the most obtrusively didactic of all of his plays, it is neither pathos nor tragedy but, rather, a dramatized essay on the same subject of universal human guilt that had been so powerfully treated in the earlier play. The characters are little more than spokesmen for different points of view, and though intellectual stimulation and a degree of dramatic intensity results from the clash of ideas, the play as such is certainly Miller's least dramatic.

It remains to be seen whether Miller's next play will reach the tragic heights of *After the Fall*. As his career now stands, he hovers between pathos and tragedy, our most important and our most serious playwright.

Notes

1. Arthur Miller, "The Family in Modern Drama," *Atlantic Monthly*, 197 (April, 1956), 36.

2. Arthur Miller, "The Shadows of the Gods," *Harper's*, 217 (August, 1958), 37.

3. "Arthur Miller Discusses *The Crucible*," as told to John and Alice Griffin, *Theatre Arts*, 37 (October, 1953), 33.

4. Henry Brandon, "The State of the Theatre, A Conversation with Arthur Miller," *Harper's*, 221 (November, 1960), 68.

5. Ibid., p. 66.

6. "Arthur Miller Discusses *The Crucible*," pp. 33–34.

7. Miller, "The Shadows of the Gods," p. 38.

8. Arthur Miller, "Tragedy and the Common Man," *New York Times*, February 27, 1949, Sec. 2, pp. 1, 3; in *Theatre Arts*, 35 (March, 1951), 50.

9. Ibid., p. 49.

10. Ibid., p. 50.

11. Miller, "Shadows of the Gods," p. 43.

12. Ibid.

13. Arthur Miller, *Death of a Salesman* (New York, 1949), p. 138.

14. Ibid.

15. Ibid., p. 59.

16. "Arthur Miller Discuss *The Crucible*," p. 34.

17. Arthur Miller, Preface to *The Crucible* (New York, 1953), p. 7.

18. Arthur Miller, *The Crucible* (New York, 1953), p. 120.

19. George Jean Nathan, "Henrik Miller," *Theatre Arts*, 37 (April, 1953), 24.

20. Arthur Miller, Preface to "A View from the Bridge," *Theatre Arts*, 40 (September 1956), 31.

21. Arthur Miller, "A View from the Bridge," *Theatre Arts*, 40 (September, 1956), 63.

22. Robert Brustein, "Arthur Miller's *Mea Culpa*," *The New Republic*, 150 (February 8, 1964), 26.

23. Richard Gilman, "Still Falling," *Commonweal*, 79 (February 14, 1964), 601.

24. "The Miller's Tale," *Time*, 83 (January 31, 1964), 54.

25. Arthur Miller, "With Respect for Her Agony—but with Love," *Life*, 56 (February 7, 1964), 66.

26. Arthur Miller, *After the Fall* (New York, 1964), p. 82.

27. Arthur Miller, Foreword to "After the Fall," *Saturday Evening Post*, 237 (February 1, 1964), 32.

28. Miller, "The Family in Modern Drama," p. 36.

29. Miller, *After the Fall*, p. 129.

30. Richard and Nancy Meyer, "Setting the Stages for Lincoln Center," *Theatre Arts*, 48 (January, 1964), 14.

31. Ibid.

32. Howard Taubman, *New York Times*, January 24, 1964, p. 18.

33. Arthur Miller, *Incident at Vichy* (New York, 1965).

Incident At Vichy

Arthur Miller Looks at the Nazis

Richard Watts, Jr. [*]

Arthur Miller, having apparently emerged from his dark period of bitter introspection, has turned to a short but intense drama of Occupied France in "Incident at Vichy." Presented last night as the Lincoln Center Repertory Company's second offering of the season at its downtown headquarters below Washington Square, it is a kind of suspense thriller with moral overtones, and, while it is hardly one of his major works, it is continuously absorbing and indicates that he is getting back into his stride as a playwright of ideas.

Its one long act takes place in the detention room of a Vichy police station in 1942. Eight men have been picked up for examination, and as they sit there waiting to be called, they wonder why they have been chosen. At first, their hopeful guess is that their identity papers are to be checked. But it soon develops that all of them are either Jews or are suspected to be. They are being examined to find whether they have been circumcised, and those who have are to be taken off in freight cars to the death camps in Poland.

Two of the prisoners and one German are the subjects of Mr. Miller's particular interest. The German is a wounded combat officer who has been forced into the police assignment and detests it. More important to his argument, though, are the other two. One is a former French officer, who has thoughts of overpowering the guard and trying to escape. The second is an Austrian nobleman, who had left Vienna in disgust after the Nazi occupation. A gentle lover of the arts, he despises the Nazis largely because they are so crude, vulgar and tasteless.

In the end, the dramatic confrontation is between these two. The Frenchman is suspicious of the nobleman because he is convinced that all non-Jews have somewhere within them a strain of anti-Semitism, while the Austrian protests that he is not merely a superficial and theoretical idealist. For a time it seemed that Mr. Miller was proclaiming the doctrine that all who are not Jews bear a share of the guilt, but it is the Austrian who makes the sacrifice to save the life of the French Jewish ex-officer.

While the subject of Nazi race savagery in wartime and its implications is

[*] Reprinted from the *New York Post*, December 4, 1964. Reprinted with permission of the *New York Post*. Copyright © 1964 by the New York Post Corporation.

not likely to become outdated for years, plays about it are in danger of seeming hackneyed unless some new angle is brought to bear on it, and it can hardly be said that Mr. Miller has found one. His arguments develop nothing that is unfamiliar or startling. Yet the earnest force of the writing, the slowly rising intensity of the dramatic action, and the manner in which the horror of the period is captured keep "Incident at Vichy" arresting if not of distinguished quality.

With Boris Aronson's setting to help out, the downtown theater for the first time seems properly equipped for drama, and the repertory players are at their best. David Wayne is especially fine as the sensitive Austrian, and there are notably excellent portrayals by Joseph Wiseman as the French officer, Hal Holbrook as the embittered German, Stanley Beck as a Communist, and David J. Stewart as an ex-actor, while Ira Lewis has a moving scene as the youngest prisoner. Harold Clurman's direction is expert. Mr. Miller appears to be returning to form.

Sept-D'un-Coup

Martin Roth°

Arthur Miller has had a great deal of trouble finding forms for his plays; he seems to want to find a substitute for dramatic form because, I believe, his literary sensibility is essentially undramatic—he is a man in the wrong profession. His most successful fusion of emotion and form to date has been the scenario of *The Misfits*, where romantic symbolism and lyric meandering are most at home. Instead of creating form, he tends to borrow outside shapes for his plays, which is fine theoretically; but instead of working out their implications individually and jointly, he simply slaps them together, because essentially no extended form is compatible with that passionate lyricism which is all that he has to express. All that he has ever cared about is the shriek (the lyric poem) that precedes drama.

The latest Arthur Miller play, *Incident at Vichy*, is an allegory of the state of mind known as anti-Semitism. The allegorical fiction—partially represented in the play by the cursing of French police, the coldness of Nazi doctors, and the agony of German field officers—is presumed to be known to us already, played out in the gas ovens of Nazi Europe. While others may be impressed with the banality of this attitude and its consequences, Miller is more taken with its symmetry: "Part of knowing who we are is knowing we are not someone else. And Jew is only that name we give to that stranger, that agony we cannot feel. . . . Each man has his Jew; it is the other." If this final solution, which is after all a piece of German science, seems rather formal and unrelated to the murder of masses of humanity, it is only because you have been spared the pathetic course of its development.

For the allegorical and ritual structure of *Incident at Vichy*, we have instructions from the author: "When lights begin to rise, six men and a boy of fifteen are discovered on the bench in attitudes expressive of their personalities and function, frozen there like members of a small orchestra at the moment before they begin to play." Five men and the boy are French; they are waiting to be finally identified as Jews. They have already been pulled in—the French police insisted that they follow their noses—and are waiting to be debagged. The seventh nose belongs to an Austrian nobleman. The point of having his proboscidean fullness mistaken for a Yiddish hook, I imagine, is to illustrate the optical confusion that follows from the grossness of the Nazi vision.

Identification, the "plot" of this play, is the reductive form of identity. And

°Reprinted from *Chicago Review*, 19, No. 1 (1966), 108–11, by permission of the journal.

the rhythms of Jewish identification presented here are ritualistic in a way never prescribed by an Old Testament God: measure the nose—in, measure the prick—out; next nose, next prick. To watch a man being swallowed up in a process is potentially dramatic whether that process is executed by Nazis or registrars. Such a formalism is capable of expressing deep social irony or comedy—Miller's, for example, is one of the major themes of burlesque.

The point is that Miller is not interested in anything subsidiarily dramatic or theatrical about his presentation. This is only one of many structures in the piece that might have made a playwright's bit, or scene, or act. But these Jews are not waiting to be identified, they-are-waiting-to-be-BURNED! They are not reacting to their scene, their interrogators, one another, they-are-reacting-to-being-BURNED! It is all catastrophe and the passion and rhetoric of catastrophe, which is not passion or rhetoric at all. At the center of Miller's plays there is always the tantrum, and everything else, anything even faintly redolent of art or craft, is simply lure—the ploy by which the grown-ups are made to pay attention. Then, sir, are you implying that Arthur Miller is a ploywright? Madam, how can you!

The leading character in the play, Leduc, is a psycho-analyst, and the play is sessionary, for *Incident at Vichy* also corresponds to the analytic process. This, like the symposium, is a rudimentary form of drama. On the other hand, in a session of group therapy conducted by a professional, all themes have a dangerous habit of collapsing into the theme of personal responsibility—history particularly is exposed as a rationalization; and this is what happens here. The method is the careful shattering of defenses: a character who insists that his presence in the detention area is due to "an absolutely idiotic accident," will be brought to understand that

> you didn't advertise your name on those forbidden books in order to find a reason to leave Paris and save yourself. It was an order to get yourself caught and be put out of your misery. Your heart is conquered territory, mister.

And of course all signs, all accidents, all slips, can be shown to cohere in a purposive design, since within the play itself there is an interpreter of symbols. There is even a superior authority for talking about dreams: "I had dreams at night—Hitler in a great flowing cloak, almost a gown, almost like a woman. He was beautiful." The outcome of all this talk is to be commitment to an institution or the freedom to act—i.e., overpowering a guard at the end of a corridor.

These are undoubtedly the kinds of confrontations that Miller has tried to put into *Incident at Vichy,* and, as allegory, drama, and symposium, it has all gone badly. The tension between analysis and drama, for example, has not even been considered, much less resolved. Even granting that detention may represent a state of mind that one can not walk away from, and that freedom from detention must, in one sense, follow from an appreciation of its meaning; nevertheless, the particular place, this detention area, is an impossible stage for analysis. On one side there is an armed guard, on the other a closed door beyond which lies the brute incomprehension of the concentration camps. (Isn't this, after all, the drama that Miller didn't write, the dramatic shape of our attempts to understand this movement of the German psyche? We are caught between the man with a gun, who must represent the violence that we desire, because we can even idealize it, and the closed door. After the Jews were inside, the door was closed; asphyxiation was attended by no images; one acted toward a building. It even stands for that other tremendously powerful cliché of not knowing what was going on, the staple principle of all childish evasion.)

To equate *this* place with the stage of the mind, the avowed locale of *After the Fall,* ignores the dynamics of waiting in such a space, the intense desire to be overlooked, to shrink into as small a compass as possible, the burning and suffocation of a space where such inexorable measurements are to be taken. In this play, truths are blurted out within Nazi hearing that are totally incompatible with a sense of danger. In effect, Miller serializes: the therapeutic dialogue is interrupted sporadically by theatrical outcries of fear and terror.

Lenny Bruce is reported to have leaped from a bar in Texas at a particularly vocal anti-Semite, screaming "Here comes Superjew." In one of his worse novels, Friedrich Duerrenmatt has his giant Samson pursuing a private vendetta through central Europe. The impulse is understandable, but hardly a matter of public bruit since we can all do so well for ourselves in that area of art. Leduc is Miller's Superjew. Von Berg, the Austrian, is an Aryan and an outsider. As an Austrian nobleman, he is literally the ideal that stands behind Nazism. On the other hand, he shrinks from contact with Nazi and Jew alike. If he could be made to share the anguish of Jews awaiting extermination, made to see the typically human resources they fall back upon in the face of incomprehensible terror; if, in addition, it could be explained to him by a master of rationalization, that he is not accidentally present, but is in fact both victim and murderer; then . . . what? . . . what a tremendous satisfaction that would be.

Worst of all there are seeds of artistry in the play: the idea of psychoanalysis as an expression of Talmudic reasoning, which flies at you in passing. Von Berg's dream of Hitler in a flowing gown and his feeling that the rhythm of acquiescence on the part of the German people is neither intellectual nor passional, but musical. On Miller's part, this is half-baked Wagner, but it is still powerful, and it is contradicted in the play by the opening stage direction.

The subject matter of *Incident at Vichy* is ancillary to a big historical fact: roughly six million Jews killed. This may be outside the limits of drama, but not necessarily. Gunter Grass has translated the period into a poetic truth of a very high order, which was inconceivable prior to *The Tin Drum.* Max Frisch has successfully dramatized anti-Semitism. Arthur Miller approaches this problem with the integrity of a counter-man in a delicatessen. Two-thirds of the play is devoted to an exploration of what detention means, and we are expected to apprehend lines like the following as meaningful explorative gestures:

> In my opinion you're hysterical. After all, they were picking up Jews in Germany for years before the war . . . are you telling me all those people are dead? Is that really conceivable to you? War is war, but you still have to keep a certain sense of proportion.

Experience tangles; life thrusts upon us situations so knotted in pain as to be hardly endured. We believed once that philosophy teaches us how to endure and tragedy to transcend these human extremes. But we also know the temptation to wallow in these moments for the curiously vital pleasure that they give. Arthur Miller is essentially a wallower who refuses to amuse himself in private. He has already confused this activity with tragedy in his essay, "Tragedy and the Common Man," and once again he cries in our faces with Lebeau, his artist: "I'm not a philosopher, but I know my mother, and that's why I'm here."

Arthur Miller's
Incident at Vichy:
A Sartrean Interpretation

Lawrence D. Lowenthal°

Just after Paris was liberated from the Nazi occupation, Jean Paul Sartre sat at the Café de Flore on the Left Bank and wrote *Anti-Semite and Jew (Reflexions sur la Question Juive)*, a fascinating and controversial analysis of Europe's most terrifying problem. Twenty years later, America's leading dramatist, Arthur Miller, wrote a long, one-act play about the holocaust, called *Incident at Vichy.* Although Ronald Hayman, an English critic, recently suggested that "a good case could be made for calling Arthur Miller the most Sartrean of living playwrights,"[1] no critic has yet pointed out that *Vichy* is an explicit dramatic rendition of Sartre's treatise on Jews, as well as a clear structural example of Sartre's definition of the existential "theatre of situation."

This affinity between Sartre and Miller is understandable when one considers the existential development of Miller's later plays. Beginning with *The Misfits,* Miller's works begin to shift the tragic perspective from man's remediable alienation from society to man's hopeless alienation from the universe and from himself. *After the Fall, Incident at Vichy,* and *The Price* are all organized around "absurdist" themes of metaphysical society, personal solitude, and moral ambivalence. Quite clearly, one presumes, the accumulated impact of international and personal tragedies has strained Miller's faith in man's ability to overcome social and spiritual diseases. Miller no longer has any illusion about a "Grand Design" whose revelation will enable man to live harmoniously as a social being. His characters now grope alone for values to sustain their dissipating lives and each value, once discovered, slips again into ambiguity. Most frightening of all is the realization that human corruption, once attributed to conscious deviation from recognizable moral norms, is now seen as an irresistible impulse in the heart of man. The theme of universal guilt becomes increasingly and despairingly affirmed. But Miller's belief in original sin in a world without God does not preclude the possibility of personal redemption, for Miller shares Sartre's insistence on free will and the possibility of "transcendence" or the re-creation of self through a succession of choices.

Miller's existential concerns are clearly delineated in *Vichy,* a play that

°Reprinted from *Modern Drama*, 18, No. 1 (1975), 29–41, by permission of the journal.

reminds us immediately of Sartre's "The Wall" and *The Victors*. In all these works a fundamental Sartrean thesis is dramatized: "A man's secret, the very frontier of his freedom is his power of resistance to torture and death."[2]

Structurally, *Vichy* answers Sartre's call for "situational drama" which, he hoped, would replace the outmoded drama of "character" so prevalent in the contemporary bourgeois theatre. In a famous article, "Forgers of Myth," written in 1946, Sartre described situational drama as "short and violent, sometimes reduced to the dimensions of a single long act":[3] "A single set, a few entrances, a few exits, intense arguments among the characters who defend their individual rights with passion. . . .[4]

Each character is displayed as a free being, entirely indeterminate, who must choose his own being when confronted with certain necessities."[5] Men do not have "ready made" natures, consistent throughout alternating circumstances—a primary assumption in the theatre of character—but are rather naked wills, pure, free choices whose passion unites with action.

The characters in *Vichy* are not simply "types" or "public speakers with a symbolic role" as one critic maintains;[6] on the contrary they are dynamic, fluid, undetermined beings, "freedoms caught in a trap," to use a Sartrean phrase. We know nothing about them, aside from their professions, until they reveal themselves through their choices of behavior, and their choices often prove to be surprising. They are all faced with undeniable limits to these choices, but within these limits they are always free to act. The Jew can resist or submit; the German can murder or rebel. The structural movement of the play is existential in that individual possibilities for evading choice are methodically decreased. As each Jew is taken into the dreaded office, the option to revolt becomes more difficult. The traditional palliatives of reason, civilization, political ideology, and culture which ordinarily stand between man and the absurd are dispelled, one by one, until each character is made to face the realities of torture and irrational death.

Miller's play, though existentialist in theme, is rationalistic in structure. Like Sartre, Miller writes about the absurd in coherent terms. Miller's intention is still to explore "sheer process itself. How things connected,"[7] and although his discovery of cause and effect patterns no longer reveals "the hidden laws of the gods" with any certainty, the disasters in the play do not spring from a mysterious void as they do in the absurdist plays of Beckett and Ionesco. The central crisis is, of course, precipitated by Nazism, but Miller's analysis of the cause of this evil is more existential than political or sociological, and is expressed in terms of the Sartrean concepts of Nothingness and Dread.

Sartrean "dread" is a state-of-being arising from one's confrontation with "contingency," or the inherent meaninglessness of the physical world. Sartre's vision of ontological chaos or the absurd is most graphically described in *Nausea*, his first novel. As Roquentin, the narrator, sits sadly on a park bench, he sees the root of a chestnut tree suddenly ooze into viscosity before his eyes. Flowing obscenely beyond its bounds, its shape, its position amidst other physical objects, the tree suddenly loses its essence as a tree and becomes merely substance, *there,* without reason or justification. The tree's abandonment of its *a priori* essence compels Roquentin to acknowledge the general fact of the world's contingency: "I mean that one cannot define existence as necessity. . . . Everything is gratuitous. . . . When you realize this, your heart turns upside down and everything begins to float."[8] Roquentin's awareness that "existence comes before essence" is the starting point of Sartre's philosophy. Beginning as an undefinable consciousness in a world of innately undefinable objects, man finds himself responsible for imposing himself on the world and creating a reason for his existence. The realization of his superfluity leaves man forlorn because "neither within him nor without does he find anything to cling to. He can't start making excuses for himself."[9]

Roquentin's psychic epiphany in *Nausea* is parallelled in *Incident at Vichy* by the phenomenon of Nazism. Both events undermine all assumptions about the necessity of human existence. The Nazis are the fulfillment of Ivan Karamazov's cry, "everything is permitted." Their boundless evil is like Roquentin's oozing tree. Like the tree's outrageous proliferation which shatters the theory that essence precedes existence, the Nazis' refusal to abide by the rules of civilization makes a mockery of all illusions about moral behavior, social order, and humanist conceptions of man. If civilized people like the Germans can suddenly become uncivilized monsters, then one's belief in the continuity of human essence is destroyed. As Von Berg says, "What one used to conceive a human being to be will have no room on this earth."[10] The effect of this transformation stuns those who retain the civilized codes, now seen as absurdly fragile artifices, and arouses the sense of "nausea" that afflicts Roquentin. Von Berg is the first to recognize the implication of the Nazi power. When told of the death camps in Poland, he says, "I find it the most believable atrocity I have heard." When asked why, he replies: "Because it is so inconceivably vile. That is their power, to do the inconceivable; it paralyzes the rest of us" (p. 61). The Nazis are like Camus' "plague" which falls upon our safe and ordered lives and alienates us from all harmonious connections with the universe. In the wake of their attack on civilization lies the void, the disintegrated wreckage of all human constructs against the threat of chaos. "Who can ever save us," cries Von Berg after his awakening (p. 107).

But Von Berg's plea is, of course, the starting point for existential ethics, for if man can no longer find refuge in external deities and beliefs, he must look for sanctions within himself. Since existence is neither inherently necessary or predefined, man is free in that he is permanently in flux: his capacity for self definition is therefore illimitable: "Man is nothing but that which he makes of himself," Sartre writes, "that is the first principle of existentialism."[11] The only solution to the devastation wrecked upon human security by the plague is a responsible and free human action, an end in itself, which will momentarily solidify the relentless flow of our inner and outer being. But it is precisely this obligation that causes dread in man. As Sartre says, "Man is condemned to be free." The constant necessity to reassert and redefine values, projects, and commitments—the perpetual challenge to justify one's life—produces anguish, the feeling that results when we confront "the absolute openness of our future, the nothingness in the center of which we live."[12] Rather than commit himself to responsible actions without recourse to outside justification, man clings to "bad faith," that "lie in the soul," as Sartre calls it, which enables him to flee from responsibility into determinism.

Bad faith appears in a variety of forms: the coward abandons freedom by fabricating excuses for his condition; the masochist accepts the congealed image imposed upon him by the Other; the "salaud" claims special rights to existence in accord with a fabricated, *a priori* system of values and assumptions. The persecutors and victims in Miller's play clearly illustrate one or more of these types.

The Nazi, to begin with, is the most violent example of Sartre's concept of the anti-Semite—the most dangerous man of "bad faith." If the phenomenon of Nazism illuminates the horror of contingency to the naive civilized man, Nazism itself can be seen as a flight from the same Nothingness. The Nazi is incapable of accepting his condition of freedom. He flees from consciousness which reveals to him the contingency of the human condition, the openness of all truth, the limitless and elusive durability of a stone.[13] He cannot tolerate the continual suspension of his existence but wishes "to exist all at once and right away" (p. 19). Sartre's concept is clearly expressed by Von Berg's analysis of the Germans, who assiduously "despise everything that is not German": "They do these things not because they are Germans but because they are nothing. It is the hallmark of our age—the less you exist the more important it is to make a clear impression" (p. 61).

Fleeing from Nothingness, the Germans find refuge in the "durable stone" of Nazi ideology. Their lives, as a result, far from being gratuitous, become absolutely necessary: they have "rights," like Lucien, the anti-Semite in Sartre's short story. "The Childhood of a Leader," but these "rights" can only be affirmed by denying them to other people. Like the actors in Genet's *The Balcony* who need the cooperation of the Other in order for the game of illusion to be maintained, the Nazi needs the Jew to affirm his illusion of personal necessity. "If the Jew did not exist," Sartre says, "the anti-Semite would have to invent him" (p. 13).

Anti-Semitism, therefore, is an ontological phenomena in that it reveals a yearning for a cohesive sense of being, a passion for essence. Because one's essence, however, is continuously nihilated by the Nothingness that separates man from what he was and what he wants to be, the anti-Semite must repress his consciousness and thereby convert a false assumption into a sacred belief. To achieve this aim, the anti-Semite divides the world into a Manichean duality of good and evil—gentiles and Jews—and to sustain this duality he must be constantly alert, wary of any sudden, rational intrusion into his fabrication.

Anti-Semitism is thus a freely chosen project which crystalizes the world and the individual anti-Semite's place in it. He no longer fears isolation, ego deflation, or purposelessness; he belongs not only to his country, a condition forever barred to the alien Jew, but also to the community of anti-Semites to which he clings. His essence is clearly defined, tangible, and, in his own mind, empirically defensible.

The Professor in *Vichy* is the clearest example of the Nazis' "bad faith." Armed with the scientific conclusions of the "Race Institute," the Professor's function is to separate "inferiors" like Jews and gypsies from the superior race. His "rights" as a superior person, sanctioned to live whereas other people are not, are never questioned: "Science is not capricious," he tells the Major. "My degree is in racial anthropology" (p. 65). The Professor is a "salaud" and he fits Sartre's description of the anti-Semite as a "destroyer in function, a sadist with a pure heart. . . . He knows that he is wicked, but since he does evil for the sake of Good, since a whole people waits for deliverance at his hands, he looks upon himself as a sanctified evil-doer" (p. 50). The Professor's "bad faith" extends beyond his scientific assertion of "rights and duties" to a disavowal of personal responsibility for the acts he performs: "I will not continue without you, Major. The Army's responsibility is quite as great as mine here" (p. 67). By diffusing all responsibility, the Professor hopes to de-individualize himself; he seeks faceless-ness in the collective unit of the Nazi apparatus because, even though he is scientifically convinced of his "rights" as a German, he is unwilling to stand alone and assume the consequences of his assertion.

The Jews themselves all face an existential crisis: "The Jew remains the stranger, the intruder, the unassimilated at the heart of our society," Sartre writes (p. 83). As Sartre says: "To be a Jew is to be thrown into—to be aban-doned to—the situation of a Jew" (p. 88). The particular situation of the Jew is to be looked at by the anti-Semite. This "look" of the other is the essence of Sartre's concept of Being-for-Others—a mode of existence clearly illustrated by the Jew's relationship with his enemy. "Conflict," Sartre says, "is the original meaning of Being-for-Others."[14] One's consciousness, Sartre says, is unreflec-tive of itself and needs the presence not only of objects but of the Other's subjectivity to realize its structure of being. We determine ourselves according to the other's image of us. But the confrontation between two individuals results in a struggle to undermine the freedom of each since the Other's look is unfortu-nately negative and enslaving.

The presence of the Other is Sartre's version of the fall, since the Other cuts off man's freedom and renders him vulnerable to feelings of shame and ossifica-tion. The loss of innocence is the consciousness of being seen and the consequent guilt one feels in the "look" of the Other. The Other freezes our possibilities for transcendence by imposing on us a "Nature," an outside, an objective identity. We are no longer in process but are fixed in the jelled image of the Other's gaze. Because the "look" is reciprocative, human relations become a relentless, see-saw battle of wills, each person attempting to wriggle out of the Medusa stare of the Other in a desperate effort to regain freedom. The antagonists often collapse into the bad faith of sadism and masochism in order to end the struggle.

In the Jew-anti-Semite confrontation, the anti-Semite sadistically objec-tifies the Jew in order to justify his own existence, while the Jew often submits to this manipulation in order to escape the struggle toward transcendence. But the masochistic Jew will always feel anguish because he knows that within his violently narrow sphere he is free to make choices. If nothing else, he is free to determine his attitude toward uncontrollable circumstances. In his situation, therefore, the Jew can either act authentically by maintaining a "lucid consciousness" of the situation and assuming the risks and responsibilities it involves (meaning, to defy the gaze of the anti-Semite), or inauthentically by escaping into the "bad faith" of cowardice and masochism.

Marchand, the wealthy merchant, acts inauthentically by removing himself from his fellow Jews and indirectly denying his Jewishness. Similar to Birenshatz in Sartre's novel, *The Reprieve*, Marchand is disgusted by the Jewishness of others and considers himself to be purely French. But, as Sartre says, "If the Jew has decided that his race does not exist, it is up to him to prove it: for a Jew cannot choose not to be a Jew" (p. 89). The Nazis release Marchand, presumably because they still consider him useful, but once they choose to manifest his "race" all his efforts to repudiate their "look" will be in vain.

Both Miller and Sartre agree that a Jew cannot be defined by religion, race, or national identity: one is a Jew if a gentile says one is a Jew, a thesis Miller previously affirmed in his novel *Focus*. Quite simply, Sartre says, "what makes the Jew is his concrete situation, what unites him to other Jews is the identity of their situation" (p. 145). The look of the gentile circumscribes the situation of a Jew and defines the choices he is compelled to make. In *Vichy* the Jews are thrust into their Jewishness. The victims in the play, aside from the religious old man, are either indifferent or hostile to their Jewishness. Each considers himself French, and each identifies himself with his profession or political ideology rather than his religion. There is no feeling of unity in their mutual crisis and even their physical movements on stage lead away from their fellow victims toward a brooding isolation. What unites them technically into a "we" consciousness is simply the fact that the Nazi, or the "third" as Sartre would call him, looks upon them hostilely as a collective unit. The Jew experiences the "look" of the anti-Semite as a community alienation, but his sense of "community" ironically arouses only fear and antagonism.

The artist Lebeau, for example, is a masochist who feels a Kafaseque [sic] sense of guilt because he is a Jew and is driven by his humiliation and despair into a death wish. He waits for slaughter like a naughty child waits for parental punishment: "I don't know. Maybe it's that they keep saying such terrible things about us, and you can't answer. And after years of it you . . . I wouldn't say you believe it, but . . . you do, a little" (p. 80). Sartre points out that this kind of inferiority complex is not actually received from the outside, but that the Jew "creates this complex when he chooses to live out his situation in an unauthentic manner. He has allowed himself to be persuaded by the anti-Semites; he is the first victim of their propaganda" (p. 94). Lebeau accepts the image of himself that he sees reflected in the eyes of the Other, and instead of transcending the Other's gaze, he allows himself to be paralyzed and destroyed. He relinquishes his freedom as a man in order to sink into the blissful passivity of a Thing. Like the Nazi, who solidifies himself in the role of "Superior One," Lebeau escapes his crisis by falling into the stone-like posture of "victim." His struggle ends in resigned submission.

Bayard, the communist, can suppress his panic only by depersonalizing himself. He is the Sartrean "man of seriousness," like Brunet, the dedicated party worker in *Roads to Freedom*, whose individual fate will be redeemed by the inevitable proletarian victory. Bayard, too, is guilty of "bad faith": like the Professor he abdicates his freedom by dissolving his individuality in a collective mass, and by turning back on the existential present for the theoretical proletarian revolt in the future. Von Berg's pointed assertion that most Nazis are from the working class damages Bayard's thesis, but he continues to delude himself in the absence of any other defense. Without his communistic idealism, Bayard explains, "I wouldn't have the strength to walk through that door" (p. 54). Like Sartre's Brunet, Bayard is an attractive character, strong, alert and ideologically sincere, but his absolute belief in historical determinism compromises his authenticity.

Monceau, an actor, puts the reality of the Absurd at a distance by fabricating an image for himself as he does on stage. He believes he can flee from his crisis into the illusion of a role. Believing that the Nazis are like dangerous animals who can sniff out the fear in their victims, he will *act* as if he is unafraid, for salvation lies simply in the ability to convince one's executioners that one is not a victim. Monceau refuses to acknowledge the absence of reason in their plight and chooses instead to delude himself into believing the Nazis cannot be as monstrous as people say and that civilization has not ended, despite all the evidence to the contrary: "I go on the assumption that if I obey the law with dignity I will live in peace" (p. 82). Pushed by Leduc to the extremity of his illusion, Monceau finally admits that if the world is mad, there is nothing he can do but submit to its madness, a conclusion which draws from Leduc the despairing remark: "Your heart is conquered territory, mister" (p. 83).

Like Lebeau, Monceau succumbs to the temptation of "impenetrability." He, too, is masochistic, an object to be casually destroyed by the hostile Other. His "bad faith" lies in his refusal to acknowledge the mutability of the world, its potentiality for alteration through human action. But action demands revolt, and, as in the case of Lebeau, the role of rebel proves more terrifying to him than the role of victim.

The dramatic core of the play is the moral debate between the psychiatrist Leduc, the German Major, and Von Berg. Their arguments revolve around Miller's central question: What is the nature and possibility of responsibility in a world acknowledged to be absurd? The German Major, according to his statement to Leduc, is a decent man who despises Nazi brutality and madness, but in order for him to protest against this evil he would have to sacrifice his life. Furthermore, his sacrifice would change absolutely nothing because, as he tells Leduc, "We would all be replaced by tomorrow morning, wouldn't we?" (p. 85). All that he would gain from helping Leduc escape would be Leduc's love and respect, but the Major cannot accept this reward as adequate compensation because, "Nothing of that kind is left, don't you understand that yet?" (p. 86).

The Major's "bad faith" is similar to Monceau's: Both men relinquish their freedom by submitting to what they insist is an overwhelming determinism. "There are no persons anymore, don't you see that? There will never be persons again," the Major shouts (p. 87). Responsibility and ethics in a fallen world become meaningless words to the Major, but his plea of helplessness is merely an evasion of his own tormenting moral impulses.

The Major, like Garcin in Sartre's *No Exit*, is guilty of essentialism. He tries to convince Leduc that he has an essence of decency which circumstances cannot violate. "Captain, I would only like to say that. . . . this is all as inconceivable to me as it is to you. Can you believe that?" (p. 85). But Miller, like Sartre, insists on defining character through action. Since essence is never given but rather chosen and constantly renewed, a man *is* what he *does*, and all the Major's civilized instincts are nullified by his uncivilized acts. "I'd believe it if you shot yourself," Leduc replies. "And better yet, if you took a few of them with you" (p. 85).

Deprived of his decent "nature" by the scornful "Look" of Leduc, the Major now tries to ensnare a new being completely outside himself. Exploding with hysterical fury, he hurls himself into the role of anti-Semite by making the Jews cower under his pistol: "Like dogs, Jew-dogs—look at him—with his paws folded. Look what happens when I yell at him, Dog" (p. 87). Submitting to the lure of sadism, the Major now decides to be nothing but the fear he inspires in others. By conforming his words and gestures to the disquieting image he sees in the eyes of his victim, he achieves a solid reality and momentarily dispels his anguish.

The Major's sadistic "bad faith" is further reinforced when he skillfully challenges Leduc's assumption of moral superiority. By forcing Leduc to admit that his innocence is coincident with his present role of victim, the Major makes clear the circumstantial nature of morality. When asked by the Major if he would refuse to be released while his fellow Jews were kept prisoners, Leduc is forced to answer "no." It becomes clear that the foundation for moral stability is precarious, and even decent men like Leduc would rather survive in disgrace than die with honor. Under these circumstances, the efficacy of individual moral action becomes buried in an infinite chain of destructive power: an executioner like the Major is himself a victim, acting in response to a gun pointing at his head. In a crisis situation, when individual moral action can only be equated with self destruction and when evil is seen as a constant in human relations, all rational motives for decency decay and the world collapses into moral anarchy.

Up to this point, Miller seems to have presented a nihilistic vision. Von Berg, however, is Miller's answer to despair. Like Sartre's Orestes in *The Flies*, he is the existential hero who wrenches himself from passivity to engagement by freely committing a sacrificial act. Von Berg's act is absurd in that it has no rational basis, but it elevates him to moral authenticity. His rebellion annihilates the nausea brought on by his understanding of the Nazi plague and his realization of his personal complicity in the holocaust, a realization unknown to him until his conversation with Leduc toward the end of the play. Leduc convinces the apparently innocent Von Berg that he harbors in his heart, unknown to himself, "a dislike, if not hatred of Jews," not like an ordinary anti-Semite, but simply as a human being who must somehow objectify his need to despise "that stranger, that agony we cannot feel, that death we look at like a cold abstraction" (p. 105). For Von Berg, the Jew fulfills Heidegger's concept of "the one" upon whom we thrust off the threat of death: "one dies," we say, never imagining the statement to apply to ourselves. "Each man has his Jew; it is the other," Leduc says. "And the Jews have their Jews" (p. 105). The hunger for survival makes accomplices of us all.

Von Berg's sacrifice, however, eradicates his guilt as victimizer and confirms his previously untested assertion that "there are people who would find it easier to die than stain one finger with this murder" (p. 104). Von Berg's present action throws Leduc's accusation of complicity into the irrelevant past. Von Berg, in effect, becomes what he does: by dying in Leduc's place he translates his guilt into active responsibility and becomes Leduc's "Jew."

Leduc is now stained by Von Berg's gift of life and must carry on the existential cycle of transmuting his guilt into redemptive action. He is free, like all men, to transcend his present action by choosing a new and redeeming project. If Leduc fights in the Resistance, he will modify the guilt brought on by Von Berg's sacrifice: the death of the weak aristocrat will then be justified by the services of the strong combat officer. Until he performs that action, however, Leduc will feel as morally debased as the Major who also saves his life at the expense of the Other.

Von Berg is the only triumphant character in the play since death will cut him off at his highest point and permanently fix his essence as martyr. His act frees him from alienation and imposes a moral coherence upon his previously contingent world.

The varied threads of the intellectual and emotional debate finally crystallize around the concrete act of Von Berg. A moral norm is unequivocally established: One's life must submit to one's conscience, despite the absence of any external moral criteria. All the characters in the play, particularly the Major, are judged by Von Berg's "Look," and since Von Berg will die, his look becomes uneradicable. Of course the possibility of the Major's moral transcendence in the eyes of others continues to exist, but under the implacable gaze of Von Berg the Major can never alter his constitution as a degraded object.

The play thus represents in its total action the essence of Sartre's philosophy, which was, and still is, the demand for authenticity, or the moral awakening to individual responsibility. But if Miller follows Sartre in the general theme, structure, and dynamics of his play, his implied conclusion to the threat of anti-Semitism differs radically from Sartre's *Anti-Semite and Jew*. Ironically, Sartre offers an optimistic proposal to the problem while Miller remains doubtful and pessimistic. In the twenty-one years between the publication of *Being and Nothingness* and the production of *Incident at Vichy* the two writers have exchanged philosophic positions—Miller subscribing to Sartre's corrosive analysis of human relations in *Being and Nothingness* and Sartre affirming Miller's former belief in human solidarity.

Despite Sartre's analysis of anti-Semitism as a cowardly search for being and, therefore, an ontological problem, he nevertheless concludes that the Jew's dilemma is social and consequently remediable.

Sartre's ordinarily complex and tough-minded Marxism seems simplisitic and contradictory in *Anti-Semite and Jew*. While allowing for the freedom of the anti-Semite, Sartre nevertheless believes that an alteration of the anti-Semite's situation will consequently alter his choice of being. Existential free will and socialist determinism are unsatisfactorily mixed. With the advent of the Marxist state, Sartre predicts, all members would feel a mutual bond of solidarity because they would all be engaged in a common enterprise, and anti-Semitism would naturally disappear. Man's fear of being would be overcome by the benevolent leadership of the unbiased proletarian, the abolition of private ownership of land, and the consequent elimination of class struggles.

As Sartre's political activism increased, Miller's early leftist enthusiasm diminished. Leduc undoubtedly speaks for the playwright when he insists that "man is not reasonable, that he is full of murder, that his ideals are only the little tax he pays for the right to hate and kill with a clear conscience" (p. 104). Leduc's description might well fit the brutal characters in Sartre's early play *No Exit*, that grim dramatization of human interaction as outlined in *Being and Nothingness*. Since the void at the heart of being is a static condition, man's attempts to escape it through sadism and masochism cannot be expected to change.

Understandably, *Incident at Vichy* has been attacked by left wing critics. Eric Mottram has accused Miller of expounding nihilistic despair: "Miller can only see the present repeated endlessly as the future. . . . Miller can suggest no argument for the future based on social change, through economic legislation, education and sexual understanding."[15] Miller would answer that he is still a liberal, but his faith in the efficacy of social reform has diminished since man's evil, he now feels, is directly related to his fear of existence, an unalterable condition even in the Marxist "utopia."

Tom F. Driver, writing from a theological perspective, criticizes Miller's loss of faith in a "universal moral sanction" and his subsequent failure to discover a conceivable basis for a new one.[16] Miller does offer a "lesson" in *Incident at Vichy* however: if man can awaken to his complicity in evil, he can exchange his guilt for responsibility, as does Von Berg. But Miller admits that "it is immensely difficult to be human precisely because we cannot detect our own hostility in our own actions. It is tragic, fatal blindness. . . . ."[17] Driver describes the existential nature of Miller's conclusions:

> There being no objective good and evil, and no imperative other than conscience, man himself must be made to bear the full burden of creating his values and living up

to them. The immensity of this task is beyond human capacity . . . to insist upon it without reference to ultimate truth is to create a situation productive of despair.[18]

Obviously, however, this moral task is not "beyond human capacity" since Von Berg succeeds in fulfilling it. It is well to remember that Miller based his play on a true story.

Undeniably, Miller's moral imperative is difficult. His attack on Jewish victims like Lebeau and Monceau, who willingly submit to their destruction, may seem callous, especially since Miller concedes the terrible plight of the escaped Jew in occupied Europe. But in the claustrophobic intensity of the drama, Miller succeeds in turning us against these inauthentic characters. He strips away all extenuating circumstances and brings each man into an irreducible conflict with his fate. There is no mitigation of the harsh necessity to choose ourselves, especially since Miller seems to agree with the Sartrean ethic that what one chooses for oneself, one chooses for all men. Miller is, in essence, dramatizing Sartre's famous account of the freedom one felt in France during the Occupation, "When the choice each of us made of our life was an authentic choice because it was made face to face with death."[19] Man is always capable of saying "no," even to his torturer.

Von Berg chooses to say "no" to the men and circumstances that threaten to degrade him, and he therefore fits Miller's definition of the tragic hero in his early essay, "Tragedy and the Common Man." Although the play is grim, it is not "productive of despair" since the heroic action of a frightened and delicate man sets the norm for all the characters. If Miller now seems pessimistic about Mankind, he is still optimistic about individual man. Solidarity between two individuals is achieved; a gentile has broken through the ontological barrier that makes an enemy or an object of the Jew; and guilt has been eradicated through heroic action. If it is clear at the end that Evil is unredeemable and that the horror just witnessed will be repeated after the arrival of new prisoners, the cycle of complicity has been momentarily broken and the human reaffirmed.

Eric Mottram has negatively described the climax of *Vichy* as "an act of courage and love within the context of nihilism."[20] But is this statement not an apt description of some of the most powerful of modern tragedies?

Notes

1. "Arthur Miller," *Encounter*, November 1970, p. 73.

2. Quoted Ibid., p. 74.

3. "Forgers of Myth," in *Playwrights on Playwriting*, ed. Toby Cole, New York, 1960, p. 123.

4. Ibid., p. 122.

5. Ibid., p. 117.

6. Robert Brustein, *Seasons of Discontent*, New York, 1967, p. 260.

7. "The Shadows of the Gods," in *American Playwrights on Drama*, ed. Horst Frenz, New York, 1965, p. 139.

8. *Nausea*, Norfolk, Conn., undated, p. 176.

9. "Existentialism," in *A Casebook on Existentialism*, ed. William Spanos, New York, 1964, p. 282.

10. *Incident at Vichy*, New York, 1967, p. 61. Subsequent references are cited in the text.

11. "Existentialism," p. 278.

12. Maurice Cranston, *Jean Paul Sartre*, New York, 1962, p. 49.

13. *Anti-Semite and Jew*, trans. George J. Becker, New York, 1962, p. 18. Subsequent references are cited in the text.

14. *Being and Nothingness*, trans. Hazel Barnes, New York, 1956, p. 367.

15. "Arthur Miller: The Development of a Political Dramatist in America," in *Arthur Miller: A Collection of Critical Essays*, ed. Robert W. Corrigan, Englewood Cliffs, New Jersey, 1969, pp. 55–6.

16. "Strength and Weakness in Arthur Miller," *Arthur Miller*, ed. Robert Corrigan, p. 65.

17. "Our Guilt for the World's Evil," quoted by Leonard Moss, *Arthur Miller*, New Haven, 1967, p. 97.

18. Driver, p. 66.

19. Quoted by William Barrett, "Jean Paul Sartre," in *On Contemporary Literature*, ed. Richard Kostelanetz, New York, 1964, p. 557.

20. Mottram, p. 54.

The Price

Review of *The Price*

Alan S. Downer[*]

The Price, although a new play, is also a revival in which Arthur Miller returns to and revitalizes that quintessential American family, the Lomans. It is true that the Franz's once stood higher on the economic ladder; they had stocks and bonds and cultural amenities and furniture that outlasted the payments, and their sons were college bound, professionally ambitious. But the father was as stricken by the Wall Street disaster of 1929 as Willy Loman by the loss of his skills and his job; Mr. Franz's suicide was a retreat to an attic room where he listened to the radio and old phonograph records, and shrewdly concealed from the son who had sacrificed a career to support him the small capital that still remained in his bank account. His two sons, when we meet them forty years later, are the Loman brothers grown older: Happy (Walter) who single-mindedly settled for a successful career, Biff (Victor) who surrendered his ambitions to a life of domestic responsibility.

This is, of course, to oversimplify. Walter, whose career has seemed ruthless and whose character has been untouched by human pathos, reveals himself as one who arrived at the bitter self-knowledge that he had made the wrong choice and who rose from the ruins of his life with a new purpose and new disinterestedness. Victor, who had chosen to be responsible for his father, discovers that he has been a dupe, that his hateful years as a civil servant were wasted generosity. In an attic crammed with the family monuments the brothers meet after years of no contact, make tentative gestures of reconciliation, retreat from the recognition of reality, are lulled by the memory of certain good days, and explode at the reiteration of viewpoints. The theme of the play is perhaps best stated by the secondhand dealer who has been summoned to dispose of the family furniture: "The price of used furniture is nothing but a viewpoint, and if you wouldn't understand the viewpoint it is impossible to understand the price." One of the daily reviewers criticized the play because, he said, nothing was *changed*, a curious complaint in a theatre that still looks up to Chekhov. What changed, of course, was the viewpoint, over and over like a revolving kaleidoscope, as the audience was drawn first to one character, then to the other; the result was one of the rarest of dramatic (or human) experiences, understanding, sympathy, with all.

[*]Reprinted from "Old, New, Borrowed, and (a Trifle) Blue: Notes on the New York Theatre, 1967–68," *The Quarterly Journal of Speech*, 54 (1968), 203–06, by permission of the journal.

In a theatre increasingly preempted by the faddish and evanescent, Miller is increasingly concerned with ultimate things: the reactions and interactions of men and women of middle stature in the situations where choice or accident have thrust them. At the beginning of his career he was certain of his position on the issues of the day and was able to manage his action within the confines of the conventional well-made play. But with *Death of a Salesman* and most particularly with *The Crucible* he sought the distancing of history. Doubtless he is as troubled by Viet Nam and drugs and the underprivileged as any thoughtful citizen, but no serious artist will try conclusions with the headlines in his work. *The Price* does not preach or editorialize; it must reject the tidy structuring of the well-made play. It is one long act of uninterrupted confrontation, of touch and go; but it is not the play of individual psychology, the case history which Miller deplores in the introduction to his collected works. Like the later plays of O'Neill, it goes beyond the tragic catastrophe to the maturity of understanding and acceptance.

It is tempting to say that Miller, like Tennessee Williams, has been consistently fortunate in his interpreters, directors, and actors. Yet the production of *The Price* was visited with so many emergencies—last minute replacements of two of the four players and, apparently, a change of directors—that it is equally tempting to discover in him the poetic dramatist: the only begetter, the assured manipulator of all the tools of his craft.

The Price is written with the greatest economy, but with no miserliness. Its single setting, a cluttered attic, though assembled on a ramped stage, is realistic, as familiar as everybody's catchall room. It is also, very specifically, the scene of the action, the architectural envelope that has caused and is to affect the life histories of the characters. In the center is the overstuffed chair of the dead father, the eternally present catalyst even in absence. Beside it is a phonograph and a pile of records: one is "The Laughing Record" which could reduce party-goers of the twenties to helpless cachinnation with no notion of what they were laughing at; the play begins and ends with the playing of the record. Around the sides of the setting are the family remains, a solid, oversized dining room table, a sculler's oar, a fencing sword, a cracked harp. The very locale is eloquent, expository; the action could occur nowhere else, no other action would justify it.

There is similar economy in peopling the set. One can imagine other characters: the cleaning woman, whose mop has been left behind, for more direct exposition; the policeman's son, the doctor's nurse, or ex-wife. But they would only have distracted from the business in hand. We are to be concerned with only four actors: the two sons (doctor and policeman), the policeman's wife, and the furniture dealer. The latter is one of Miller's most engaging characters, a ninety year old Russian Jew who has maintained his accent and his integrity with fierce loyalty to himself. Although an outsider he becomes a kind of surrogate for the father. In their reactions to him the sons relive their relationships with the destroyed businessman and so reveal themselves, the policeman willing to be led, the doctor preferring to connive. The policeman's wife is the tritagonist; because of her the play remains a drama and never descends to debate.

Although the theatre will no doubt continue its reckless commitments to expendability, *The Price* should be around for a long time. Because of its economy it is essentially a theatrical experience; it is not movie matter. But the repertories and those academic theatres that have not surrendered wholly to the cruelties and absurdities of the moment will keep it alive, perhaps with better performances than the original. Arthur Kennedy is an actor shaped to Miller's hand. From Chris Keller to Biff to John Proctor to Walter Franz he has grown with the playwright, the modestly sensual man who has the courage to learn from experience. Harold Gary, a last minute substitute for the furniture dealer, judiciously combined the shrewdness of commerce, the wisdom of age, and a dusting of Willie Howard, with never a hint of the stand-up comedian reaching for a punch line; those who follow him in the role must be fully aware of its temptations. As the policeman's wife, Kate Reid remembered too often her success in *Who's Afraid of Virginia Woolf?* Mrs. Franz is a frustrated middle class housewife, but her love and admiration for her husband are apparent in her most distraught moments. Miss Reid, slatting Marthalike about the stage and face-making during the tense arguments of the two brothers, seemed always on the verge of some outrageous action or obscene comment. Esther is no Juno Boyle, but she was created by a playwright who respects women. Pat Hingle's policeman was an unmade bed. In quieter moments, his nasal voice, bumbling movements and general appearance of partly raised dough made him touching as adolescence is touching, though one wondered about the suggestion of "dese and dose" coming from a man of such family pride. When the tension increased, however, when in a moment of anger he hurtled himself like a mortar shell across the table at his brother, his voice became grating, his gestures undisciplined, and his posture shapeless.

Yet, after all the passion, in the final peaceful moments of the play, Hingle was infinitely moving. He had only to take the money from the dealer, adjust his uniform, glance about the attic, and set off for the movies with his wife. The simple actions of survival. If the play's subject is the death of a family, it ends with the birth, or at least the confirmation, of an individual.

The Other Arthur Millers

Walter Kerr[*]

"We invent ourselves" was the desperate summary Arthur Kennedy made of two possibly wrongheaded lives in Arthur Miller's *The Price*. We choose the role we mean to play—the role may call for martyrdom or rebellion or whatever occurs to us at the moment of choice—and then wear the costume until it fits so snugly that it may, in the end, serve as a winding-sheet. And all the while it may not have represented us, really; it may even have killed what was most generous and best in us. A man may well wonder, as he looks down at the dusty policeman's uniform he wears or at the skilled surgeon's hands that now tremble a bit, what other uniform might have become him, what other work the tiring hands might have done. Thus the near conclusion of Mr. Miller's interesting inquiry.

It was interesting, in spite of its very evident thinnesses, for a special reason. Sometimes during his career as one of America's most admired playwrights—or at least as a playwright of whom much was expected and then demanded—Arthur Miller would seem to have been very busy inventing Arthur Miller, carefully and most consciously wrapping about himself the cloak of seer, prophet, founding father and dormitory prefect. We rather expected this Arthur Miller to pontificate; we may have wondered whether it was proper to applaud or to genuflect upon leaving the theater. With *The Price*, though, the master moralist had suddenly relaxed in two ways, and while I am in no position to say who the real Arthur Miller or the secret Arthur Miller or the total Arthur Miller may be, it was fascinating to catch a glimpse of two faces of the man we hadn't quite seen before. Fascinating, and attractive.

The first of the unfamiliar faces was an astonishingly droll one. Mr. Miller has never been much of a man for leavening his work with comedy, certainly not with comedy that is gentle and even forgiving toward an essential cynicism. Mr. Miller has never really liked cynics, compromisers, manipulators. But in the person of an ancient used-furniture dealer, going on ninety and carrying eggs, salt, and Hershey bars about with him for energy, he had literally opened an attic door to let guile in, guile with a scalawag charm to it.

The dealer shuffled in at the attic door, making his way through the dust on unsteady stork's legs that seemed to settle twice with every step, because two

[*]From Walter Kerr, *Thirty Plays Hath November* (New York: Simon and Schuster, 1969), pp. 217–20. Copyright © 1969 by Walter Kerr. Reprinted with permission of Walter Kerr.

estranged brothers had come briefly together to dispose of the family belongings, remnants of the market crash of 1929. The building was to be torn down, and everything—the gaudy cracked harp in the corner, the Motorola radio, the gramophone with its Okeh Laughing Record still on the turntable, the chandeliers and fencing foils and tightly rolled rugs—had to be got rid of. The dealer was asked to name a price.

He was wonderfully patient about not getting to it, nibbling at the treasure trove he kept stored in his bulky overcoat pockets, admiring the family he so benevolently wished to serve, displaying such candor about his tactics that the tactics came to seem heavensent favors. When Kate Reid, wife to one of the brothers, pointedly announced that with every little delay she could hear the price going down, he clapped his hands for joy. "I like her, she's suspicious," he exclaimed, a seraph who had always surreptitiously admired devils. Suspicion was fine, it added zest to life, even though it was rather wasted on such an elderly fellow, a fellow who'd really retired and whose name—as he suggested—must have been got out of a very old telephone book. "I smoked all my life. I drinked all my life, and I loved every woman who would let me—so what do I need to steal from you?" was his philosophical answer to the urgencies of money-minded folk. Money was not for him. And the price went steadily down. The writing was softly sly, trickily inverted, and—this is what's important—affectionate. If Harold Gary was extraordinarily funny in the role, playing it as though he'd slept in it and had just turned out for a stroll, Mr. Miller himself displayed a becoming strain of wry kindliness.

The second and not altogether familiar face Mr. Miller offered us was one of uncertainty. His play had no real ending, and that was a dramatic defect in it. Two brothers badgered one another, all but knifed one another, all evening long; the fencing foils in the corner would have come in handy for the emotional work they meant to do. But when the work was done, and a hundred home-truths had been rooted out of them, they were no different. Whatever they had learned in the scorching match was powerless to alter the cut of the costumes they had so long ago adopted; they left as they had entered, blind enemies, and the effect upon us was dry and unresolved, rather as though we'd followed a good detective-story for nineteen chapters only to discover that someone had torn out the twentieth and last.

But his very inability to imagine a handy solution had a kind of retroactive effect upon Mr. Miller's management of the situation in mid-flight. It made the author rather more troubled and rather more human and it put him to the task of making each detective-story twist and turn—as two people dug for their identities—independently arresting, inch-by-inch vigorous. Occasionally there was too much vigor: certainly director Ulu Grosbard or the author himself ought to have suggested to contestants Pat Hingle and Arthur Kennedy that a roar becomes more exciting when it is interrupted by an undercut. Someone should have come in fast but low once in a while. Some of the surprises that were tossed in to keep two angry men regularly off balance were less than plausible, the Erle Stanley Gardner line "All right, I'll *tell* you what happened!"

occurred too often for complete comfort, and the characters continued to have that sensitive cigar-store-Indian flavor that haunts Mr. Miller's work. Mr. Hingle was a boulder, Mr. Kennedy shivering steel; they were more nearly natural elements than observed people, and they spoke across a valley.

Nevertheless they made us listen; we wanted to dog them through each step in their bullheaded bout of self-discovery. We wanted to know why there was a cold reserve in Mr. Kennedy's eye when he was at his most gracious, why Mr. Hingle seemed ready to dissolve only to flare into fresh, implacable distrust. Mr. Kennedy was the son who abandoned the family when the Depression wiped it out. He had gone on to become a successful doctor and had paid the price of his isolation: his wife and his health were gone. Mr. Hingle was the son who'd stayed, cared for a destroyed father, given up his own schooling and wound up profitlessly patrolling a beat: self-appointed martyrdom had come at a price, too. Now neither could be certain that he'd done what he did honorably. But neither could abandon a role adopted at such cost. Two men were in a bind, writhing to get free of it.

It was the bind itself that generated the energy of the play, not any promise of salvation. Which meant that Mr. Miller had come down from that mountaintop he has sometimes seemed to inhabit and got into the ring. If participation—with no conclusion foreseen—pushed him into melodrama, all right. If it forced him into patches of disbelief, so be it. Let's see how the footwork might go.

The sheer theatrical footwork went very well. And the necessity of slugging it out, without a clear moral planned beforehand, brought the playwright just a shade closer to us. We observed him feverishly at his work; we even caught him out at his work. But we knew he was involved in other men's troubles.

What Price Arthur Miller?:
An Analysis of *The Price*

C. W. E. Bigsby°

In many ways Arthur Miller's new play, *The Price*, seems to mark a return to the world of Joe Keller and Willy Loman. Once again, it appears, we are invited to witness the struggles of a man who has "the wrong dreams" and who embraces too completely the ethics of a society intent on success at any price. But in the twenty years since *Death of a Salesman* Miller has become aware of more fundamental influences than those exerted by Horatio Alger Jr. and while he continues to expose the vacuity of the American dream he is more concerned with probing the nature of human freedom than with exposing the social charade. His latest play, therefore, owes more to *After the Fall* and *Incident at Vichy* than to *All My Sons* and *Death of a Salesman*.

The line between *Incident at Vichy* and *The Price* is disturbingly direct. Miller has said that he is fascinated by the Nazi era because it constituted a turning point in man's perception of human nature. The war and the Nazi occupation of Europe produced not merely "a chilling of the soul by the technological apparatus" but also "the obstruction of the individual's capacity for choosing, or erosion of what used to be thought of as an autonomous personality."[1] While this was carried to its extreme by the Nazi regime, however, Miller sees his contemporary society as "struggling with the same incubus."[2] Indeed, in a sense, as Miller has suggested, *Incident at Vichy* itself is "about tomorrow morning,"[3] and *The Price*, in turn, about man's continued surrender of identity and submission to a false concept of human nature.

As in *Death of a Salesman* and *After the Fall* we are at a point in time when the main characters are made suddenly aware of the futility of their lives thus far. For Willy Loman it had been an imperfect perception—a dull sense of insufficiency and failure. For Quentin it was a sudden realisation that his life had been dedicated only to self-interest. In *The Price* the crisis emerges from a meeting between two brothers. Both men are at a crucial stage in their own lives. Victor, a frustrated and bitterly disappointed policeman, looks back over his life and sees no meaning and no hope for his remaining years. He is poised. He lacks the courage to retire because this means that he will be forced to acknowledge his failure to create anything worthwhile through his career.

°Reprinted from *Twentieth Century Literature*, 16, No. 1 (1970), 16–25, by permission of the journal.

Likewise he lacks the will to start again—to change a destiny which he has already rationalized away as the consequence of the economic determinism of the nineteen-thirties. His brother, Walter, is in a similar position. Although successful he can find no purpose or meaning behind his frenzied pursuit of wealth and fame. His personal life is in ruins, his professional integrity compromised. But after a serious nervous breakdown he feels at long last that he has begun to understand himself and as the play progresses it becomes apparent that he is determined to put this new, imperfect, knowledge into practice. For the first time he feels genuinely alive to the possibilities of a life built on something more substantial than mutual recrimination and obsessive guilt. Seized with a naive excitement he struggles against his old nature and fights to explain his new perception to his brother.

The play is set in the attic of a Manhattan brownstone house. With the building about to be torn down Victor and his wife, Esther, arrive to negotiate the sale of his father's furniture. The room is as it has been for sixteen years, since the time that is, of his father's death. The sight of his former home and the various reminders of his youth provide an appropriate background for the revelations of the past which now follow.

We soon learn that Victor's marriage is breaking up. His wife is embittered by his failure and contemptuous of his weakness. Rather than face the reality of her position she resorts to alcohol and when her husband discovers an old fencing foil the mock thrusts which he makes are a weary re-enactment of their antagonisms.

Into this tense situation there intrudes the figure of the furniture dealer— eighty-nine-year-old Solomon. He it is who acts not merely as a chorus but also as a moral arbiter between Walter's seemingly callous realism and Victor's apparent good nature. Dragged out of retirement, he grudgingly admits to satisfaction that he should be working again for only then does he regain a sense of purpose in his life. Thus when he resists Walter's attempts to take the business away from him he is literally fighting for his survival.

Walter himself is a highly successful surgeon who has made money by sacrificing his vocation to simple greed. Having avoided his brother for many years he is conscious of the importance of their present meeting. But the bitterness which has long existed between them quickly wells to the surface and in the course of the accusations and confessions which follow we gradually discover the truth about a past which both of them had embroidered to suit their own purposes. At the end of the play each brother is finally left "touching the structure of his life."[4]

Tennessee Williams has said of American businessmen that, "Disappointed in their longing for other things, such as tenderness, they turn to the pursuit of wealth because that is more obtainable in the world."[5] This "reverse sublimation" clearly characterizes the protagonists of *The Price*. Shocked by the failure of love and bewildered by the treachery and cruelty of human relationships, they retreat into illusion. Victor, as we have seen, adopts the role of victim while Esther turns to the bottle. Walter, as Williams had suggested, substitutes the ethos of business for genuine human relationships. Even Victor, like Willy Loman before him, embraces the cynical competitive ethic of a commercial society. Having failed himself his main hope rests in having produced "a terrific boy," but his proud boast that "nobody's ever going to take that guy" exposes the true nature of his values. Trapped in an illusory world none of them have been able to discover or create any meaning. But Walter, like Quentin before him, is suddenly forced to re-examine his life and to test the presumptions on which his actions have been based. What he now understands and tries to convey to his brother is that human failure can be traced not to some indefinable hostility in the universe or to the destructiveness of a particular social system but to the failure of individuals to recognise the paramount importance of some kind of genuine human relationship. The misery of their own family life, for example, was not a sign that "there was no mercy in the world" but rather that there was "no love in this house. There was no loyalty. There was nothing but a straight financial arrangement." (p. 109) His mother had blamed her husband for destroying her musical career; his father had watched while his son unnecessarily sacrificed his future for him. Victor has refused to face this particular reality by creating an elaborate fantasy but has forced himself to sacrifice sixteen years of his life in order to give substance to this illusion. But Walter now insists on the need to face the real world with courage and determination and when Esther asks, "But who . . . can ever face that" he replies, "You have to." (p. 109) Like Quentin before him he finally comes to feel that only when the individual is prepared to confront reality and to cease defending himself by indicting others does he really take his destiny into his own hands. In his own words, "I don't look high and low for some betrayal any more; my days belong to *me* now." (p. 109)

The Swedish dramatist, Peter Weiss, has talked of the urgent need for "getting over" a concern with the "guilt laden, doomed and damned bourgeoisie."[6] While his own Marxist leanings make this primarily an apology for a more clearly political drama his rejection of bourgeois 'problem plays' puts him in line with the mainstream of modern drama. To many critics Arthur Miller has long been the exception to this development, remaining obsessed with precisely that "guilt laden" bourgeoisie rejected by Weiss. Nevertheless there is evidence that with his more recent work he too has come to concern himself with more fundamental aspects of the human condition. He has turned his attention from the symptoms to the disease itself.

In an article written in 1960 Tom Driver could say with considerable justice that Miller lacked "that metaphysical inquisitiveness which would take him to the bottom of the problems he encounters." Miller's chief fault, according to Driver, lay in the fact that he tended to see the issues "too soon . . . in their preliminary form of social or even moral debate" and not "in terms of dramatic events that disturb the audience's idea of basic truth, which is the foundation for its moral attitudes."[7] The justice of this comment is underlined by his failure, in many of the early plays, to trace moral and social failures to their source in the human character. In the person of Chris Keller, in *All My Sons*, he demonstrates the cruelty of the idealist without attempting to understand its cause while in the same play he draws a picture of a war-profiteer without questioning a human nature which could evidence such cruelty and deceit.

Again, in *Death of a Salesman*, he seems uncertain as to whether Willy is the victim of his own weakness or of a brutally simple-minded society. We know, finally, that Willy is fatally illusioned but discover little about the true nature of reality or the potential freedom of moral or social action which depends not only on Willy's state of mind but on the nature of the human situation. Part of the reason for this, as Driver points out, is that at this time Miller was himself confused as to the reality of human nature. At one moment he could declare that "there are people dedicated to evil in the world" and regret not having made Judge Danforth, in *The Crucible*, more of a villain; while in the same breath he could say that "man is essentially innocent" and that "the evil in him represents but a perversion of his frustrated love."[8]

However, after a nine-year silence, following *A View from the Bridge*, Miller, benefiting perhaps from the impact of a revived European theatre, consciously attempted to examine both the nature of his own life and the source of personal and social antagonisms. With *After the Fall* and more recently with *The Price* he has probed not only behind the bland facade of success but also behind the social and psychological rationalisations of earlier plays. Discovering somewhat belatedly an existential ethic he recognises the imperfection of human nature but insists on man's responsibility for his own fate. Earlier he had said that "The great weight of evidence is upon the helplessness of man. The great bulk of the weight of evidence is that we are not in command." But significantly, even then, he felt constrained to add that "we surely have much more command than anybody, including Macbeth's Witches, could ever dream of and somehow a form has to be devised which will account for this. Otherwise the drama is doomed to repeating and repeating *ad nauseam* the same pattern of striving, disillusion and defeat."[9] In spite of this panegyric in favour of man's power to act few playgoers can have seen much evidence of this in Willy Loman's sure progress towards death or even in Biff's belated and untested declarations of faith in a realistic future. Even *The Crucible* proved only that men could be brave in the face of their fate, not that they could do much to avoid unjustified persecution. To recant or to remain obdurate was still to be subject to circumstances not of one's own making. It is only with his most recent work that Miller has been able to reconcile man's freedom to act with the determining factors of his own nature. In *After the Fall* and in *Incident at Vichy* he draws, with Sartrean finesse, the lines which connect individual choice with social injustice and immorality. He probes, for virtually the first time, the real nature of evil and the human origin of cruelty and deceit.

Both Miller and Peter Weiss attended the Auschwitz trials which were held in Frankfurt a few years ago. They went, separately, as Jews who had escaped the persecution and agony of the Nazi onslaught. Weiss's family had escaped from Germany during the so-called *Kristallnacht*. They lived out the war in Sweden where Weiss still works, writing in his native language. Miller spent the war years in America, safe from any threat of invasion and thus direct persecution and remote from the incomprehensible brutality of Nazi terror. With the end of the war he was left to face a number of paradoxes and his attempt to resolve them is the story of his development as a writer. The treachery and brutality of the war years forced him to reassess his vision of human nature. The naive optimism of the prewar world, the pathetic faith in political solutions bowed before the realities of Auschwitz and Hiroshima. The world was open to ambiguity again and Miller was sensitive enough to reflect this.

As a Jew who had survived and indeed suffered little inconvenience he felt an ill-defined sense of guilt. This guilt appears throughout his work in a sublimated form. In *All My Sons* it is the guilt of the war-profiteer; in *Death of a Salesman* and *The Crucible* that of a man who has deceived a faithful wife; and in *A View from the Bridge* a man who informs on his daughter's lover through envy.† To many critics he seemed to be consciously avoiding specifically Jewish characters while continuing to use a Jewish idiom. Only with *After the Fall*, his painfully autobiographical work, do we discover the real source of this guilt as Quentin, Miller's protagonist, confesses to feeling the "guilt of the survivor." To be a Jew and to have survived is to be inexplicably favoured and hence to be a hostage to the past. This play, then, resolved many of the problems which had vexed Miller throughout his writing career. It served to exorcise his personal sense of guilt but, more significantly, provided evidence that he had finally evolved a consistent concept of the relation between human freedom and human limitations. In a sense *The Price* could scarcely have been written before *After the Fall* had successfully laid some of Miller's more persistent personal ghosts. Only now could he create a character such as Solomon; only now could he maintain the tension between determinism and freedom with conscious and subtle control and yet finally permit a synthesis which retains conviction.

In *The Price* we are presented with several characters who are made suddenly aware of their direct responsibility for their own actions and of their freedom of action—a demonstration, perhaps, of his earlier comment that "The only thing worth doing today in the theatre . . . is to synthesize the subjective drives of the human being with what is now demonstrably the case, namely that by an act of will man can and has changed the world."[10] If Victor, the unsuccessful policeman, offers little proof of man's power to transform his surroundings this is because he refuses to acknowledge his own freedom of action. He conspires to create his own irrelevance and as such becomes a depressingly apt image for what Miller sees as a nerveless and deluded society. Indeed Miller would agree with the Swiss dramatist, Friedrich Dürrenmatt when he says that, "True representatives of our world are missing; the tragic heroes are nameless. Any small-time crook, petty government official or policeman better represents our world than a senator or a president."[11] Miller has no need to claim tragic proportions for Victor, as he had earlier for Willy Loman. In an essay written after *Death of a Salesman* he had defined his understanding of tragedy. It was,

†Catherine is, of course, Eddie's niece, not his daughter.—Ed. Note.

he insisted, a quality which exalted the "thrust for freedom" and which "auto-
matically demonstrates the indestructible will of man to attain his freedom." As
a description of his earlier play this was inappropriate enough; here it is simply
an ironical comment on Victor's failure to recognise his own freedom of action.
Unlike Miller's own conception of the tragic hero he does "remain passive in the
face of . . . a challenge to his dignity."[12]

In these most recent plays, then, man is unequivocally in control of his own
destiny. If he chooses to see himself as a victim this is evidence of his failure of
nerve and not of the impossibility of positive action. Man's absurdity, in other
words, is of his own making. Indeed, in the hands of dramatists like Gelber and
Albee the absurd has become a more clearly social concept than for Beckett and
Ionesco. For the latter the absurd emerges from man's desire for order in a
chaotic universe. For the former, and here also for Miller, it derives not from
the human condition but from the failure of social and personal values. This is a
society in which, as Victor points out (with a faint echo of Clifford Odets),
"there's no respect for anything but money." (p. 48) For the American dramatist absurdity is rooted precisely in this perversion of the puritan ethic and in
what Walter calls "the slow, daily fear you call ambition." (p. 83) But Miller has
long since "come to a kind of belated recognition that the great faith in social
change as an amelioration or a transforming force of the human soul leaves
something to be wanted."[13] Unlike the European writer, however, he does
believe in the possibility of change but that not in the form of social organisation
but in the nature of human response. Aware that "the social solution of the evil
in man has failed"[14] he insists on the need to state a belief in life and the
existence of a viable system of values. Miller, indeed, has declared a basic
commitment to the need "to organize life and not to present the case for death
and despair."[15]

Peter Weiss has said of *The Investigation* that "It is capitalism, indeed the
Western way of life, that is on trial."[16] Essentially the same remark might be
applied to *The Price* whose setting is "New York. Now." But while Miller has
characteristically reserved an acerbic criticism for the moral and spiritual
blight which accompanies the American dream his real concern is more fundamental. He recognises the distortion of the soul which accompanies a frenzied
pursuit of wealth and success but he also acknowledges the weakness of a
human nature which, in any society, defends spurious innocence at the cost of
indicting the rest of humanity. There can be little doubt, either, that Weiss's
remark is a rather unhelpful analysis of his own play. He is chilled by the
ruthless efficiency of an ambiguity at the root of the human mind. Victim and
oppressor are defined by circumstances and political accident. The possibility
of a reversal of roles is a constant reminder of the possibilities of imperfect man.
It is precisely this existential truth which offers a point of real contact between
Weiss and Miller. *The Investigation* was designed to "show the possibilities of
human beings, either to let themselves be suppressed and exterminated; and on
the other side, the possibility of the accused now slowly to develop this men-
tality of mass murderers which they weren't born to be."[17] *The Price* offers

similar evidence not only of this reversal of roles but also of the need to acknowledge man's freedom of action. Victor tries to justify his failure by reference to personal and social necessity, but under Walter's ruthless questioning it
soon becomes apparent that his failure was entirely his own responsibility. His
refusal to acknowledge this existential truth constitutes an almost classic example of *mauvaise foi*. He denies his freedom rather than accept the price which
goes with it.

The paramount need to accept the consequences of one's actions; the need
to "take one's life in one's hands,"[18] as Holga had put it in *After the Fall*, is
underlined in *The Price* by Solomon. At eighty-nine he had thought his life
finished until contacted by Victor. Now, faced with the prospect of disposing of
the furniture, he seems to get a new lease on life. He is suddenly aware that
there are "more possibilities." This, indeed, is the very heart of the play. Victor
has been living his life as though there were no alternatives. He is trapped, in
Saul Bellow's words, in a perpetual state of 'becoming' rather than 'being.' Like
Quentin, he has been mortgaging the present to the future. In *After the Fall*
Quentin had finally come to realise this, confessing of his personal future that,
"I've been carrying it around all my life, like a vase that must never be
dropped."[19] In *The Price* it is Victor's wife, Esther, who points out that "all
these years we've been saying, once we get the pension we're going to start to
live . . . It's like pushing against a door for twenty-five years and suddenly it
opens . . . and we stand there . . . everything's always temporary with us. It's like
we never were anything, we were always about-to-be." (p. 18) The furniture
itself, stored for sixteen years in a single room and left untouched, is in many
ways an appropriate image for Victor himself. When Solomon says of the
furniture that its main drawback lies in the fact that is has "no more possibilities" the comment could obviously apply equally well to Victor's own self-
image. But even after the need for some kind of positive action had been
demonstrated both by Solomon and Walter he is still unwilling to concede the
truth of Esther's comment that, "You can't go on blaming everything . . . the
system or God knows what else! You're free and you can't make a move." (p. 78)

The original version of *Death of a Salesman* was to have been a mono-
drama with the action taking place entirely in Willy Loman's dispirited mind.
As such all the characters were to be seen through Willy's eyes and were in a
sense an extension of his personality. While Miller eventually abandoned this
plan there is still a sense in which individual characters are an expression of
Willy Loman's own nature. This is particularly true of the two brothers, Happy
and Biff, who reflect the two sides of Willy's warring personality. Happy values
only material things. He looks for some kind of consolation in his relationship
with women and, though vaguely conscious of some insufficiency, measures
himself solely by reference to his success in business. Biff, on the other hand, is
aware of other values than the purely material and is capable finally of the kind
of genuine humanity which Willy only approaches in moments of rare
sensitivity.

In *The Price* Miller makes use of a similar device. The two brothers repre-

sent profoundly different approaches to life—approaches which not only coex-
ist in the world but which constitute the basis of most individual lives. This is the
significance of Walter's remark that "we're brothers. It was only two seemingly
different roads out of the same trap. It's almost as though . . . we're like two
halves of the same guy. As though we can't quite move ahead—alone." (p. 110)

The qualities of the two brothers are ambiguously presented. At first sight
it appears to be simply a contrast between heroic self-sacrifice and callous self-
interest. But beneath this public face is what Pirandello used to call the "naked
figures." This apparent reversal of moral force is evidence of Miller's wish to
penetrate to "the pantheon of forces and values which must lie behind the
realistic surfaces of life."[20] Victor is revealed as a weak and irresolute individual, unwilling to concede responsibility for his own life and consciously
avoiding painful realities by retreating into illusion. Walter, on the other hand,
is a man who, like Biff, has gradually come to recognise the inconsequence of
wealth and success and who now tries to pass his insight onto others. He recognises the need to acknowledge the reality of human weakness and to accept
responsibility for one's own action.

When Edward Albee presented a similar contrast between those who lived
in a fantasy world and those who insisted on the primacy of reality, in Who's
Afraid of Virginia Woolf?, he suggested that illusion, far from destroying
man's loneliness merely exacerbated it. Only when George and Martha have
ritualistically destroyed their illusions does real contact between them become a
possibility. The same is essentially true here. As Walter points out, "It is all an
illusion and if you could walk through it we could meet." (p. 110) To Albee, this
conflict between illusion and reality has a political and moral dimension, for
continued refusal to acknowledge reality is as lethal on a national and international scale as it is for the significantly named George and Martha. This further
dimension is a significant part of Miller's play too, for in a production note he
insists that, "As the world now operates the qualities of both brothers are
necessary to it." (p. 117) But while accepting their necessity in the world "as it
now operates" he admits that "their respective psychologies and moral values
conflict at the heart of the social dilemma." (p. 117) This conflict is not simply
defined by the individual brothers in some kind of moral polarity. If Walter has
a clearer understanding of reality and the need to accept responsibility for one's
actions he lacks Victor's moral sensitivity. Yet the struggle is to find an interpretation of existence which depends neither on a naive endorsement of human
perfectibility or a cynical pose of alienation. The real problem lies in acknowledging the imperfection of man and the inadequacy of society and yet continuing to place one's faith in human potential. In the words of the wise Solomon,
"It's not that you can't believe nothing, that's not so hard—it's that you've still
got to believe it. That's hard. And if you can't do that . . . you're a dead man."
(p. 37) As a piece of moral philosophy this is no different in kind from Quentin's
final perception, in After the Fall, that is is perhaps enough to know that "we
meet unblessed; not in some garden of wax fruit and painted trees, that lie of
Eden, but after, after the Fall."[21] To accept imperfection in individuals and in

society is not to capitulate before despair. Rather it is the first stage in the reconstruction of meaning and purpose. But there is a price to pay for such a revaluation. It means granting the death of innocence; it necessitates the acceptance of responsibility for one's actions. However, the price for ignoring the challenge is even greater. It involves the destruction of human relationships and the erosion of identity—a price paid by both Victor and Walter. At the end of the play, however, purged of all illusions and forced to face the reality of their lives they have at least a chance to recreate not only themselves but also the society which they in part represent. In this way the social element of Miller's work is traced to its origin in the nature of individual experience and the essence of the human condition.

Like the earlier *After the Fall*, *The Price* has a further intriguing dimension in that it offers an insight into Miller's sense of his own role as a successful playwright. Gunter Grass has said that "art is uncompromising and life is full of compromises" adding that "To bring them together is a near impossibility, and that is what I am trying to do."[22] Miller's attempts to reconcile art and reality have reached some kind of climax in his recent work as the personality of the artist itself has progressively become a matter of central concern to him. For many critics the autobiographical nature of *After the Fall* was crass and unwelcome and while too many disregarded the play's genuine virtues there can be little doubt that it is an intensely personal document, commenting not merely on the vicissitudes of his private affairs but also on the problems of the writer. When Quentin confesses that "I felt I was merely in the service of my own success,"[23] this can be seen as not merely the complaint of a lawyer suddenly made aware of the inadequacy of his life but also as the comment of a playwright desperately reassessing the nature of his personal and artistic career. The advocate, indeed, is an appropriate image for the writer but so too is the surgeon. It comes as no surprise, therefore, to find that *The Price*, like *After the Fall*, has an equally personal dimension; a parallel which is enforced when Walter accuses himself of becoming "a kind of instrument . . . that cuts money out of people and fame out of the world." (p. 82)

The parallel between the surgeon and the writer is apt enough. For both are concerned with penetrating beneath the surface in order, as one of Albee's characters has put it, to get down to "the bone, the marrow." Both are trying to discover the true nature of a disease which manifests itself in external symptoms. This is the implication of Miller's remark that "I am trying to account as best I can for the realistic surface of life."[24] Both playwright and surgeon are also faced with a choice of motives. Do they act from personal ambition or from an objective integrity? The question, as we saw in *After the Fall*, has long haunted Miller. When Walter admits that he has been trying to "pull off the impossible. Shame the competition" (p. 84) one is even reminded of Hemingway's fisherman, in *The Old Man and the Sea*, whose suffering symbolised the writer's own anguish and whose attempt to achieve more than others was the cause both of his unique success and of his apparent failure. Yet Miller acknowledges a doubt which never seems to have troubled the self-assured Hemingway.

For like his surgeon protagonist he fears that "In dead centre, directing my hands" is none other than "my ambition—for thirty years." (p. 84) Thus, the playwright shares the physician's fear that his craft has become subordinate to ambition and wealth. In Walter's words, "I wanted to be tops—I ended in a swamp of success and bankbooks." (p.84)

Miller's own dissatisfaction with his Broadway success is well known. *After the Fall* was first produced at the Lincoln Center because, as he himself put it, "the first order of business in this theatre is to open the theatre to a wider audience, an audience of students, of people who are not totally oriented to the most vacant kind of entertainment."[25] While he would scarcely classify his own work in these terms he is aware that for many critics and writers Broadway success is taken as evidence of inconsequence. While he has not shown the attraction for off-Broadway productions of his work that Tennessee Williams has evidenced it is clear from his own comments that he feels somewhat uneasy about a success built on an audience which is "totally strange to the aims and the preoccupations of the artists."[26] Success, like failure, then, has its price.

The Price marks a sharp improvement over his last two plays. It avoids the pretentious dialogue of *After the Fall* and the simple-minded manipulation of *Incident at Vichy*. It acknowledges, too, a sense of ambiguity lacking even from his earlier success. Despite the somewhat contrived nature of the debate between the two brothers and the unconvincing nature of the minor characters—Solomon and Esther never become anything more than caricatures—there is some justification for feeling that Miller has at last emerged from the personal and artistic difficulties which he has experienced since the mid-fifties.

Notes

1. Walter Wager, ed. *The Playwrights Speak* (New York, 1968), p. 13.

2. Ibid., p. 13.

3. Ibid., p. 16.

4. Arthur Miller, "Author's Production Note," in *The Price* (New York, 1968), p. 117. All future references to this work will be incorporated into the text.

5. *The Playwrights Speak*, p. 216.

6. Ibid., p. 192.

7. Tom Driver, "Strength and Weakness in Arthur Miller," in *Discussions of Modern American Drama* by Walter Meserve (Boston, 1965), p. 110.

8. Ibid., p. 112.

9. Arthur Miller, "Morality and Modern Drama," in *Death of a Salesman: Text and Criticism* (New York, 1967), p. 181.

10. Ibid.

11. Friedrich Dürrenmatt, "Problems of the Theatre," in *The Context and Craft of Drama* (San Francisco, 1964), p. 265.

12. Arthur Miller, "Tragedy and the Common Man," in *Death of a Salesman: Text and Criticism* (New York, 1967), pp. 144-7.

13. "Morality and Modern Drama," p. 173.

14. Ibid.

15. Ibid., p. 185.

16. *The Playwrights Speak*, p. 194.

17. Ibid., p. 202.

18. Arthur Miller, *After the Fall* (London, 1965), p. 33.

19. *After the Fall*, p. 91.

20. *Discussions of Modern American Drama*, p. 107.

21. *After the Fall*, p. 127.

22. *The Playwrights Speak*, p. 6.

23. *After the Fall*, p. 12.

24. *The Playwrights Speak*, p. 7.

25. Ibid., p. 10.

26. Ibid.

The Creation Of The World And Other Business

Arthur Miller's 'Creation' Opens At Shubert Theater

Richard Watts[*]

By taking on the Book of Genesis as his starting point, Arthur Miller has tackled quite an ambitious subject for himself, and I'm sorry to say I can't believe he has carried it off successfully. His "The Creation of the World and Other Business," which opened last night at the Shubert Theater, has imagination and an unexpected vein of humor, and it starts out with a good first act. But by the end it seems to me to have become both confused and confusing.

It begins inevitably in the Garden of Eden, and God Himself is on hand chatting with Lucifer, an ambitious young fellow who would like to go into partnership with Him. The offer is rejected, although God rather likes him because he is the only person around with whom He can carry on an intelligent conversation. Being a bit lonely, He creates Adam, who has the gift for naming things, and gives him Eve as a partner. Then there is the business of being told not to touch that apple and the expulsion from Eden, but you already know about that.

Perhaps I should at least add that the narrative continues through Cain's murder of his brother Abel, who was their mother's favorite son. Then God, angry over the stubbornness of the people He has created, tells them He is leaving and will never drop in on them again. I suppose this was intended as a threat, though God, as Miller depects Him, seems to be so disagreeable and demanding, and so given to making a mess of things, that Adam's family might have considered it a welcome promise. For He isn't really a very appealing God.

Indeed, I thought Lucifer came off rather better. Mr. Miller appears to have a rather ambivalent attitude toward him. At times, God's antagonist makes quite a lot of friendly practical sense and at others he behaves literally like a Devil's Advocate. When he discovers that Cain is going to kill his brother, he at first seems genuinely disturbed and tries to make peace between them. A few minutes later he is busily egging them on, and gloating over his victory. But I may be prejudiced on his behalf because he struck me as the play's most engaging character.

[*]Reprinted from *New York Post*, December 1, 1972. Reprinted with permission of the *New York Post*. Copyright © 1972 by the New York Post Corporation.

A year or so ago, Pierre Boulle, the French novelist, wrote a charming little fantasy in which Eve upset God's designs for the world by stubbornly refusing to eat the apple. I wouldn't think of suggesting that Mr. Miller should have dramatized the Boulle story, but at least it had freshness and a good ironical point, while "Creation of the World" appeared to me uncertain of the viewpoint it was driving at and far from clear about its aim. It is an intelligent and inventive comedy of ideas but not a very satisfying one.

The cast is excellent. Best of all, I thought, was the unfailingly brilliant George Grizzard, who is a delightfully sly Lucifer. But Stephen Elliott is a really impressive Deity, Zoe Caldwell is an attractive Eve, and Bob Dishy is downright lovable as a bewildered Adam. Boris Aronson's setting of Eden and the world beyond it and Gerald Freedman's direction are admirable. "The Creation of the World" should, I think, have been much better than it is.

Miller's 'Creation of the World' is a Plodding Comedy-Drama

Douglas Watt[*]

Musing tiredly, and according to Genesis, on the wonder and mystery of man and his beginnings, Arthur Miller has wrought a play devoid of wonder, mystery or even the satisfying caress of fancy. In three acts, it is called "The Creation of the World and Other Business," and it opened last night at the Shubert.

Uncertain in its approach, it tries to be both playful and serious-minded, failing in both instances. Its jesting is awkward and heavyhanded, its statements are preachy, and the writing, taken as a whole, is surprisingly flat and mechanical. If this is how we began, we shall all end in apathy.

In trying to unravel an eternal mystery, or at least shed some interesting light on it, the author has become so perplexed and perplexing that he can offer no solace other than the lame one that, well, at least Adam and Eve have each other. As the final curtain falls, even they don't appear too satisfied with the conclusion.

The play is an ever-shifting debate between God and Lucifer in which Adam and Eve are used for both comic and thinly romantic relief.

Cast from heaven for showing Adam and Eve how to multiply, Lucifer imagines his role thenceforth to be that of God's representative on earth, demonstrating that good and evil are contained in all men. Or maybe I'm getting this wrong, because Miller changes directions so many times, even once proposing that good and evil are the same, that his course is unclear. the two do wind up antagonists and God does stalk off finally, vowing never to show his face again. This, at the close of an act in which God and the Devil have been joining in the action as both visible and invisible beings, and so interchangeably that the effect is both confusing and laughable.

Adam gets a vision of the Sabbath by dreaming of scrambled eggs with "warm croissants" on the side. Lucifer suggests to God that his title should be Minister of Perverse Affairs. God tells Lucifer, "If it weren't for the law of conservation of matter, I'd destroy you." Adam, looking distastefully at the ungainly Eve in her final days of pregnancy, says, "Why did you let yourself

[*] Reprinted from New York *Daily News*, December 1, 1972. Copyright © 1972 by the New York News Inc. Reprinted by permission.

go?'' Such are the jokes. Even so, they are a relief from the evening's weightier reflections.

The scene, a rather magical, slanted clearing designed by Boris Aronson and serving for both the Garden of Eden and earth, kindles the imagination as, inevitably, do the figures that come to occupy it—God, Lucifer, Adam, Eve, some angels and, eventually, Cain and Abel. And the principal actors are good ones, full of promise they are never allowed to achieve.

Bob Dishy is a most lovable Adam—shy, matter of fact and funny on his own. Zoe Caldwell is amusingly tantalizing as Eve. Stephen Elliott, though handicapped by a kind of ethereal version of a hospital orderly's uniform, is a rich-voiced and imposing-looking God with nothing of much interest to utter. And George Grizzard could obviously make a fascinating Lucifer given half a chance. They are all, indeed, characters in search of an author.

In smaller roles, Barry Primus struggles vainly as a Cain in the grip of both God and Lucifer, and others, having little else to do, try hard to exert personality.

Gerald Freedman has staged the dragging play as simply as possible and Tharon Musser has suggested more mystery with his lighting than Miller has with his script. Hal George's costumes improved (except for God's) as the evening went along, starting with flesh-colored leotards for Adam and Eve on which their more private parts were outlined in comic strokes.

Miller's best business has always been with the present or recent past. Perhaps the least fanciful of our major playwrights, he has provided us with a lethargic evening by toying with myth. In fact, his world gives the impression of having taken longer to create than God's.

. . . And Other Business

"All in a Boiling Soup":
An Interview with
Arthur Miller

James J. Martine*

[The transcript of this interview, recorded in New York City on 13 February 1979, is presented here in the hope that it may be useful to critical scholars and the larger audience of Miller's works.

Miller was lean, tan, healthy, immaculately attired, and looked twenty years younger than his age. He was more than courteous and cooperative. He is unpretentious and instantly likeable. Our conversation was immediately informal, and he makes one feel very comfortable. We chatted as though we had spent our youth in the same neighborhood, which in a sense is true, although the neighborhoods were in separate cities.

Re-reading this transcript, I am not sure that Miller's inflection, his intonation, his wit and comic sense are done justice. There are places in which Miller and I were both enjoying things. I know I was. But, by and large, he spoke carefully and reflectively.]

QUESTION: You have said many times that Ibsen was important to you. Would you say something about your own reading as a young man at Michigan?

MILLER: Ibsen's importance at Michigan when I was a student there was actually second to when I stumbled across the Greeks. I suppose they're both parts of one unified ideal which I didn't feel at the time, but which in later life I saw was unified. Both of these kinds of drama are densely formed. They are attempting to communicate, obviously, but at the same time they are *private*, to be sure. Ibsen was, like any writer of any value, a private man and was not simply a public speaker. But the purpose of the form was not self-indulgence but to express to his fellow citizens what his vision was. The same thing is true of the Greeks.

At Michigan, of course, we were in a moment of great social stress, when the virtues of being totally cut off from man and from society were nonexistent. One didn't consider that—at least I didn't. Art had a purpose, which was communicative. And I fell heir, so to speak, to the notion of the dramatist being a sort of prophet. He was the leading edge of the audience. This was implicit in the whole notion of literature in the 1930s.

But, of course, it was also part of the Ibsen and Greek notion too.

* This interview was completed specifically for this volume and is published here for the first time by permission of Arthur Miller.

Aeschylus, on his tombstone, after all, doesn't speak of himself particularly as a writer, but as a defender of the state and the democracy against the Persians. That's how he wanted to be remembered. I'm sure that infiltrated into all his work too. It certainly did into the *Oresteia* and many other works as well.

Anyhow, as a general statement, I think I drew from these two sources for my form—certainly for my ideas of the theatre's purposes. That was *very* important.

QUESTION: What do you read now? What is worthwhile today generally in literature: novels, poems, essays?

MILLER: Well, I read completely at random. I usually, unless I get caught up in something which will really sweep me along for periods, I read bits and pieces of a lot of books. I get books every day from publishers. So, I dip into them. Occasionally, I find one that's interesting for a couple of chapters. But I find, that the older I get the more I wish to cut. I get impatient with writing, whether it be prose or dialogue or verse, which is overwritten. So I get impatient with a lot of things that I read.

Now as for what I would be reading, let me think. I'm just reading now *The Coup* by Updike. I was reading a book by a philosopher named Kaufman on religion about two days before. I was reading Rilke this morning just before I came here. It's a hodgepodge. But I pick up, if not ideas, then stringencies. A good writer makes you feel how slack you are. I get more strict with my own thinking as a result of reading anything that's well done. I was reading Conrad the week before.

Then, I read a lot of newspapers, which is fundamentally a waste of time. It makes you feel that there was only one newspaper, and that all of these are reprints of that newspaper—for ever and ever and ever, in all countries, at all times. Still, you have to find out what the latest version of the old disaster is.

I should keep notes of what I'm reading. I can't think at the moment whether . . . oh, I just picked up from a book shelf Grace Paley's book of short stories which were really wonderful. I'm reading them again: *The Little Disturbances of Man*. Then, I was reading seed catalogues—a lot. What else? I read a pamphlet put out by the government on grafting apple trees. I have land up there, and I'm always resolving to be a farmer, and then it goes away after a little while. I do a lot of work on the land, but not professionally.

I read poetry I suppose more than a lot of people do—just for pleasure. I have a large number of books of poetry in my house, and I just keep going back to them. And they would be anything from Wordsworth to May Swenson to Muriel Rukeyser to . . . it wouldn't matter. It depends on my mood.

QUESTION: Would you evaluate other American writers, particularly playwrights such as O'Neill, Williams, and Inge?

MILLER: I can't evaluate writers. What I can do is say what, if I've gotten something from somebody, because we're all, I think, in a boiling soup. What one man or woman is doing is . . . we change the flavor by what we add, and it changes all of us.

QUESTION: Your thoughts on Ibsen are well known. What of Pirandello (never mentioned by you in earlier interviews)?

MILLER: I must say that I didn't appreciate Pirandello—I didn't know about Pirandello, I don't think, in college. In the last fifteen years, though, I've come to regard him as maybe one of the most important writers of the Twentieth Century. He really formulated for the stage at least, the temporal concept which is be-deviling everybody. That is, the question of what is real in terms of space and time, when the human subconscious is so powerful and recreates reality wherever it turns its attention. He started out, I suppose—I'm just imagining this—I imagine that early on in his career they must have regarded him as a trickster and as rather amusing and comical when, of course, he was a tragic writer. He was looking at the whole thing from a tragic viewpoint—which is, I think, possibly why it seems so lasting. His work is quite lasting. How popular it is, I don't really know, but I don't see that many productions—at least in New York. They should be. *Henry IV* is a really massive piece of work.

QUESTION: Is there any common denominator—a consistent factor that great playwrights share?

MILLER: I think the one thing which they share, which is difficult to evaluate after they're gone, is, to use that awful word, their relevance for the moment—because the theatre is a very passing show. Most of the time, it is a matter of fads and fashion, as to what seems to be important. The most discouraging thing anybody can do is to look up the list of Pulitzer prize winning plays of the last decades and you see what I mean. I'm sure that however many there are, ninety-five percent or more you wouldn't even know the titles of anymore. It's quite amazing. So that, paradoxically enough, in order to last very long they have to be very temporal. They have to be applicable right then and there. Most plays don't get a second chance; I've said that frequently. If they fail the first time, they dispirit and discourage all imitators—that is, all the amateurs, the other producers. And it takes generations before somebody fresh with no preconceptions looks at the script and thinks that he understands what the author was about. And sometimes that's true. It even happened with Shakespeare for a long time. So I would think that the first thing that—I don't know about "great," but—*significant* playwrights need is a relevance to their time. Otherwise we probably just would never think about them, never hear of them, if you haven't heard of them when they're going, when they're alive. They just become part of the debris of history, and God knows how many plays we've lost because they didn't seem to pertain to anything at the moment. Who knows? But that's one thing they'd have to have.

I personally prefer to think that the ones that I know who have lasted—the ones I know about—have shared a kind of tragic vision of man. The ones that are too happy about it all seem to fade away. Now I'm thinking of, as a contradiction to that statement, Wilde—Oscar Wilde—who is a formidable writer of comedy. But, of course, his view of man is, underneath the laughs, a pretty tragic view. He's giving you the bright side of that disastrous vision he had. So, it's maybe not inapplicable even in his case.

QUESTION: Have you been able to discern *your* influence on newer playwrights and the theatre?

MILLER: I really haven't, excepting I've noticed from time to time—I used to, more than now; I don't think it's so fashionable now—that there was a tendency to misuse flashbacks. They thought I was using flashbacks in *Death of a Salesman*. And they're not flashbacks, in my opinion. There was a lot of imitation of that play. Beyond that, I can't say. I don't go to the theatre that much.

QUESTION: You've said that the theatre can't die because "we must have, in order to live at all, some kind of symbolization of our lives," [*Theater Essays*, p. 308] and you speak of an art which expresses "the collective consciousness of people." As well, anyone who has seen your plays—almost every one treats this in one way or another—and read your essays recognizes the central fact and importance of the word "community" to you. Would you expand for a moment on your concept of "community" and "the collective consciousness of people"?

MILLER: The concept of community, I think this is a vital notion, is a very slippery one and difficult to talk about. But, to be boringly obvious about it, the community, meaning the audience for all intents and purposes, in the theatre, and the atmosphere outside the theatre, *lean* on plays directly. If tomorrow morning we had suddenly an atomic strike on New Mexico, and the United States were confronting doomsday, it's perfectly clear, isn't it, that the theatre simply couldn't go on the way it's going on now. There's no way that it could do that.

QUESTION: How might this concept of community be said to apply to your major protagonists, Willy Loman, Eddie Carbone, or John Proctor, all men, if we are to understand them, seen in the context of the community in which they live?

MILLER: I suppose that I have assumed the collective or the community, not in any one member necessarily, but as a whole, contains the ethos that the character is working with and against. They contain the source of all the moral energy in the play. It may be a community that is perfectly visible as it is in *The Crucible*, after all, and it is in *A View from the Bridge*. Or it may be not visible as in *Death of a Salesman* where we don't have a crowd on the stage; we only have what they believe on the stage. The men are in the society, there is no question about it. They are working, whether openly or implicitly, in relation to the ethos of the time that they are in—and the class of people that they're in even. I don't figure this out. I mean, this is nothing I have to diagram. It is just the way I feel anyway. I think that man is a social animal; there's no getting away from it. He's in society the way a fish is in the water, and the water is in the fish. I can't possibly disentangle them, and I think those plays indicate that. As a matter of fact, I've tried, I think, in the interest of truthfulness, to take as far as I can that awareness of my own in these dramas—because I'm under no illusions that people really invent themselves. They do to a degree, but they're working with a social matrix.

QUESTION: If part of *your* matrix, then, is the Greeks, and part the product of the Thirties, how important do you feel ethnic background is for an American writer? Has it influenced you at all? What of socio-economic background?

MILLER: These are vital for a writer, in America especially. Obviously, they form his vocabulary—in a way. You can't conceive of Faulkner except as a part of that society, a part of that region, even though he transcends it. But any writer worth discussing, that's true of. That again forms one pole of the tensions that a writer works with. He's both trying to express it, at times he's trying to transcend it, in certain cases he might even try to disguise it. But it's there; it is part of his equipment, part of the given that he has to work with. There's no doubt about it. Of course, the final question, as always, is how good a work he has done. But that he has been openly expressing some ethnicity is beside the point really. We've got writers like Bernard Malamud who is essentially a Yiddish writer, a Jewish writer in America. But Bellow probably isn't. He's one step, or several steps, beyond that. I'm Jewish, but I have a different attitude · toward these problems in my work—toward that situation. And there are as many Roth—there's still another—. Updike is sort of an ethnic. He has responded, I think, in subtle ways to the ethnicity of so many of the Jewish novelists around him and of the influence of Jewish critics, and has asserted himself as what he is. It makes for more richness to me. I think it just enriches the whole scene.

QUESTION: You have said [in a 1958 interview with Philip Gelb published as "Morality and Modern Drama"] in response to John Beaufort's claim that Willy Loman is not the average American citizen, that Willy can't be the average American man, but that Willy Loman is a person "who embodies in himself some of the most terrible conflicts running through the streets of America today."

If we agree with "Tragedy and the Common Man" (1949) that "tragedy is the consequence of a man's total compulsion to evaluate himself justly, [and] his destruction in the attempt posits a wrong or an evil in his environment . . ." and, further, that the "under-lying struggle is that of the individual attempting to gain his 'rightful' position in his society"—would Willy have been better off in the 1960s? Or today? Is the social environment better or worse today? What would have happend to Willy Loman today? Are there more Willys today than ever before? Have the conflicts deepened or lessened?

MILLER: This has to be a subjective answer, because I'm not a pollster, and strictly off the cuff because I don't think in those terms really. I mean that Willy is for me a dramatic character. He's not a sociological entity. He's not a real citizen—put it that way. He doesn't vote or have problems outside the ones that I deal with in the play. He's fiction.

But I suppose I would have to say that I think that the society around him now, as opposed to when I was writing, would be even more amorphous than it was then. And part of the problem he had was amorphousness. He not only couldn't climb the ladder, he couldn't find it. And now I think it's possible life is even more abstract than it was then. I have just the gut feeling now that maybe people haven't even the security to believe that *they're* right and that something is wrong. We've *dismissed* the whole society, which means we've *accepted* the whole society. I mean everything now is up for grabs. But at the same time, the kind of alienation that exists now seems to me to be quiescent, it isn't actively taking up psychological arms against anything. People fundamentally feel defeated. You see, Willy is not defeated. Everybody thought he was in those days, but he isn't. If he were, then he would be sort of sitting on a rocking chair and telling you some of his troubles. He would be quiescent. And I get the sense now that there is a feeling abroad that the situation is either so complicated that nobody can solve it or that there's simply no use in making broad, generalized outcries—such as that play makes. And, maybe, maybe Willy still had, and this I realize is paradoxical, but he may still have carried forth a kind of beautifully naive insistence on certain values—even some which never really existed. He keeps talking about the old days when people acted better toward each other, and I strictly doubt that that was true, but nevertheless he feels they were. There was a comradeship among people of the same *métier*, the same kind of work. Perhaps that's true. I don't know. But the separation now of human, intimate psychological need and the marketplace is cool, almost total. You see, Willy is demanding of the market and of his job some real return psychically. He simply can't settle for being this robot that apparently people now believe is inevitable. Many of them even seek it. They want to be a robot; they don't want to be forced to feel anything. He's revolting because he's being told not to feel anything. And I'm wondering whether it hasn't gone way over the edge, comparatively speaking, now: where the technocratic idea has won that the human being is there to serve the machine. Simply. And that this is now accepted as inevitable and probably even as a social good. And that the person who isn't able to be absorbed into the machine is a misfit, and has to be psychoanalyzed into accepting this proposal. So things have gone farther than they were then probably.

QUESTION: You have said several times [as late as 1967 in "It Could Happen Here—And Did"] that the paranoid politics of McCarthyism could happen again. Is our society farther from such a possibility following the events of the past few years?

MILLER: Well, of course, I'm of the belief that paranoia is just beneath the skin of almost all of us. We can be persuaded without too such difficulty that hidden, undefined dangers are imminent and can overwhelm us. And consequently the next step is to believe that there is a group in the society carrying explosives to blow us all up. As we all know, paranoia is based, in part, on reality. Let's face it, there are people walking around with bombs who really would like to blow us all up. The question is how many and when. One simply has to learn how to forget this fact. That's normality. The paranoid is simply somebody who can't forget it, who can't forget what we all know to be true. The rest of us lapse into some persuasion that we're living in a more or less reasonable situation and that if we step on the starter of our automobile it is not going to set off a time bomb. The paranoid knows goddamned well that it is going to set off a time bomb.

QUESTION: Then the playwright as *vates*, as prophet, sees things getting worse?

MILLER: Yeah, oh yeah, in that sense.

QUESTION: Which is a significant sense.

MILLER: Which is a hell of a significant sense. But, yes, it is.

QUESTION: In 1972, you said [in "Arthur Miller vs. Lincoln Center" in *The New York Times*] that "our cultural life seems to be drying up, we're becoming a utilitarian society in the crudest sense, namely, that which is not bought cannot be art." In the half dozen years since then, has our cultural life improved, gotten worse, or remained the same?

MILLER: This is a question I would rather not answer, I'd rather ask it because when I compare the present with what I knew of the past, I think there are probably more opportunities now than there used to be—and in more places—to see some kind of art, to hear some kind of music, and to participate, even, in some kind of art be it amateur or semiprofessional, a symphony orchestra or theatre company or something like that. I don't know the statistics; I have a feeling that there are more, and that the chances are better now.

Let's not forget that when I started in theatre there was no off-Broadway theatre, of any description. You arrived in New York, if you were stupid enough to come here, with a play which a commercial producer would put on Broadway or you didn't ever see your work done. Even in colleges when I was at school, the drama department only did the latest Broadway hits. My first play—nobody at Michigan would do it. Not because they didn't like it, but because nobody ever did a student's plays, and it was finally done by the Hillel Foundation which had no theatre. But they had a building with an auditorium which was for meetings, and they let me use the auditorium. And we got a gang of actors from the drama department who put the play on there. And this was not particularly reactionary. There were very few places in the United States—I think Carnegie Tech was one; there was a drama school there, but I suppose you could count them on one hand—where a new play by a student could be produced. Of course, this goes on all over the place all the time now. Not only in colleges but in New York. So it's better that way than it used to be.

QUESTION: *All My Sons* does [as you say in the Introduction to the *Collected Plays* (1957)] "lay siege to . . . the fortess of unrelatedness." Has this sense of social unrelatedness worsened or been ameliorated in the years since that play was first written?

MILLER: Just as a remark, I would say that the whole notion of going into a theatre and sitting with a lot of other people and watching a spectacle, especially now when you can watch television or the movies with greater convenience, tells me that, apart from the fact that it's a little more exciting to see a live actor on the stage, it's also exciting to sit next to human beings. I think people need that; they have to feel that when they laugh together there is a relatedness. They learn what's funny.

It's an old story, for example, that if you've got a comedy, and you play that comedy to five or six people who are usually partisans of the play, I mean they'd be the producer and the staff, it's a totally different procedure than if you'd play it to a house full of people. Part of the reason is that we laugh because others are laughing. They form part of our judgment as to what is funny. We also react emotionally, in part, because of the way others are reacting. We are social beings; there is nothing degrading about that. It's rather an elevated thought, in fact. It's what will save us if anything does.

I think that the theatre does break down an unrelatedness in people—to a degree. It refreshes the spirit which now experiences the reactions of other people, if only through looking at a common spectacle.

QUESTION: In 1966, [in the *Paris Review* interview] you didn't quite seem overdelighted at the movement in theatrical criticism away from reporters who had no references in aesthetic theories of drama to academic critics or "graduates of that school." Yet you have apparently an excellent relationship with "academics" and are considerate of them. Are, then, criticism and scholarship two separate entities in your mind as they might be said to apply to your work? Do you read criticism of your work?

MILLER: The question of criticism is very important; maybe it's too important for me to speak off the cuff about. Important only in this respect: it can lead or mislead the young and burden people sometimes for years and years and years with misconceptions about the value of things so that they overvalue or dismiss out of hand plays, writers, actors, actresses because some critic who has their ear for the moment has taught them to do so. A critic, like any other professional who is not fundamentally a creative artist should try to make himself unnecessary. That is, he should try, if this is conceivable, to so educate the taste of his public that they don't need him anymore. This, of course, is the worst thing you can say to any living critic that I know of—and understandably. But I do believe that. I think that a critic is a teacher, should be a teacher. He shouldn't be a kind of clown who is trying to distract you from what you're supposed to be concentrating on. There's been a kind of undergrowth of performing critics—critics who one is supposed to observe as though they are doing a number. Those people, I think, get in the way of the act.

The first thing I would love to see in a critic is a certain modesty, because we now have far more critics than artists—because there's far more white space to fill. The arts almost exist in order for these people to write about them. And that's going a little far. I think that the whole question of why somebody likes something is not even discussed anymore. It's all a question of temperament. This critic has a temperament which prefers English to American whatever it may be, from tweed to tragedy. Another one really wants musicals. This is like having doctors who don't like measles, but they like tuberculosis—incompetent where it comes to measles but know everything there is about tuberculosis. There's something obscene sometimes about the showing-off, which is usually at the expense of some artist who may well be contributing something, for all one would know. Of course, one will never know because they close up shows too quickly.

I'm afraid that I have to agree with Chekhov who said that if he had listened to the critics he would have ended up drunk in the gutter. This goes on forever.

QUESTION: How important were the critics to you?

MILLER: They were very important to help me find an audience. This is what I'm talking about. I owe a great deal to Brooks Atkinson with whose work I often times disagreed deeply. His standards, his feeling about the theatre was oftentimes not mine; however, without him I would have had a much more difficult time at a crucial point in my life and that is when I wrote *All My Sons*. I was unknown, and so was the director, Elia Kazan; so were most of the actors in the play like Arthur Kennedy who was a young, upcoming actor but not very well known. And Karl Malden, whom nobody had heard of. The reviews in general were okay but not enough to really run that play for very long. Atkinson came back in a Sunday piece and he really did a tremendous reconsideration of the play, and that made it. From that day, the audience came and they listened, and it won all the prizes, and I won an audience. Without him, I probably wouldn't have, at least not then, and I'd have had to try all over again. Having won that audience, it made it easier for me to take off with *Death of a Salesman* and to try new approaches to the theatre, and to break up some of the reigning realism—I should say naturalism; it wasn't realism.

QUESTION: Do you ever read academic scholarship on your own work?

MILLER: I don't, unless somebody sends it, and I happen to be opening that mail right at the moment when I can read it. The only reason is—I have no disrespect for academic people at all—it's just that I think reading too much criticism of oneself makes you self-conscious—for a few hours. I'm not really all that interested in the past, in my own past. I have problems tomorrow morning. I've got a lyric I want to finish, or I've got a story I want to write, and that criticism can't help me do that at all.

QUESTION: In 1967, you were prouder of *The Crucible* than anything else you had written. Does that remain so a decade later?

MILLER: I'll tell you about *The Crucible;* first of all, it's the most produced of my plays, more than *Salesman* or anything else. I'm proud of it in the sense that it seems to reach the young very well. They do it all over the place. And I get very moving letters from them sometimes about where it has sent their minds in relation to liberty, in relation to the rights of people. It seems to affect their living as citizens. Which is terrific. And I kind of feel proud about that. They're stronger in their belief in the best things in America because of that.

Equally, it makes a statement abroad. *The Crucible*, I think I've said once, when it gets produced in some foreign country, especially in Latin America this has been true, it's either that a dictator is about to arise and take over, or he has just been over-thrown. I'm glad something of mine is useful as a kind of a weapon like that. It speaks for people against tyranny, and that's nothing to be ashamed of.

QUESTION: When Philip Gelb asked you about "the discipline whereby you sit down and write regularly," you responded that "I don't know how to write regularly. I wish I did. It's not possible to me." Yet, very few serious American playwrights have produced the quantity of your plays. How, then, do you work? To what do you attribute the magnitude of your canon?

MILLER: About my work, working habits—frankly, I think like most writers who last at all I work all the time, that is, even when I'm not working. It's like Chekhov in *The Sea Gull:* Trigorin, when Nina says to him how marvelous it must be to be a writer, and he says something to the effect [that] Oh God, yes, it's marvelous, but you're never relieved of it; I look up at the sky right now, and there are some clouds going by and I think, well, I must make a note that that cloud looks like a grand piano. [Miller is paraphrasing Trigorin's long speech to Nina in Act II of *The Sea Gull.*]

I just never stop. But the amount I've written discourages me. I think I should have written far more. I destroy, I'm afraid, a large proportion of what I write. I can't satisfy myself—I can't find really what I'm trying to say, and there's an enormous amount of destruction of material that I go through, trunkfuls of stuff which I dread even thinking about. So, if it does seem that I've written a lot, I assure you I've written much more, but I'm afraid that I will never come to complete it.

QUESTION: What do you do in addition to your writing? What are your hobbies? That is, what do you do to relax, to escape the pressures of the muse?

MILLER: Well, I live in the country; I have really almost twenty years now, all the time. I've always had a place in the country, but I've lived there winter and summer for almost twenty years. I'm a pretty good cabinet maker, and I make furniture now and then. I also keep a good garden. I resolved to do some sculpting, but I haven't gotten to it yet. I play tennis. And, I guess I wander around wondering why I'm not writing—most of the time.

QUESTION: You are the winner of the Hopwood Awards of 1936 and 1937 (University of Michigan), the Donaldson Award, two Antoinette Perry Awards, The New York Drama Critics Award, the Pulitzer Prize, and the Gold Medal from the National Institute of Arts and Letters. As well, you were the recipient of a doctorate (L. H. D.) from the University of Michigan (1956). What is your feeling about this kind of recognition? What is your attitude toward prizes generally? Do you think of the Nobel?

MILLER: Prizes. Well, I just wish they would stop giving any at all. But, of course, I'm an old man now I guess. These prizes, most of the time most prizes are given so that we will recognize the prize-giver, and he will achieve some distinction by giving out the prize. The Nobel Prize, for example, the list of writers who never got it is certainly as grand in its achievement as the ones who did get it. I'm not even going to bother running down the names of the left-out in the last fifty years.

QUESTION: What of television? TV has done nice productions of *Crucible, Price, Vichy,* and *Fall.* Do you like what television has done with your plays? What of the recent "Fame" production?

MILLER: Television cuts plays, and I don't like that about it. Incidentally, *Vichy* had the best production I've ever seen of that play, apart maybe from the original that we did on Broadway—or off-Broadway rather. That production directed by Stacy Keach was a marvel, I thought. On the whole, the others are not as good, I have to admit, even though I like the people who did them. I'm afraid that most of it is due to the fact that you can't cut plays without losing something, especially plays like mine which were cut already. You lose—you cut the sinews, and things dangle that were once muscularly connected and vigorous. You weaken them, and I'm afraid that this is true of both mine and other plays I've seen on television.

As for the "Fame," they missed the whole first twelve minutes of that, and I'm sorry that that happened. The rest of it was very good—was very well done. They did not know how to do a *crucial* scene in the beginning which set the whole play up. I'm sorry I wasn't there; it would have been very simple to do it.

QUESTION: What of television's famous impact for good or ill—your opinion? Do you watch any television? What?

MILLER: I watch television. Yes. I live in the country, and sometimes you want to see what's happening in the big world. I can't say I watch it at any length. It tires me out, and it's usually terribly superficial no matter what it's doing. It's being chased by the two arms of the clock. There's something hysterical about it always.

Unfortuantely, I'm afraid, it is the only art probably most Americans ever get to see—if you want to call it an art. That's where they get the news, and that's where they get their opinions apparently. I personally would love to take it more seriously if the institutions would permit it, but they don't on the whole.

Now, I think, for example, the *Holocaust* program, which was done like a soap opera, I simply have to admit a fact, and that is that it brought to consciousness something which otherwise was not there. I've just talked to my brother-in-law who works in Germany, and he brought me some press comment on the *Holocaust*, which just happens to have gone on recently, and apparently it was a most devastating event in German history since World War II. Forty-seven percent of the German people watched that program. Now, forty-seven percent of the German people have not done one thing together—whatever it was. And he said that it had probably the most profound effect of any event in the public history of the German Republic. A whole generation knew nothing about this—the young generation. The older one, that knew, wasn't talking. The teachers had never been taught this. It was like you dropped out ten years of your life and lost them.

So, television is maybe the single most important artistic fact—God save the term—in the United States today. They say—I can't believe this—but I read somewhere the average American looks at it—I can't remember now whether it was—six hours [daily]. Well, what are we doing all the time? Don't they work or something? Apparently not. But I imagine in some homes it's on all the time with nobody watching it. But, anyway, it's a formidable fact. I mean, certainly the Bible at its most popular hour was not studied six hours a day.

QUESTION: What remains to be done? What are you working on at the moment?

MILLER: I'm just completing a rather shortish play—I don't know really how long it's going to take to perform, maybe an hour and a half—which I began in 1969, which to my astonishment is ten years ago. But these numbers are meaningless at this point.

I just did a film which is based on a memoir of a woman who was a member of the orchestra of the Auschwitz concentration camp called *Playing For Time*. That's in the process of being set up.

QUESTION: Does the play have a working title?

MILLER: Yes. It's called *Smoke*. I don't know whether it'll continue to be called *Smoke*, but I kind of like that title now.

They're doing a new production of *The Price* on 42nd Street in the Harold Clurman Theatre, which is just off-Broadway I suppose you'd call it. Which has a hell of a cast, and I have high hopes for that; Fritz Weaver is in it and Mitch Ryan and Joe Buloff and Scotty Bloch.

QUESTION: Will you be involved in the production?

MILLER: Well, I'll be involved in the sense that I'll go down after a couple of weeks of rehearsal and see what they've done, and give them my invaluable advice. But I'm not going to direct it or anything. I'm seriously considering directing my new play, though, which I may do in the same theatre.

QUESTION: Do you have a projected date for it?

MILLER: If I get done in the next couple of weeks, I may do it soon after that—if I can cast it properly, and I think I can.

QUESTION: How about the musical?

MILLER: The musical is called *Up From Paradise* and is supposed to go into production in the Fall.

QUESTION: Hasn't it been produced before?

MILLER: We did that in a sort of workshop performance in Washington last year. However, it wasn't complete; a lot of the music and lyrics hadn't been written yet, but now it's complete. It has a producer named Charles Hollerith, and I think we'll go ahead. So it seems anyway.

QUESTION: You are doing the lyrics.

MILLER: I do the lyrics and, of course, the book. It's based on *Creation of the World and Other Business*—vaguely. It's quite different.

And I've written and published two short stories this year in *Esquire* and in *Atlantic*. And I've written this book on China; well, it's really forty thousand words. It's a long essay or a short book, and, I don't know, other odds and ends. So that's where it is.

QUESTION: How do you want to be remembered? What is you estimation of your legacy? How well do you think your intentions and reception jibe? How will literary history treat Arthur Miller? Are you satisfied with that?

MILLER: I really don't know how to answer that, frankly. As for literary history, it just doesn't seem like anything I ought to think about even. I've seen so many writers, frankly, that had some effect on their time or even seemed permanent whose names would probably hardly be known now except to historians. There's always something new under the sun. There's always a change. Who can ever hope to predict any of this?

I've hoped that I've done my work honestly—and well. That's all I can really do.

Miller's Roots and
His Moral Dilemma:
or, Continuity from Brooklyn
to *Salesman*

Daniel Walden°

Arthur Miller, born in 1915 (the same year Saul Bellow was born) to a middle-class Jewish family in New York City, grew up in a religious framework nominally orthodox but more likely liberal conservative in fact. His father manufactured ladies coats, his mother, a former school teacher, devoted herself to Arthur, Kermit (his older brother), and Joan (his younger sister). Like a growing number of middle-class American Jewish boys he was, quite at variance with the tradition of his Eastern European heritage, an indifferent student but a promising athlete. In 1928, the year of his bar mitzvah, when his father's business suddenly declined, the family moved to Brooklyn, to a neighborhood in which many of his relatives already lived. Although the Jews shared the neighborhood with the Italians and the Irish, there was relative harmony. Unlike Henry Roth, who suffered a lifelong trauma when his family moved from a Jewish neighborhood to a disharmonious one, Miller grew up in a multi-ethnic homogeneous ethos.[1]

At James Madison High School and then at Abraham Lincoln High, Miller admitted that "we were none of us encumbered by anything resembling a thought." On the other hand, reality began to close in as the Depression hit his friends and neighbors. Once he noticed a crowd about the Bank of the United States a few blocks away. He noticed the effect mortgage payments had on his block. He observed the closed stores and the classmates who dropped out of school to work. He heard quarrels in homes. He saw the lot that was used for football games turned into a junkyard. After graduation, at sort of dead end, he applied for admission to both Cornell University and Michigan University. When he was refused he went to work for his father.[2]

Working in his father's factory was a revelation. If the economic effects of the Depression had begun to awaken his social conscience, the social conditions in the Seventh Avenue district shocked him. The arrogance, cruelty, hardness and vulgarity of the buyers, in particular, affected him in a way he never forgot. He saw his father and the company's salesman treated like dirt. In a sketch

°This essay was written specifically for this volume and is published here for the first time by permission of the author.

written at that time, "In Memorium," he described a salesman named Schoenzeit who committed suicide by jumping in front of a subway train.[3] Schoenzeit, which breaks down to "es is shayn zeit" in Yiddish, means "it is already time" or more literally and ironically, "a nice time." Because Miller knew Yiddish and spoke Yiddish as a young man, it seems certain that the salesman in the sketch for whom he felt sympathy in the 1930s was the basis for the salesman on whom he based Willie Loman some seventeen years later.[4] Reacting to the broken, poverty stricken man who asked him for subway fare, he felt "both rage and pity for this decrepit soul who, it seemed, aged many years as he turned to me. I know then that he felt as though his life was ended, that he was merely being pushed by outside forces. And though his body went on as before, his soul inside had crumpled and broken beyond repair." As Miller put it much later, from this shattering experience he had learned "the heroism of those who know, at least, how to endure [hope's] absence." He had begun to put things together, to see "how things connected."[5]

At the University of Michigan, to which he was finally admitted, conditionally, on his second try, he first was exposed to the articulation of the despair and confidence and analysis of the Depression and the New Deal. In contrast to the harmony that had prevailed in his early years, he met and took part in debates, and in passionately held arguments. At the end of his sophomore year, needing money badly, he wrote a play in four days for which he won the Avery Hopwood Award of $250.00. The play was called *Honors at Dawn*. The next year his *No Villain* again won the Hopwood Prize. Both plays, reflecting the influence of the decade, and of Clifford Odets, were social protest plays, stressing the necessity of integrity and responsibility in a time of crisis. In *Honors at Dawn*, sibling rivalry and familial strife were part of a thirties, quasi-Marxist struggle between the evils of capitalism and the goodness of the people. *They Too Arise*, which followed, an expanded and revised version of *No Villain*, was a play about a middle-class Jewish family reminiscent of both Odets' *Awake and Sing* and Miller's family. Based on the tension between loyalty and principle, the play followed the outlines of autobiography closely. Abe Simon, the owner of a small wholesale clothing firm, was once a salesman and is now struggling to keep his head above water and the family together. His wife, frustrated and yet infinitely good-hearted, tries to persuade son Ben to marry a rich manufacturer's daughter to save the family from ruin. Meanwhile, Abe, caught in the middle, is criticized for not being able to provide for his family. At this time, son Arnie, just back from the Universtiy of Michigan, crosses a picket line at his father's place, not knowing the situation, and is beaten up. Feeling betrayed by his father, Arnie joins the strikers. At the end, torn between family loyalty and his belief in the nobility of labor, he chose his principles. In turn, Abe, seeing both sons choose independence, becomes critical of the treatment the other bosses give to the working man. "I can't see that it's the way for Jewish men to act," he complains; his wife agrees, saying, "a lotta things we gotta learn."[6]

They Too Arise is the work of a playwright at the beginning of his career.

Essentially autobiographical, it focused on a family driven by Jewish values and American values. The drive for success, so eagerly assimilated by the Jewish immigrants, was matched by the hold of the Old World's principles and teachings. Needing to hold his family together, Abe relied ultimately on the American Dream. As he told Ben: "I wanna see you on top. You can do it, Ben, without me. You gotta do it, Ben. It ain't fair that I should give my life like this and go out with—nothing Ben."[7] Unfortunately, like so many of Miller's characters, Abe couldn't communicate with his sons and didn't understand why. Proud to see them go off to college he was uncomfortable with the results of their education. Rejoicing in their ability to learn, in the Jewish tradition, he was ill at ease in the face of their moral commitment. Having staked his life on the expectation of success and the certainty that he would pass on his patrimony, he was unable to contemplate any other scenario. As he told his son, "It ain't right it should end like this." With the need to hold on to some dignity he pleaded: "But as long as we got something—as long as we got what's left—whatever it is— Benny, we gotta hold on to it." But it was Arnie who articulated the triumphant refrain. Criticizing his father for his shortsightedness, as in *All My Sons* and *Death of a Salesman*, Arnie told his father that he had abdicated his responsibility to humanity but "the time has come when things don't get better unless you make them better."[8] In effect, as a result of Arnie's tirade, Abe has to struggle for his name, for his integrity, even as John Proctor did in *The Crucible*. In this way, repeatedly, it seems to me, Miller enunciated his Jewish heritage, his belief in the family and the millenia-long values of the Jewish people. As Benjamin Nelson has put it, "It is the cry of the individual conscience for its self-respect."[9] As it says in most Jewish prayerbooks on the Day of Atonement, "A good name is his here below, and the crown of immortal life beyond."

In 1938 Miller graduated from the University of Michigan. For a few months he worked for the Federal Theatre's WPA Writing Project. For the next few years he drove a truck and worked as a steamfitter in the Brooklyn Navy Yard. In 1940 he married Mary Slattery, whom he had met at the university. Significantly, Miller has consistently affirmed his Jewishness as an individual, especially in the first and most important phase of his career, while he, also consistently, sought the comfort of the mainstream with an Irish American intellectual, a world famous actress and beauty, and a talented photographer from Germany. Meanwhile, writing radio scripts was good practice although of necessity the medium demanded more circumspection than he cared for. He knew that though he was refining his skills he "was writing about what lay outside" him.[10] In 1943 he began a new play called *The Man Who Had All the Luck*. Although it closed a week after it opened in November, 1944, it served as a preparation for the future. In writing it, according to Miller, "the crux of *All My Sons* . . . was formed; and the roots of *Death of a Salesman* were sprouted." [11] Again, material America was pitted against the older morality. In Alger-like fashion, David Frieber, a mechanic, achieved wealth, married his sweetheart, but, unlike Alger's heroes, continued to expect divine wrath for his run of luck.

Only at the end, through a series of unbelievable accidents, did David become aware of his responsibility for his life. Incidentally, sometime before the opening on Broadway, David Frieber became David Beeves, possibly a dramatic improvement but almost certainly a conscious or unconscious move toward universalism.

In 1945 Miller published his only novel. *Focus*, originally conceived of as a play, tells the story of Lawrence Newman, a nondescript, middle-class office worker who, on getting a pair of glasses, suddenly appears Jewish. As a result, he loses his job, his neighbors shun him, and, after he marries a woman, also Gentile, who looks Jewish, he is harassed unbearably. At the end, after confronting anti-Semitism in a violent form, he discovered his own identity. Meeting Finkelstein, the neighborhood's Jewish grocer, whose family had fled the pogroms in Poland, he accused Jews of having no principles. "Did I ever cheat you in my business," asked Finkelstein. Newman answered: "It's not what *you've* done, it's what others of your people have done." In other words, says Finkelstein, "when you look at me you don't see me." Unable to answer, Newman fled. The next time he met the grocer, however, Newman advised him to move. Not long after, Finkelstein rescued Newman from some pro-Nazi hoodlums, and together they fought against them. At the police station, when Newman lodged a complaint, the policeman asked how many of "you people" are there on the block? There are the Finkelsteins, Newman replied. Just you and them? the cop continued. Yes, just them and myself, Newman agreed. But telling the story, "Newman felt as though he were setting down a weight which for some reason he had been carrying and carrying."[12]

Focus was a didactic novel, a novel with a message. It depended on a trick, that the reader believe that putting on a pair of glasses could make a person appear Jewish. In part derived from an incident that happened to Miller, just after high school, the book owed most of its impulse to the vicious anti-Semitism in the New York area in the 1930s and 1940s, fomented by various Nazi front groups. As a result, in Miller's mind, the novel was a story about irrational hatred and prejudice. It was also a nightmare experience, symbolic of the moral crises of the 1940s. It was a story about human character and the possibility that Newman was a victimizer as well as a victim, the same point made by Bellow in *The Victim*. It also represented the way in which a clear image appeared to Newman, and how he was able to break through his stereotypical thinking to the point of dealing with and recognizing just one Jew, Finkelstein.[13]

The idea for *All My Sons*, his next play, came to Miller one evening when a relative told the Millers about a family in her neighborhood in the Middle West whose daughter had turned in her father because he had shipped faulty parts to the Army. As Miller remembered the event, "The girl's action astounded me. An absolute response to a moral command." Suddenly the hints in *The Man Who Had All the Luck* came together. Suddenly "Something was crystal clear to me for the first time since I had begun to write plays," he said, "and it was the crisis of the second act, the revelation of the full loathsomeness of an anti-social action."[14] As in *They Too Arise*, family loyalty and success were the twin goals.

In this case, Joe Keller, who has shipped faulty parts to the Air Force, and succeeded on having it blamed on his partner, justified his actions saying he did it for the family. His life had been based on achievement and acquisition, on the American Dream of success, and his belief that he could pass on his business and his principles to his sons. After finding out that his son Larry had died because of his choice of success and family loyalty over morality, he is stung by his other son Chris' denunciation: "What the hell do you mean you did it for me? Don't you have a country? Don't you live in the world?"[15]

Originally the play was titled *The Sign of the Archer*, a reference to Mrs. Keller's penchant for astrology. Shifting the emphasis to where the conflict was, Miller followed the line of his essential thinking and orientation. As Joe admitted at the end: "Sure he was my son. But I think to him [Larry] they were all my sons. And I guess they were."[16] In short, in pointing to the theme relating to "all my sons," he was searching for a way to deliver his message but in a more universal context. "Why shall I continue to feign ignorance of cause," Miller argued in 1941. "Why try to make heroes of the damned and the pathetic? They strive for no [thing but the] scene that has passed. The hero today fights to the death for that which is to come. And now in my strength so do I."[17] The point is that though *All My Sons* is not saturated with the Jewish atmosphere of *They Too Arise*, or is directly related to anti-Semitism as in *Focus*, it is concerned in the best sense with man's capacity for suffering for his ideals and integrity, for humanism, subjects which Jews historically know a good deal about. In Miller's words, "possibly the greatest truths we know have come out of suffering. The problem is not to undo suffering or wipe it off the face of the earth, but to make it inform our lives so that we regard it as a necessary part of existence and try to pluck from it what growth and wisdom we can, instead of trying to cure ourselves of it constantly, and arrive at that lobotomized sense of what they call happiness in which nobody learns anything but an ultimate informed indifference."[18]

Death of a Salesman, Miller's most celebrated play, derived from "In Memoriam," written in 1932, and an unfinished play written in 1936. Explaining that playwrights often do not know what is beneath the surface or what they have already done, that explanations are often rationalizations after the fact, Miller said:

> The best proof of it is that I started writing *Death of a Salesman* one day in Connecticut. I wrote the whole play. Then, in one of my annual fits of neatness, I decided to clean out closets, suitcases, and so on, and make what I call order. . . . And in the course of that I discovered old notebooks, and in one old notebook which dated back to 1936 when I was at college, there was a play about a salesman of which I'd written an act and a half. All these characters were there in a different form, but they were the same people, and obviously I had been striving as a student to start to grapple with the material. I had completely forgotten that I had written an act and a half of the play. . . . I'm saying the obvious, which is that we're bound by a certain unconscious continuity.[19]

To most people *Death of a Salesman* is a play about human beings, about a salesman, his values, his family, and the American system. I would contend that *Salesman* is a play about a sane and rational human being, originally a Jewish salesman, who comes to grips finally with the existential question, Who am I? and who faces the truths of his life. For Miller, because there is in him "a sensitization, so to speak, in relation to the rest of mankind or to the rest of my cohabitants of this area anyway,"[20] there is the compulsion to wrestle with the forces surrounding him. Arguing with Eugene O'Neill's interest in the relation of man to God, Miller wrote that his religion had no Gods but godlike powers: "The powers of economic crisis and political imperatives which had twisted, torn, eroded, and marked everything and everyone I laid eyes on."[21] In turn, maturing in a Jewish household in the 1920s and 1930s, he internalized the values of his heritage. "You have to suffer to discover anything," he once said, as he added "I sometimes sense a want of suffering." At base then, "The ultimate questions involved in any study of man, either psychological or esthetic, are questions of value, of course." Remember, he explained, that Sigmund Freud's achievements were the result of cultural or moral commitment of a sort, because of the fact that Freud "lived in a certain culture, that he was a Jew, that he was what he was and that society was what it was."[22]

In seems to me that Arthur Miller, in the first phase of his creative life, up to and including *Death of a Salesman,* was a playwright intensely concerned with and close to his Jewish heritage. True, as Leslie Fiedler put it, he "creates crypto-Jewish characters who are in habit, speech and condition of life typically Jewish American, but who are presented as something else—general-American, say, as in *Death of a Salesman.*"[23] On the other hand, looked at dispassionately, it seems to me that the general-American, or middle American, referred to is a two-level creation of life, at once Jewish and American. Recalling the thought patterns, values, syntax, and mode of his early years, Miller recreated the essence of those days in the framework of the tension of his maturing years. Committed to a system of values he had inherited and assimilated, he had to struggle against the newer system he knew, to which he had been acculturated, that might be intrinsically good but had gotten off the track.

When *Death of a Salesman* opened in Brooklyn, in 1950, in Yiddish, the reviewer wrote that "this Yiddish play is really the original, and the Broadway production was merely—Arthur Miller's translation into English."[24] With Willy Loman as an outsider in the culture, trying to hold his family together, it was the epitome of the questions Miller asked: "How may a man make of the outside world a home?" Or, more explicitly: "How may a man make for himself a home in that vastness of strangers and how may he transform that vastness into a home?"[25]

During the years that Miller was growing up, Ernest Hemingway was refining an aesthetic of simplicity and a code hero. Concentrating on individual conduct and individual relationships, he developed a "code" based on the needs of men as they manifested themselves in the basics, food, drink, sex, and physical exertion. Insofar as individuals had a responsibility it was to themselves, so long as their actions and drives were conducted with discipline and dignity. Not surprisingly, given America's historical past, including the shattering effects of the Depression on top of the catchpenny values of the preceding decades, many Americans hoped to emulate Hemingway's heroes.[26] It was the exception when Hemingway's social conscience intruded, as in *For Whom the Bell Tolls*.

For Miller, however, writing in a secular society in which our society's structure related to materialism, the development of values came out of his heterogeneous experience, religious and secular. Given that his family and his roots were always with him, given that the fact and the image of his work experiences—as in "In Memorium" and the half-finished play of 1936—were in his subconscious, it seems that an emotional-religious-psychological conflict raged just beneath the surface. In his early works he was able to dramatize those value conflicts that were close to him and almost on the surface. In his richer works, in *All My Sons* and *Death of a Salesman*, the past came rushing in, "dynamically with the inner logic of his erupting volcanic unconscious," as Dr. Daniel Schneider wrote of Willy. In psychiatry, says Schneider, this was "the return of the repressed," when a mind breaks under the invasion of primitive impulses no longer capable of compromise with reality.[27] In short, as I see it, in his career up to and including *Salesman*, Miller's Jewish heritage was in conflict with his American present. Believing in the values he assimilated from his earliest years right through his University of Michigan years, when he was a Jewish boy from New York in Ann Arbor, it was the moral dilemma of his times that was his subject.[28] As a man and playwright, he saw group identity smashed by external forces and by the demands of individualism and success. On the other hand, at the same time he perceived the ideal world as one in which "the individual was at one with his society; his conflicts with it were, in our terms, like family conflicts, the opposing sides of which nevertheless shared a mutality of feeling and responsibility."[29] In this sense, Miller proceeded from his roots. Not certain of who he was but certain of his values he tried to set forth what happens "when a man does not have a grip on the forces of life and has no sense of values which will lead him to that kind of grip . . . the implication was that there must be such a grasp of those forces, or else we're doomed."[30] These are the reasons behind Miller's portraits of Willy and Joe Keller, for example, for at base Joe's trouble was not that he could not tell right from wrong, "but that his cast of mind cannot admit that he, personally, has any viable connection with his world, his universe, or his society."[31] It seems undeniable that in attempting to deal with his moral dilemma, Miller's roots were the barb or spur reflecting his Jewish heritage and sensitivity, and responsible for his continuity of thought and treatment from Brooklyn to Broadway, from adolescence to *Death of a Salesman*.

Notes

1. Benjamin Nelson, *Arthur Miller* (New York: David McKay, 1970), pp. 13–14; and Arthur Miller, "A Boy Grew in Brooklyn," *Holiday*, 17 (March 1955), 119.

2. Miller, *Holiday*, p. 120; Nelson, *Miller*, pp. 16–18.

3. "In Memoriam" (1932), an unpublished sketch at the Humanities Research Center, University of Texas, Austin.

4. According to Mrs. Lucille Rochester, who knew Miller in his youth, Arthur had a good knowledge of Yiddish: in Joel Shatzky, "Arthur Miller's 'Jewish' Salesman," *Studies in American Jewish Literature*, 2 (Winter 1976), 9, n.3.

5. "In Memoriam," p. 3; Shatzky, p. 2; Arthur Miller, "Introduction," in *Collected Plays* (New York: Viking, 1957), p. 49; also see Miller, "The Shadow of the Gods," *Harper's*, 217 (August 1958), 36.

6. Arthur Miller, typescript, p. 38, 63; in the Theatre Collection, New York Public Library, Lincoln Center.

7. Miller, typescript, p. 57.

8. Miller, typescript, pp. 33, 47.

9. Nelson, p. 38.

10. Miller, "Introduction," p. 14.

11. Miller, "Introduction," p. 15.

12. Miller, *Focus* (New York: Harcourt Brace, 1945).

13. Nelson, p. 70.

14. Miller, "Intorduction," p. 17.

15. Miller, *All My Sons*, in *Collected Plays*, p. 116.

16. Miller, *All My Sons*, p. 126.

17. Notebook entry, October 8, 1941; in the Humanities Research Center, University of Texas, Austin.

18. Richard I. Evans, *Psychology and Arthur Miller* (New York: Dutton, 1969), p. 78, a dialogue. Although this book involves assumptions made by Dr. Evans, with which Miller aruges, there are some valuable passages that have been ignored.

19. Evans, p. 42.

20. Evans, p. 47.

21. Miller, "The Shadows of the Gods," *Harper's*, 217 (August 1958), 35–43.

22. Evans, pp. 69, 63.

23. Quoted in Eric Mottram, "Arthur Miller: Development of a Political Dramatist in America," in *Arthur Miller: A Collection of Critical Essays*, Robert W. Corrigan ed. (Englewood Cliffs, N.J.: Prentice-Hall, 1969), 23–57.

24. George Ross, review of "Death of a Salesman in the Original," *Commentary*, 11 (February 1951), 184–86.

25. Miller, "The Family in Modern Drama," *Atlantic Monthly*, 197 (April 1956), 36.

26. George De Schweinitz, "Death of a Salesman: A Note on Epic and Tragedy," *Western Humanities Review*, 14 (Winter 1960), 91–96, has an interesting discussion of America's changing value structure. Also see Charles C. Alexander, "America Rediscovered: Literature in the Thirties," in *Nationalism in American Theatre 1930–1945* (New York; Rand-McNally, 1969), pp. 25–59.

27. Daniel C. Schneider, *The Psychoanalyst and the Artist* (New York: Farrar Straus, 1950), pp. 246–55.

28. Miller, "University of Michigan," *Holiday*, 14 (December 1953), 68–70, 128–43, establishes this point beyond question.

29. Miller, "Introduction," in *A View from the Bridge* (New York: Viking, 1955), pp. 1–15.

30. Miller, "Morality and Modern Drama," interview with Philip Gelb, in *The Educational Theatre Journal*, 10 (October 1958), 198–99.

31. Miller, "Introduction," p. 19.

'What Comes Easier—'
The Short Stories
of Arthur Miller

Allen Shepherd°

As he once observed in an interview, Arthur Miller feels guilty about writing short stories, despite the considerable critical acclaim which his first collection, entitled *I Don't Need You Any More*, evoked on its appearance in 1967. "To me the great thing is to write a good play, and when I'm writing a short story it's as though I'm saying to myself, Well, I'm only doing this because I'm not writing a play at the moment."[1] In his foreword to the collection he speaks somewhat more positively, even affectionately, of the short story as "a friendly and familiar form of art,"[2] one permitting, even encouraging, a modesty of tone and sense of connection with the reader which the more aggressive and more public form of the drama denies. The great strength of a good short story, as Miller defines it, is that it can hold events and character development frozen, that it can "see things isolated in stillness" (x), rather than accelerating and condensing them, as is done in drama.

In brief, then, the short story is for Arthur Miller an occasional form, of secondary importance though not simply a diversion. It has—or may have—certain affinities with a play, economy and formal decorum, but its primary resources lie in its differences, its delineation of "[t]he object, the place, weather, the look of a person's shift of posture" (x), the intimacy of thought difficult to convey in a play.

In opening his foreword to the collection Miller speaks of "a certain continuity" (ix) evident in these nine stories written over fifteen years, 1951-1966. The title of one story, "The Misfits," might be taken as generic, for in almost every story the protagonist feels himself to be standing alone, outside, cut off from other men or from himself. So it is with 5-year-old Martin in "I Don't Need You Any More," burdened with his terrible secrets, guardian, as he thinks, of his parents' innocence and "alone outside the circle of a fine family" (22). Occasionally a resolution or reintegration is offered, as in "Monte Sant' Angelo," in which an American Jew, Bernstein, discovers in a remote Italian town a home and a past. There may be, too, a model for emulation, as in "A

°Reprinted from *Illinois Quarterly*, 34, No. 3 (1972), 37-49, by permission of the journal and the author.

Search for a Future," in which an old man, enfeebled by a stroke and incarcerated in a nursing home, one night escapes, living still for a future on the strength of will. Most often, however, as in "A Search," a saving sense of wholeness, of relation, is apprehended and desired by the protagonist but is beyond recovery.

The stories vary considerably in length, complexity, ambition and accomplishment, from a negligible sketch of less than three pages, "Glimpse of a Jockey," to an intense and sometimes incisive psychological study of almost forty pages, "I Don't Need You Any More." Although there are three such novella-length pieces, and although they apparently represent major efforts, Miller is most effective in medium-sized stories. The sketches tend to be very slight, or maudlin, as one viewer called them,[3] and the longer stories seem to carry considerable extra bulk. "The Misfits" clearly displays Miller's central thematic concerns as well as a number of his more notable fictive resources, and consequently merits detailed examination.

I

"The Misfits" is an account of a mustang-hunting expedition, carried out by plane and pickup truck by three men, the catch to be sold at 6 cents a pound for dog food. For some time the reader is uncertain just what is being planned as Miller establishes a sense of place, of a "vast prehistoric lake bed thirty miles long by seventeen miles wide, couched between two mountain ranges" (74). Although they are not actively hostile or threatening, these boundless wastes dwarf both the characters and the action they perform. Periodically, as the hunt progresses, Miller shifts focus so that the characters sink to the size of dots, and they are seen "isolated in stillness."

Scene setting is interspersed with character introduction; each of the three principals is methodically given a biography: Gay Langland, 45, Perce Howland, 22, Guido Racanelli, about 50. There is one other character, Roslyn, never seen but much on the minds of two of the men, Gay and Perce. She is an Easterner, middle-aged, college-education, with whom Gay has been living and to whom Perce has recently been introduced. Although the two men cannot share this woman, the three men do share a creed, one of independence, self-sufficiency, masculine camaraderie, a creed whose first commandment is intimated by Gay's confidently asking of their present endeavor, "Better'n wages, huh, Perce?" (64) But as comes clear later in the story, theirs is a marginal existence, and these great-grandsons of the pioneers are doomed as surely as the few remaining wild horses they hunt. Both are on the edge of extinction.

Gay is last seen driving the truck peaceful and content now that Perce has agreed to accompany him on another hunting expedition. Yet there is no escaping a Roslyn, no way to explain to her or anyone else why he had spent three days earning $35 nor any hope to overcome the "terrible longing to earn money working" for wages (73). Three men, stoic by intent, sharing a creed, discovered in a wild setting far from civilization as they prepare for a hunt, might seem to recall hunting stories of William Faulkner or Ernest Hemingway. Yet here there is no mystical buck or bear, no communion with Nature, no initiation. Hemingway provides the more likely analogue, given the terse understatement of "The Misfits," Gay's recognition that "you never kept anything" (73), Roslyn as the "rich bitch" of the piece, the animals born free but unsentimentalized. For Gay, however, there is no victory, not even that of Francis Macomber, no dramatic apotheosis. Gay drives off and the story closes with the mustangs anchored to the old lake bed, dragging for a few yards enormous truck tires.

The association of men and horses as misfits is pointed up by the balance of the story's opening and closing. As it begins, Gay "turned his head and then his body in a full circle, looking into the deep blue sky for sign of a storm" (62). As it ends, "[t]he colt turned its head and returned to her [its mother] and stood at her side with vacant eye, its nostrils sniffing the warming air" (90). The connection and the point of the connection are consistent, even inescapable. Something of the success of the story lies in the fact that in the process the men are not animalized and the horses are not humanized. Gay and his companions are not brutes or Marlboro men; the mustangs are beautiful, even momentarily pitied, but are worth, in their world, $125.

II

"Please Don't Kill Anything," as the title would suggest, seems to espouse a contrary philosophy. As reviewers unfailingly noted, the story offers a portrait of Miller's late wife, Marilyn Monroe, distraught at the presumptive fate of twenty or so trash fish discarded on the beach by commercial fishermen, to whom they are of no value. The woman, who is left nameless in the story, is full of wonder, tenderheartedness and alarm, and is possessed of a "startling shape" (58), which seems like cheating. Sam, her husband, for a time resists her pleas to save the sea robins and a passing dog happily retrieves some that Sam has thrown back, but all ends pleasantly: " 'Oh, how I love you.' she said with tears in her eyes. Then they walked home" (61).

"Please Don't Kill Anything," with its biographical genesis, presents some uncommon questions of taste and literary judgment to the critic. One sees who is who but such portraits, however warm and breathing, don't make a good story, not in and of themselves, certainly. Nor do they necessarily make a bad one, be it noted. The nub of the story lies not with the narrator's observation of the woman, but rather in the conflict which Sam experiences. He has been through this before and knows, among other things, the limits of rational persuasion. His observation concerning the miles of unprotected, unpatrolled beach is pointless before a Blakean faith that everything that lives is holy. Nature may be red in tooth and claw and fin (one of the sea robins, when picked up, disgorges a minnow) but the consequences Sam knows and fears are, in descending order, the woman's suffering, their separation, his own appearing or being foolish, and finally, even the fishes' fate. The measure of Sam is that he does not insist on a lesson being learned, and the relative complexity of his response is what gives body to the story.

Such appears to be the meaning of the story, assuming that it asks more of the reader than simple identification of one or both of the principals. The female lead might well be called a misfit, in the sense that under most circumstances she, with "her fierce tenderness toward all that lives" (59), would stand alone and know it. Here, however, in this small peaceable kingdom a resolution is at hand, romanticism is saved by realism. Whatever its virtues, the story is a sentimental one, easily envisioned with pastel illustrations by Jon Whitcomb. Its sentimentality resides, as sentimentality usually does, in simplification, in the writer's pulling hard for a response. "Then they walked home."

III

Biographical genesis and sentimentality are again potential issues in one of the longest stories in the collection, "Fitter's Night," not published previously. The scene is the Brooklyn Navy Yard in World War II and Miller's tenure there as a steam fitter during the war is reflected in an encyclopedic account of all that the protagonist's job entails. Tony Calabrese, Shipfitter First Class, is as he enters the story, a tough and bitter man who knows what the good life is and who knows he has missed it. He had had his chances.

> But at the last moment something in his make-up had always defeated him, sent him rolling back into the street and a job and a paycheck, where the future was the same never-get-rich routine. He knew he was simply not smart enough (141).

The end of Tony's hopes dates from two related happenings, his marriage and his effective disinheritance. Grandfather, the great man of the family, who owns fishing boats, announces that he is coming from Calabria to stay in America, if he approves, coming moreover with his fortune which Tony is to inherit. Mother puts the screws to Tony, telling Grandfather he has been in and out of jail since he was 12, will not work at a regular job, and is dishonoring the fine Calabrian girl he is engaged to. Grandfather demands that Margaret be married, and subsequently, that she be impregnated. Grandfather's trunk full of devalued lire is found to be worth $1,739, Margaret produces twins, and Tony's life is over.

Present events at the Navy Yard are set in counterpoint to what Tony recalls as his betrayal, "the resentment that held his life together" (149). The vision of Margaret, whom he has not touched for twelve years, and of the Italian lire, "the bills covered with wings, paintings of Mussolini, airplanes and zeros, fives, tens, . . ." (161), is what gives his life coherence and focus, in the absence of love, money and power. Tony is summoned from his safe retreat in a distant ship's compartment and to his rage and disgust sent out on a frigid winter night on an almost impossible and highly dangerous job, to straighten two bent depth charge rails on a destroyer scheduled to join a convoy in several hours. With

practiced skill and force Tony explains to the young captain the nearly in-
superable difficulties, that he, Tony, is not "supposed to work unsafe condition"
(167), that no one can possibly blame the captain. Then comes the point to
which all the story has led:

> Standing a few inches from the captain's boyish face, he saw for the first time that
> there was no blame there. No blame and no command either. The man was simply at
> a loss, in need.
> For the first time in his [Tony's] life he had a kind of space around him in which to
> move freely, the first time, it seemed, that it was entirely up to him with no punish-
> ment if he said no, or even a reward if he said yes. (167)

He says yes, succeeds, and is rewarded with a vision to replace that of Margaret
and Grandfather's lire, the look in the captain's eyes "when he had poured
Tony's coffee, his closeness and his fine inability to speak. That lit face hung
alone in an endless darkness" (177).

Thus the heartwarming conclusion of "Fitter's Night." It is a conven-
tionally realistic story, as all of them are, for Miller, though a competent craftsman, is not an innovator in the genre. It succeeds, for several reasons. Miller
deftly controls the story's principal structural device, that of counterpoint,
cutting from present to past and back so that gradually the relevance of what at
first seem interpolated blocks of biographical data comes clear. Tony's divided
nature is early established: often he takes real pleasure in his job, particularly in
his considerable skill, but is alternately much depressed by the thought of the
good life gone beyond hope, by "his real failing, a lack of stern dignity, leadership, force" (142). Two subsidiary characters, Hindu and Looey Baldu, Tony's
helpers, personate his two sides and two prospects: Hindu, larger, stronger,
expert in women and avoiding work, Baldu, young, earnest, patriotic, who aids
Tony after Hindu refuses. The chief function of these two is to register the
developing change in perspective in Tony: Baldu, initially scorned and derided,
Hindu the envied confederate. The ultimate reversal is acted out as Hindu with
narrow-eyed affront is ordered into the open back of the pickup truck, Baldu
into the heated cab.

Tony the misfit is vouchsafed brief illumination, senses the possibility of
freedom, reveals—happily—not a heart of gold, although the likelihood of such
sentimentality shadows the latter part of the story, but simply that he has seen
not "things" but a man "isolated in stillness," the "lit face" hanging "alone in an
endless darkness."

IV

Meyer Berkowitz, of "Fame," suffers—initially—from none of Tony Calabrese's woes. Meyer is a notably successful playwright, his name in lights, who
walks on thinking of the $675,000 coming to him over the next ten years.
"Fame" is very short, very neat, slick and in its way satisfying. Meyer is carried
through a carefully delineated, un-Baconian reflection on fame, exposed on the

way to various external stimuli. Thus, early, a rope of pearls displayed in a jeweler's window catches his eye. "My God, he thought, I could buy that! I could buy the whole window maybe. Even the store!" (132) People are the problem, however. He finds his arm grasped with "annoying proprietary strength" and himself turned "to an immense chest, a yachtsman's sunburned face with a chic, narrow-brimmed hat on top" (132), over which he triumphs by admitted that yes, he does *look* like Meyer Berkowitz.

And so it goes through nearly a dozen such sequences, Meyer feeling grateful at being recognized, uncertain of his ability ever to write anything again, thankful for his thousands, alarm at his own rumpled and undistinguished appearance, unexplainable disgust at his awkward attempt to respond to a cabdriver's greeting. These preliminaries over, Miller devotes the second half of the story to what might be called a recognition-reversal-recognition, in which irony is paramount. Meyer, seated in a bar with a drink on the house (recognized again from the "Today Show"), is approached by a short, pleasingly prosperous man who asks the now expected question, but who is put off and then angry by Meyer's inability to remember him. He is Bernie Gelfand, Meyer's best friend at De Witt Clinton, four years together in English. Meyer, feeling he has offended the man, obediently asks what he does. He's in shoulder pads, "General Manager, head of everything up to the Mississippi" (137). And then the question toward which the whole story has built, addressed to Meyer: "What do *you* do?" (137) Stunned at first, Meyer can think of nothing to say. He goes on, answer by answer, weighing the possibilities, not only to crush Gelfand but also to yield himself wholly to "this very hateful pleasure which he knew now he could not part with anymore" (138).

Meyer Berkowitz is decidedly not Tony Calabrese's kind of misfit; he has, in fact, most of what Tony long despaired of. Yet Meyer is a misfit: he has lost connection with himself, has been invaded by an essentially alien presence, must have what he despises. "Fame" illustrates what Miller identifies as the strength of the good short story—it captures nuances of speech, focuses on the speaking gesture, conveys the thought process, twisting, stopping short, doubling back, freezes character development in Meyer's acceptance of his hateful pleasure. It is a well told story, nicely managed, fully realized, a good, perhaps even a model story in these senses. It is, however, very slight, without much depth or resonance, a story in which content is overshadowed by technique.

V

The title story of the collection, "I Don't Need You Any More," an O. Henry Award-winner, is, if not the best, certainly the most ambitious of the lot. It recounts a long hard day in the life of 5-year-old Martin, one studded with discoveries and adventures, almost all of them unpleasant or frightening, as the ordered world he knows breaks down around him. From the unrelieved intensity of Martin's responses it is an exhausting and at times irritating story to read. Irritating because Miller attempts to outdo Salinger's wise child, because he undertakes, by dint of essentially decorative imagery, to raise to the level of metaphysical tragedy what is, virtually by definition, the poignant-pathetic experience of a little boy. Almost in self-defense, one doubts the insight, suspects ersatz sensitivity.

The scene of the story is a New Jersey beach community, the time early twentieth-century. There are four speaking parts: Mother, Father, Martin, and Ben, Martin's older school age brother. God, beard streaming in the ocean, is a dominant presence. The sentence of the title is angrily addressed by Martin to his mother, who late in her pregnancy is less responsive to her younger son's hyperimaginative tales than he could wish. "For him nothing happened if he could not tell it, and lately it was so complicated to tell anything" (4). The details of Martin's initiation need not be catalogued for they have a certain generic validity. Essentially what happens is that Martin is compelled to sort out and rationalize to a degree his relation to four now discrete entities, Mother, Father, Ben and God. He must determine, in other words, who he is.

Mother, closest to him, is hardest to deal with. Defensively, he strikes out at her, literally and figuratively. His father, though apparently a somewhat ineffectual parent, provides a supportive refrain, "Be a man", and to Martin's surprise, moves momentarily to the attack. " 'When are you going to stop bothering him!' he bellowed into her face" (35). Tacitly opposed to his father is his older brother Ben, shocked, grieved and righteous, who confirms Martin in his sense of his own badness. The story closes at night with Martin on the beach alone, awaiting God's word. What it is he cannot articulate, but he knows "that secretly, unknown to anyone but known to the night, he was the guardian of Ben's and his parents' innocence" (39).

This is, if one will let it become so, a very affecting story. It has several very funny scenes, with Martin overcome by a racalcitrant matzoh ball, which heralds a cascade of steaming soup ("He's burning! Get your pants off!") (21), and indeed one is aware throughout that if the perspective were changed slightly, the whole story would be comic. But what principally concerns Miller is a detailed rendering, with full intensity, of the mercurial variousness of his protagonist, his being almost submerged by torrents of emotion—anger, bitterness, fear, delight, hatred, horror, terror, shock, devotion, and ultimately a sense of obligation and strength. One cannot say that it is an untrue account; what happens does not offend one's sense of human nature. But one can resist being played upon, prefer the understated indirection of "The Misfits" to the no-holds-barred assault of "I Don't Need You Any More."

VI

Between the unrelenting intensity of Martin's initiation and the technical virtuosity of Meyer Berkowitz's self-discovery in "Fame," falls a story which seems to possess the better qualities of both. This is "Monte Sant' Angelo," earliest published (1951) and best of all stories. Vinny Appello and Bernstein, the protagonist, are making what is for Vinny a triumphal tour through rural

Italy where as it seems the Appellos have for centuries been and presently remain a family of real consequence. Vinny is on his way to locate another part of his history in Monte Sant' Angelo, a remote and primitive hill town. One early exchange between the two friends, who "had sensed they were opposites" (44), indicates the mood:

> "You're crazy, you know that? You've got some kind of ancestor complex. All we've done in this country is look for your relatives."
> "Well, Jesus, I'm finally in the country, I want to see all the places I came from. You realize that two of my relatives are buried in a crypt in the church up there? In eleven hundred something."
> "Well, don't you have any feeling about your ancestors?" (43).

While this is Bernstein's story, it benefits from the presence of Appello, because the change in Bernstein, his discovery, is registered in the context of a fully developed, equal relation to another person, rather than in his own feverishly active mind alone, as is essentially the case in "I Don't Need You Any More." Approximately the first half of "Monte Sant' Angelo" is devoted to a delineation of the "opposite" friends, with emphasis upon Vinny's delight, even as his unannounced appearance inspires speechless terror in an aged aunt, and Bernstein's sense of rootless solitariness, his uneasy sophistication. Enter at this point a mysterious stranger.

The two friends are sitting in a restaurant, uneaten portions of rather hairy lamb before them, as Bernstein experiences "an abrupt impression of familiarity" (48) with a man who has just greeted them. "He knew this man. He was sure he knew him" (49). Unaccountably agitated, Bernstein urges Vinny to engage him in conversation, about anything. Then comes the first part of Bernstein's recognition. "He's Jewish, Vinny" (51). The stranger, Mauro di Benedetto by name, is puzzled but polite when Vinny, at Bernstein's urging, tells him that Bernstein is Jewish. "Are they Catholics? the Hebrews?" (52) Here is the second part of Bernstein's recognition, that the man is Jewish but doesn't know it, does not even know what Jews are. Before he departs, di Benedetto speaks briefly of his route over the surrounding country, selling cloth, carried in a bundle on his shoulder, as had his family for generations. He walks out, in "a manner of the family" (52), so as to be home with his warm loaf of bread before sundown on this Friday night. The evidence, as interpreted, is conclusive and there remains for Bernstein only the third part of his recognition, who and what he is himself, no longer the outcast, the misfit, but a man with a proud though vicarious history, for "beneath the brainless crush of history a Jew had secretly survived" (54). As the story closes, Vinny discovers the Appello crypt. "Vinny held still for an instant, catching Bernstein's respectful happiness, and saw there that his search was not worthless sentiment" (54).

The tone of the story might well be called modest, undramatic, the structure firmly controlled but not manipulated, the recognitions and reversal logical and affecting, the concluding illumination "isolated in stillness." "Monte Sant' Angelo" accomplishes more fully than any of the other stories that combination of insight and outlook whose absence damages longer, more ambitious, more intricately wrought narratives.

VII

Finally, what is the weight of this collection; how good are the stories? They are notably uneven and collectively are not distinguished. Miller always knows what he is doing, that is, the point he wants to reach, but he will sometimes butcher events for the sake of argument. Although he may be presumed to know Broadway actors and playwrights and perhaps even Runyonesque jockeys, he doesn't write of them well. One actor story, "A Search for a Future," displays Miller's inclination to skewer a single character and watch him wriggle on a spit of ethical conundrums. The "certain continuity" Miller detects in these nine stories illustrates his interests over the fifteen years of their composition—his humanism, his running dispute with American values, his inquiry into personal responsibility, these concerns familiar to readers of the playwright. There is not evident in *I Don't Need You Any More* a developing mastery of the form; indeed, the first published story, "Monte Sant' Angelo," is as good as if not better than any of its successors. As Miller said in 1966, "I think I reserve for plays those things which take a kind of excruciating effort. What comes easier goes into a short story."[4]

Notes

1. *Writers at Work: The Paris Review Interviews*, Third Series (New York: Viking Press, 1967), p. 201.

2. *I Don't Need You Any More* (New York: Bantam, 1968), p.x. Subsequent quotations from this edition will be identified in the text.

3. Oscar Handlin, review of *I Don't Need You Any More, Atlantic Monthly*, 219 (March, 1967), 143.

4. *Writers at Work*, p. 201.

The Vestigial Jews on Monte Sant' Angelo

Irving Jacobson[*]

Arthur Miller's short stories "Monte Sant' Angelo"[1] and "I Don't Need You Any More"[2] share a supplementary relationship to his essay on "The Family in Modern Drama."[3] All develop themes that prove essential for an understanding of Miller's imagination, and all deal with man displaced from the enveloping context of the family. The meaning of this displacement includes the loss not only of mother, father or brother but also a psychological state of being, a cultural and religious inheritance, a position in the community and in human history. "I Don't Need You Any More" illustrates the process by which a child becomes isolated from his family, losing that state of equilibrium, identity and completeness that Miller defined in his essay as man's fundamental state of satisfaction.[4] "Monte Sant' Angelo," however, presents a set of experiences by which an adult comes to feel himself at home in the larger world outside the family structure, reconstructing that earlier state of satisfaction with later materials and experiences.

Bernstein senses an increasing distance between himself and his friend, Vincenzo Appello, as they travel through Italy together. An essential disparity in the ways they respond to the same experiences intensifies his sense of his own deficiencies and makes him resent Appello for having what seem to be better credentials for being happy in the world. Not knowing Italian makes him feel isolated and dependent, but the major factor that accentuates their separateness is the vast difference in their family backgrounds. Abroad, Apello maintains his identity as an American but also enjoys status as a "son of Italy" with an assured place in a long family line of some prominence. He can trace that line from town to town and receive immediate recognition for the very fact of his name. In Monte Sant' Angelo he can visit a church built with the help of his ancestors in the twelfth century and raptly imagine them riding down a mountain on horseback and in armor.

Yet beyond issues of status, family affiliation in itself appears to add something to men and evoke a special response from others. For men in families, identity ceases to be an entirely personal matter. When Bernstein chides his

[*]Reprinted from *Studies in Short Fiction*. 13 (1976), 507–12, by permission of the journal and the author.

friend for having a kind of "ancestor complex," Appello responds, "Well, Jesus, I'm finally in the country, I want to see all the places I came from" (p.43). Positive associations and attributes cluster about Appello from all the places and people he "came from," and these seem to enlarge his stature, giving him a certain strength and ease that Bernstein feels lacking in his own makeup. Furthermore, Appello responds to others in kind, extending a special warmth reserved in his nature "for members of families, any families" (p. 51).

Bernstein initially perceives a concern with family heritage as rather childish, yet "as incident after incident, landmark after landmark, turned up echoing the name Appello, he gradually began to feel his friend combining with this history, and it seemed to him that it made Vinny stronger, somehow less dead when the time would come for him to die" (p. 43). Turning to his own family background in Europe, he can find only emptiness and indignity, anonymity and death. What little he remembers of what his father told him about the town he came from gives little comfort: "a common barrel of water, a town idiot, a baron nearby. That was all he had of it, and no pride, no pride in it at all" (p. 47). In consequence he perceives himself as only partial, as though some part of him were "broken" or "not plugged in." Dissociated from an historical past, he senses himself dissociated from a personal past as well. Just as Martin, in "I Don't Need You Any More," when asked to demonstrate his spelling to his family "could not bear the indignity, the danger, that lay in having to produce something in exchange for their giving him a place among them,"[5] so Bernstein feels insecure in not being able to assume that his place in the world is his by birthright, an absolute position from which he might expand his resources with freedom and ease.

Visits to Appello's aunt and to the town church reveal an inward-driving protectiveness in Bernstein that isolates him from experience and other people. The aunt represents an exaggeration of his own isolation and an illustration of its possible consequences. An analogy relates her to the town, described at the beginning of the story as comically situated, "like a tiny old lady living on a high roof for fear of thieves" (p. 41). Built out of an archaic fear that no longer corresponds to the conditions of life, the town seems grotesquely overprotected. A joke made by the taxi driver reveals the implications of this kind of isolation: "They are very far from everything. They all look like brothers up there. They don't know very much either" (p. 42). Isolation breeds abnormality, here associated with incest and idiocy. Appello's aunt relates to the rest of the town much as the town relates to the rest of the world. She lives in an isolation so extreme that almost no one even in Monte Sant' Angelo knows who she is or where to find her.

When the visiting Americans do find her house, the brief scene that follows seems irrational at best and, at worst, permeated with implications of insanity, hysteria, and death. The only coherent gesture she makes is to bless her nephew, but the two men's responses are entirely different. Appello seems to receive nothing but a calm satisfaction from retrieving one more link with his family past, one that he accepts with pride. For Bernstein, also, she is an associative link to a family past—but a less pleasant one. He is frightened by her erratic emotionalism, which reminds him of an aunt who once forced him to eat, pinched his cheeks, and smiled at him incessantly. Further, there is a certain deathlike quality in her room which, though flooded with sunlight, remains "stone cold."

Their responses during the first visit to the church vault are equally disparate. Appello actively hunts in the darkness, walking along twisted corridors and on water-covered stone floors, trying to find inscriptions of his family name on the stone tombs. Whereas after a half-hour of failure, Appello still feels a "fascinated excitement," Bernstein can only respond with the blunt declaration that "This is no place for me to get pneumonia" (p. 47). He refuses to enter the corridor at all but only waits at the doorway and watches. Were his protectiveness strictly practical, his holding back might appear to be common sense. But more than that, he cannot participate in someone else's emotions—no more at the church vault than with Appello's aunt—particularly when they give him a sense of his own deficiency.

In this context it becomes clear that Mauro di Benedetto functions as a catalyst for transformation in Bernstein's life. The similarity between his own neglected and Benedetto's vestigial Jewishness forms an emotional bridge between him and Europe. Revitalizing a positive sense of his own family past, the common ethnic background between Bernstein and Benedetto functions as Bernstein's equivalent for Appello's family line, releasing his capacity for excitement and giving him a new sense of placement in the world.

Bernstein responds to the man with an unusual feeling of attraction long before he can deduce the reasons: "It struck him as being insane. The whole place—the town, the clouds in the streets, the thin air—was turned into a hallucination. He knew this man. He was sure he knew him. Quite clearly that was impossible. Still there was a thing beyond the impossibility of which he was drunkenly sure, and it was that if he dared he could start speaking Italian fluently with this man" (p. 49). Part of the cause for this intense and immediate a response might be the marked contrast between Benedetto and Appello's aunt. Whereas Bernstein left the aunt's house afraid of the violence of her emotions and alienated by the strangeness of her behavior, in the restaurant he responds positively to her opposite: Benedetto is male, rugged, amiable, polite, in the prime of middle age, and entirely self-possessed in his surroundings. Yet Bernstein's certainty that "he knew him" can only suggest that something about Benedetto corresponds closely enough to someone he *does* know, or to some significant factor in his own psychological makeup, to strike deep chords of intimacy and warmth.

Bernstein's deduction that the man is Jewish accounts for part of this. Although it is not entirely clear from the story itself why Bernstein reddens when Benedetto says he sells cloth, it seems possible that Bernstein associates the trade with being Jewish. An historian, Howard Morley Sachar, notes that Jews in Europe were traditionally active in interurban trade because of special legal and social factors.[6] Also, Appello translates the name, Mauri di Benedetto, as Morris of the Blessed, or Moses. Further, the man says that he follows the same route and pattern his family has followed for generations, making certain he is home by sundown each Friday night—the beginning of the Jewish Sabbath. But the key factor that leads Bernstein to a conclusion about Benedetto, and the one that draws the most direct lines of connection between them, is the meticulous way the man unknots his bundle and then wraps a loaf of bread in it. This makes Bernstein announce to Appello, with "a new air of confidence and superiority in his face and voice" that Benedetto is Jewish. He explains: "It's exactly the way my father used to tie a bundle—and my grandfather. The whole history is packing bundles and getting away. Nobody else can be as tender and delicate with bundles. That's a Jewish man tying a bundle" (p. 51).

Yet not only is Benedetto unaware that he is Jewish, but he hasn't the vaguest idea what the two Americans' eager questions about his background mean. "Are they Catholics? The Hebrews?" (p. 52). He responds with polite confusion, sensing that they have associated him with something exotic, but he has no knowledge of what a Jew or Hebrew is. In that sense, he can be called a vestigial Jew, maintaining in his life pattern remnants of behavior that had religious significance for someone in the past but which have become merely a "manner of the family," an eccentric set of habits.

Thus, some part of the intensity with which Bernstein responds to Benedetto might be explained by *his* being a vestigial Jew, almost as unconscious of his own background as Benedetto. The encounter brings him to the realization, at the end of the story, that "his life had been covered with an unrecognized shame," a denial of his own religion and, with that, his own access to history:

> He did not move, seeking the root of an ecstasy he had not dreamed was part of his nature; he saw the amiable man trudging down the mountains, across the plains, on routes marked out for him by generations of men, a nameless traveler carrying home a warm bread on Friday night—and kneeling in church on Sunday. There was an irony in it he could not name. And yet pride was running through him. Of what he should be proud he had no clear idea; perhaps it was only that beneath the brainless crush of history a Jew had secretly survived, shorn of his consciousness but forever caught by that final imprudence of a Saturday Sabbath in a Catholic country; so that his very unawareness was proof, a proof as mute as stones, that a past lived (p. 54).

The effect of the experience is to remove Bernstein from an isolation that has been, in part, self-imposed, and it places his life in the kind of context within which he can form relationships. He can both understand what he had once called Appello's "ancestor complex" and feel the past to be his own as much as Appello's. It is at his suggestion that the two Americans return to the church vault and this second visit reveals the extent to which Bernstein's emotional outlook has been transformed. This time, he does not remain at the doorway, or even hesitate, but enters with his friend. Although the setting is as wet, dark and cramped as before, his response is different: "I feel like—at home in this place. I can't describe it" (p. 53). This new sense of belonging makes it possible for him and Appello to achieve a new kind of rapport, a new commonality of spirit: "Vinny held still for an instant, catching Bernstein's respectful happiness, and saw there that his search was not worthless sentiment. He raised the candle to see Bernstein's face better, and then he laughed and gripped Bernstein's wrist and led the way toward the flight of steps that rose to the surface. Bernstein had never liked anyone grasping him, but from this touch of a hand in the darkness, strangely, there was no implication of a hateful weakness" (p. 54).

Just as it becomes possible for him to yield and participate in the emotionalism of his friend, Bernstein's experience in Monte Sant' Angelo makes it possible for him to yield to his own emotions. In Miller's story there is a sense in which Appello represents the emotional and expressive aspects that are lacking or repressed in Bernstein's personality. At one point in the story, Bernstein is struck by how much he and his friend resemble one another. They are both tall, broad-shouldered, dark. Yet Appello's eyes reveal him as the more aggressive and sensual, "they glistened black, direct, and, for women, passionately." Bernstein, however, tends to gaze rather than look; he turns his eyes away or stares downward, evasive, "defensively cruel and yet gentle" (p. 44). Appello's aggressive sensuality is set off against Bernstein's inhibitions and defenses, his tendency to be distant. Miller describes their relationship thus: "They like each other not for reasons so much as for possibilities; it was as though they both had sensed they were opposites. And they were lured to each other's failings. With Bernstein around him, Appello felt diverted from his irresponsible sensuality, and on this trip Bernstein often had the pleasure and pain of resolving to deny himself no more" (ibid). Thereby, in a general sense, when Bernstein can yield to his friend's hand without protectiveness, that part of the human personality which he has lacked or repressed becomes integrated into his own with the new bond between him and Appello.

Bernstein comes to feel "at home" in the larger world outside the family structure. Significantly, the means by which he accomplishes this relate intimately to his own sense of family. Mauro di Benedetto is not only a Jew but one, more specifically, who reminds Bernstein of his own father and grandfather. By association, he can be interpreted as a paternal figure—not merely an interesting or admirable man who also seems Jewish, but a kind of father. Suitably, then, he is both Jewish, like Bernstein, and Italian, like Appello. Just as a pattern emerges in "I Don't Need You Any More" by which the protagonist moves from the mother toward the father, a pattern emerges here by which the protagonist responds negatively to the feminine images of Appello's and his own aunt and positively to a man who reminds him of his own and his father's father. To an extent, also, Bernstein and Appello are metaphorically brothers. In *The Price*, Walter says to his brother, Victor: "It's almost as though—*he smiles warmly, uncertain still*—we're like two halves of the same guy. As though we can't quite move ahead—alone. You ever feel that?"[7] With Bernstein and Appello "both stooping slightly under the low, wet ceiling" of the womblike church vault in Monte Sant' Angelo, one can see their acceptance of a common past—and with their hand-linked exit outside again, their acceptance, perhaps, of a common future. Although Bernstein can live in the social world outside the family, the images and processes of family life, re-discovered in that world, are necessary for his ability to feel emotional gratification.

In both "I Don't Need You Any More" and "Monte Sant' Angelo," the isolated ego, incapable of thriving alone, seeks to strengthen itself through relationships with other men. Given his father's concern and approval, Martin if only temporarily, feels supported by a community of manhood. Reminded of his grandfather and father by a stranger, Bernstein feels revivified by the sense of an honorable past that supports his personal existence and makes a new rapport with Appello possible. Both Martin and Bernstein, as Jews, see their male relatives as links to a cultural, religious, and, in Bernstein's case, an historical inheritance. For Martin this presents the possibility of learning a Law that will guide his behavior, help him to avoid mistakes and guilts, and allow him to participate in the respected masculine community's relationship with God. For Bernstein it means a place within history that remedies his sense of isolation in the world.

Notes

1. Arthur Miller, "Monte Sant' Angelo," *Harper's*, 202 (March, 1951); rpt. in *I Don't Need You Any More: Stories by Arthur Miller* (New York: Bantam, 1968), pp.41-55. All quotations are from the latter edition

2. Arthur Miller, "I Don't Need You Any More," *Esquire*, 52 (December 1959); rpt. in *I Don't Need You Any More*, pp. 1-40.

3. Arthur Miller, "The Family in Modern Drama," *Atlantic Monthly*, 197 (April, 1956), 35-41.

4. See Irving Jacobson, "The Child as Guilty Witness," *Literature and Psychology*, 24 (November 1974), 12-23.

5. "I Don't Need You Any More," p. 31.

6. Howard Morley Sachar, *The Course of Modern Jewish History* (New York: Dell, 1958), pp. 38-40.

7. Arthur Miller, *The Price* (New York: Bantam, 1969), p. 112.

INDEX